Denise M. Rousseau

Psychological Contracts in Organizations

Understanding Written and Unwritten Agreements

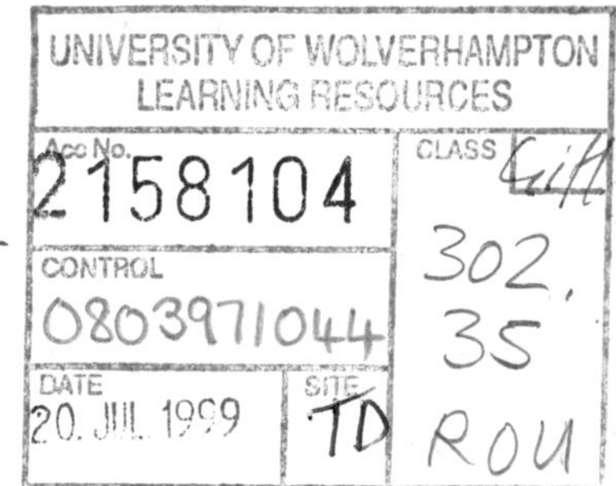

SAGE Publications
International Educational and Professional Publisher
Thousand Oaks London New Delhi

For information address:

SAGE Publications, Inc.
2455 Teller Road
Thousand Oaks, California 91320

SAGE Publications Ltd.
6 Bonhill Street
London EC2A 4PU
United Kingdom

SAGE Publications India Pvt. Ltd.
M-32 Market
Greater Kailash I
New Delhi 110 048 India

Printed in the United States of America

Library of Congress Cataloging-in-Publication Data

Rousseau, Denise M.
Psychological contracts in organizations: Understanding written and unwritten agreements / Denise M. Rousseau.
p. cm.
Includes bibliographical references and index.
ISBN 0-8039-7104-4 (alk. paper).—ISBN 0-8039-7105-2 (pbk. : alk. paper)
1. Organizational behavior. 2. Contracts—Psychological aspects. 3. Commitment (Psychology) 4. Industrial relations. I. Title.
HD58.7.R68 1995
158.7—dc20 95-11730

This book is printed on acid-free paper.

99 10 9 8 7 6 5 4 3

Sage Production Editor: Gillian Dickens
Ventura Designer: Danielle Dillahunt

Contents

Acknowledgments

Many friends and colleagues provided thought-provoking feedback on various versions of this book: Jean Bartunek, Max Bazerman, Joe Baumann, Art Brief, Martin Greller, Richard Guzzo, Jean Hirsch, Paul Hirsch, Wayne Kriemelmeyer, David Messick, Don Prentiss, Ben Schneider, Cathy Tinsley, and Kim Wade-Benzoni. Katie Schonk, who edited the manuscript, deserves particular recognition for her ability to tease out confounded concepts and errant constructions. Carole McCoy saw it through to final product. Thank you all very much. My family was especially supportive, despite living with this book for several years. My thanks to my husband, Paul, and daughters, Heather and Jessica.

Introduction

It is time to reassess our assumptions about contracts. Traditional employment contracts have been challenged by the restructuring of corporations and the decline in organized labor. Promises about the future are the essence of contracts—yet promises are increasingly difficult to make (and keep). The purpose of this book is to offer a behavioral theory of contracts to help scholars and managers address the fundamental roles contracts play in organizations. A behavioral perspective on contracts is critical to understanding and managing change in contemporary organizations.

THE PERVASIVENESS OF CONTRACTS

Contracts, unwritten and understood, are a pervasive aspect of organizational life:

- A person taking a job with the government or a family business because of the security it offers
- Terminated employees with high seniority receiving extensive outplacement and severance packages (typically in contrast to experiences of their more junior coworkers)
- Customers buying a particular brand of computer for the service the manufacturer provides
- The "moral tenure" of a nontenure track instructor who continues to teach the same classes year after year
- A working relationship with a supplier, consultant, or partner in which any formal contract is left in the desk drawer
- Mission statements saying that "our people are our most important asset"

The choices people make in taking a job or planning their retirement, purchasing a product, or commissioning a service all involve some understanding of promises made by employers, product makers, and service givers.

Nonetheless, it's common to think that corporate turmoil and economic competition have made loyalty, trust, and commitment things of the past. Employees are told to "pack their own parachute" (Hirsch, 1987) and corporate attorneys advise their clients to avoid making any statements that might be construed as a promise of long-term employment. Yet the movement toward strong corporate cultures and escalating interdependence belies claims of contract avoidance. Federal Express requires a strong commitment to service and innovation to deliver "by ten the next day," necessitating both a team culture and an employment relationship that resembles more than a simple transaction. In the past 5 years, Motorola has gone from 5,000 suppliers to 200 in an effort to better manage its relations with vendors. Team cultures and dedicated supplier relations are not managed at arm's length. They involve very different contracts with employees, vendors, and customers than those found in a more bureaucratic or opportunistic organization. Managing more extensive ties to many people requires new commitments—in employment, services, alliances, and communities.

PARADOX AND CHALLENGE IN CONTRACTS

New types of contracts are necessary for new and future types of organizations. But there's a paradox in current organizational contracting. Reverberations from the downsized and restructured corporations of the 1980s have led to a "no guarantees" attitude among many organizations and their erstwhile members. The unraveling of many long-standing contracts—internal labor markets of firms such as IBM, Digital, or Xerox—and the move toward more temporary employment—from Accountemps to Manpower—has to do with a "fear of commitment" in many organizations in the United States and abroad. But new organizational forms may foist on many enterprises a 180-degree turn toward more extensive commitments, at least to some (future) workers. Charles Handy, in his provocative book *The Age of Unreason* (1989), argues that future organizations will be "shamrocks." Essentially, shamrock organizations are based on a core of essential executives and workers supported by outside contractors and part-time help. They are not a new form (construction work and farming have been shamrocked for generations), but a complex one in terms of creating contracts that people understand and can keep. Future organizations might have it both ways—commitment and flexibility. To make this happen, we must understand the commitments and obligations that make organizations possible.

People in contemporary society are often uncomfortable with concepts of commitment and obligation—consistent with the negative stance corporate attorneys have toward commitment and open-ended agreements. In contrast, obligations and duties constitute much of social life in traditional societies (tribes, clans, or feudal systems). Tribes people such as the Navaho and aristocrats like the Japanese *dai-myo* are to their obligations born. In a traditional world, nothing is particularly voluntary about obligations and duties. They are the fabric of social life. But in a modern world, the striking feature of *contractual* obligations is that their basis is individual freedom of choice.

Contracts are a product of free societies. Choice underlies the existence and meaning of contracts. Freedom gives new meaning to promises and gives contracts a special significance. Motivationally, having a choice can engender a great personal commitment to carry out a promise. As the trend toward democratization continues worldwide, more countries will wrestle with what it means to make and keep a contract. In the former Soviet Union, for instance, the notion of an implied contract or understanding had virtually no meaning. As stated in an appropriately titled article, "Nobody's Grandfather Was a Merchant," unless the terms were in writing, they were not honored or binding:

> All contracts between American firms and Soviets are generally governed by Soviet law, which does not recognize oral agreements. . . . Written contracts then supersede all previous unwritten agreements and implied assumptions . . . the Soviets insist on writing down . . . things taken for granted in Western nations such as verbal confirmations of receipt of goods and telephone reorders. (Rajan & Graham, 1991, p. 45)

Ability to compete effectively may depend on creating contracts consistent with the expectations of customers and the flexibility demanded by both technological changes and the marketplace. Contracts arise when people believe themselves to have choice in their dealings with others. Commitments obtained by coercion are not legally binding—shotgun weddings are readily annulled. When a person voluntarily agrees to be bound to a contract, he or she gives up some measure of freedom. Working for a newspaper can mean reporters and even their spouses may shop only at stores that advertise in that paper. Similarly, corporate consultants may be forbidden to take clients with them if they quit. Contracts are made when we surrender some of our freedom from restrictions in exchange for a similar surrender by another. But by giving up something voluntarily, each gets more than might be possible otherwise.

Contracts are poorly understood and used in one of the most pervasive areas of modern life—contemporary organizations. Professional managers are often less well prepared for contract making than are other professionals. For years, marriage counselors, organizational development specialists, and therapists have used techniques of contracting to create or renew relationships. To grow and develop in such circumstances involves spelling out mutual obligations to develop trust and commitments with long-term implications. Husbands and wives may renew a troubled marriage by establishing specific commitments that, when kept, restore trust. Therapists encourage overweight teenagers or substance abusers to create contracts with themselves, including promises that bring rewards when fulfilled and sanctions when broken. Contracting makes possible new models for future behavior, a sense of confidence that these behaviors can and will occur, and the creation or renewal of trust and self-confidence. As William James once wrote: "Our faith in an uncertified result is the only thing that makes that result come true" (as quoted in *Bartlett's,* 1980, p. 649). Effective organizations have learned how to make and keep the contracts their technology, markets, and strategies prescribe.

OUTLINE

This book proposes a behavioral theory of contracts. The following key issues are addressed:

Contractual Thinking. We describe ways in which people think contractually and the way commitments are made and understood.

Contract Makers. We detail ways in which organizations send messages that are understood as promises, whether they are intended to be or not. Prominent in our understanding of contracts are the role of promises and the many ways they can be communicated (in words, by actions, and by organizational signals).

Contemporary Contract Forms. Just as Shakespeare's Hamlet once said, "There are more things in heaven and earth . . . than are dreamed of in your philosophy" (1.5.166), there are more forms of contracts that organizations are party to than managers and members are fully cognizant of. This book details the workings of each, how they are created, maintained, broken, and changed.

How Contracts Are Violated and What Happens Then. Violation is a reality of contracting, although most contracts that are kept involve some forms of breach as well. How violations play out, whether the contract is ultimately broken or endures, are shaped by the relationship's history, interactions between person and organization, and the aftermath of violation.

How Contracts Change. Contract change often borders on violation, and poorly implemented changes become contract breach. We describe how the type of change affects the processes needed to effectively redesign a contract.

How to Link Strategy to Contracts. Employment contracts and the customer relationships they foster are a product of the link between an organization's strategy and its human resource practices. The chapters describe how broader strategic management concerns affect employment relationships.

The Changing Social Contract. Finally, an assessment of societal trends augurs large-scale changes in future employment contracts.

STARTING POINT

Much of our difficulty in understanding how contracts operate in everyday work settings, customer service encounters, and vendor-supplier relations comes from confusing legalistic thinking (how people use the law to think about their behavior) with how people think contractually (how they make, keep, and rely on promises; Macaulay, 1963). Legalistic thinking focuses on the formal and the procedural, what's in writing, what's readily measurable, and what can be reduced to dollars and cents. Such thinking is often demonstrated in traditional economics: "We have a puzzle: much behavior in the labor market seems to be explicable only in terms of long-term labor contracts, and yet such contracts are *rare* [italics added]" (Bull, 1987, p. 147). The rarity of long-term agreements depends on whether we mean a formal written contract or view beliefs about seniority or informal agreements as creating obligations. In contrast, Nobel laureate Herbert Simon (1951) has argued,

> [Classical economic theory's] way of viewing the employment contract and the management of labor involves a very high order of abstraction—such a high order, in fact, as to leave out the most striking empirical facts of the situation we observe in the real world. (p. 293)

We begin here by investigating the "facts of the situation" as they play out in the psychological and social processes that underlie making, keeping, breaking, and changing contracts in organizations.

1 Contracting: A Modern Dilemma

Ten years ago, who would have thought we could lay off 10% of the workforce. . . . Today it's amazing how easy it is.

—*Chief executive*

Employees are scared. They don't trust and don't take risks. . . . Where are new ideas and innovations going to come from?

—*Middle manager*

Contracts seem to be at odds with contemporary organizational life. Contracts are *voluntary*—commitments made freely. But downsizing and restructuring have imposed on workers employment arrangements they did not choose. The ideal contract details expectations of both the employee and the employer. However, typical contracts are *incomplete* due to bounded rationality, which limits individual information seeking (Simon, 1958/1976), and a changing organizational environment that makes all conditions impossible to specify up front (Williamson, 1979). Both employee and employer are left to fill in the blanks and they do so in somewhat unpredictable ways. Contracts become *self-organizing*. People working with a contract work more efficiently and with less supervision than if there were no contract. Organizations in a free society require a committed workforce. Organizations in a turbulent environment require contracts flexible enough to change without breaking. But once created, contracts tend to resist revision, making response to change difficult.

Our focus here is on contracts in organizational settings, particularly those contracts that exist between workers and the organization. A contract is an exchange agreement between employee and employer. The contract may include written terms (e.g., union agreement, job offer letter), orally communicated terms (e.g., promises of training, support, and best efforts), as well as other expressions of commitment and future intent (e.g., tradition, custom, and culture). Our purpose here is to go beyond strict legal interpretations of contracts to address the organizational, social, and psychological meaning of contracts in organizations. Critical legal scholars have acknowledged that "all contracts are psychological" (Macneil, 1985). In organizational settings, contracts can be social (shared by the larger society) and organizational as well.

This chapter first describes why contracts have not been understood well by managers or scientists, and why they need to be. It introduces the four forms organizationally relevant contracts take and what makes them important for modern organizations. Finally, it sets the stage for later discussions of contract creation and change by outlining the basic features of promissory contracts that must be taken into account when creating contracts that can be kept.

WHY CONTRACTS AREN'T WELL UNDERSTOOD

Contracts provide an intuitively appealing and culturally acceptable way to describe employment relationships. They are also a lively subject for dispute. Consider the following letter to Dear Abby, headlined "Court Makes a Turkey of a Decision":

> Dear Abby:
>
> Grandma created quite a stir among your readers concerning her usual $50 birthday gift to her selfish descendants who, after a while, thought they had it coming.
>
> Did you know that it is a legally established fact that the practice of voluntarily giving gifts over a period of time implies an obligation to continue that practice?
>
> Several years ago, when the mills of the American Rolling Mill Co. in Middletown, Ohio, were really rolling, the company, out of the goodness of its corporate heart, began giving free turkeys to its employees at Thanksgiving.
>
> Then the company fell on hard times, and in the early 1980s it decided to discontinue the distribution of some 15,000 turkeys as an economy measure.
>
> The Steelworkers Union set up a howl and took the company to court. Believe it or not, the court took the position that through the company's generous practice over a period of years, it did indeed owe the employees their Thanksgiving turkeys! Small wonder they call them "gobblers"?
>
> —Jim

> Dear Jim:
>
> Thanks for an interesting story. It serves to reinforce the fact that that which is legal is not necessarily moral or even fair.[1]

As this letter suggests, there is disagreement about what constitutes an obligation, a contract, or a deal. Whatever a contract is, is bound up in what is legal and/or fair. Contract making is not a deliberate process for most managers and has received little attention from organizational researchers until recently. Managers and social scientists each have their own reasons for neglecting contracts.

For managers, contracts are downplayed for the following reasons:

- Contracts are seen as something to avoid.
- Contracts are conceptualized in bargaining terms.

An increasingly legalistic and litigious American society has led employers toward making widespread disclaimers of contractual obligations (e.g., "at-will employer" printed at the bottom of an employment application). Legal maneuvering to avoid enforceable commitments follows expanded entitlements in U.S. courts, which have permitted increasing numbers of exceptions to at-will employment practices (Bradshaw & Deacon, 1985). Legal recognition of contracts implied in employment frightens employers into defensive postures when the term *contract* is mentioned (McLean Parks & Schmedemann, 1994). Because the legal approach tends to assume constancy in contracts over time, a legalistic view of contracts can lock employee and employer into commitments that become obsolete.

The "let's make a deal" view of contracts treats employment as a bargaining process in which all parties have their own interests and try to obtain the most for the least. Well-publicized sports contracts and mega-money deals of rock stars and movie idols create the image of an auction ("to the highest bidder"). This competitive, transactional view of employment is market oriented, treats both labor and employment like a commodity, and adopts a short-term and limited view of what employee and employer offer each other. Attention is focused narrowly on monetary terms, downplaying the value of the relationship.

Social scientists have done little to investigate the psychological and social underpinnings of contractual thinking and behavior as they affect enduring employment relationships. A review of textbooks in social and organizational psychology reveals few if any listings under "promises," "commitments," let alone "contracts." When the term is used, the concept of a contract is employed in microeconomics to characterize one-shot transactions in which economists assume that principals (owners) are honest, agents shirk, and workers are opportunistic (Alchian & Demsetz, 1972). This one-sided view of contracting is at odds with the evidence that managers tend to act in good faith (Castanzias & Helfat, 1991) and that people tend to keep commitments they have voluntarily made (Shanteau & Harrison, 1991).

An interesting sideline to the one-sided view of contracting offered by economics is the accumulating body of literature reporting that *economists* themselves tend to cooperate less and act opportunistically. Frank, Gilovich, and Regan (1993) mailed questionnaires to over 1,000 college professors randomly chosen from professional directories in a variety of disciplines, asking them to report on the annual dollar amounts they donate to private charities. Economists had the largest proportion of free riders, those who report donating no money at all to charity. Despite their generally higher incomes, economists were also among the least generous in terms of gifts to larger charities such as viewer-supported television and the United Way. Similar self-serving behavior is observed in economics students in group exercises and interdependent games, even when the benefit from cooperation is quite high. That economics might teach noncooperation is a concern for both management professionals and academics:

> In an ever more interdependent world, social cooperation has become increasingly important—and yet increasingly fragile. With an eye toward both the social good and the well-being of their own students, economists may wish to stress a broader view of human motivation in their teaching. (Frank et al., 1993, pp. 170-171)

The fact is, most employment relations involve more than the self-interest displayed in single transactions. Traditional economics is not based on how real people act but on assumptions regarding how people *should act* if personal profit were their only aspiration and if all other people were untrustworthy and deceptive. Employment contracts *tend* to endure over some period of time and encompass socioemotional concerns such as mutual identification and trust. An implication of traditional economics' oversimplified view has been an emphasis in professional management training on bargaining, competition, and arm's-length transactions—rather than information sharing, realistic expectations, and good faith dealing, the very essence of those contracts that can be kept.

Why have contracts been difficult for economists and other social scientists to understand? The elusiveness of contracting derives from the preferences of most academics and researchers to think in terms of the following:

- A unified reality, therefore a contract's terms have one meaning (disagreements reflect error or bias, not fact or important information)
- Disinterest in unique experiences (individual or divergent interpretations are ignored)
- Little tolerance for ambiguity, with a focus instead on terms that are readily monetizable (neglecting socioemotional terms such as *trust* or *loyalty*)

We will need to use a variety of means to gather information on the nature and functioning of contracts. Interviews with individuals are important to capture the dynamics of contractual thinking. Archival data, public policy information, and social trends must be examined to address broad patterns and social agreement. In assembling information from diverse sources, we have two goals here:

- Understanding the dynamics of contract making and contractual thinking
- Predicting individual behavior and organizational results from the creation, change, and violation of contracts

As such, we will need to challenge the usual assumptions made by scientists and many real-world managers in understanding organizations. Our working assumptions include the following:

- Contracts are inevitable, not something to avoid but fundamental to productive relationships.
- Contracts reflect multiple realities and interpretations, within individuals and between groups (no simple unilateral view will suffice).
- General principles will operate across contracts, but predictions about individual behavior and organizational results will need to account for specific situational factors (organizational, social, and personal dimensions are important to understanding any particular contract).
- Fuzziness and ambiguity are often built into contractual arrangements, creating both their valued flexibility and their inevitable conflicts.

WHAT WE KNOW ABOUT CONTRACTS AND WHAT WE NEED TO KNOW

Despite the limited attention given to the behavioral nature of contracts in organizations per se, social scientists know a lot about factors related to contracts (Table 1.1). We know that voluntary commitments lead to more consistent fulfillment than coercion does (Latham & Saari, 1979). Basic models of motivation, expectancy theory (Vroom, 1964), or operational conditioning (Skinner, 1969) maintain that employees behave in ways they expect to produce positive outcomes. Contracts are built around obtaining positive outcomes. Unless outcomes are seen as beneficial, there is no motivation to make or comply with a contract. People will resist any change in a contract that creates losses. And because contracts are beneficial, changes tend to create losses. Limited information processing capacity creates bounded rationality, which limits information seeking (Simon, 1958/1976). It is typically efficient to create mental models or schemas that organize experiences so that many actions are governed by automatic processes (e.g., do it again like we did yesterday) than by careful deliberation (e.g., deciding every day over and over again how to do the job; Sims & Gioia, 1986). Once mental models are formed yielding anticipated rewards, they become relied on and resist revision. Contracts are stable and enduring mental models.

This basic knowledge about contracts can be used to get answers to some key questions:

- How do people come to think similarly or differently about the kinds of contracts they are party to?
- How do contracts change when people or their work settings change?
- How are employment contracts and business strategy bound?
- How can a contract be changed without violating it? And what happens when a contract can't be kept?

To provide answers in this book, we must first take a closer look at the nature and types of contracts relevant to organizations.

BASIC TYPES OF CONTRACTS

The most general description of a contract is the belief in obligations existing between two or more parties. Obligation is a commitment to some future action. But what that commitment means exactly, when its fulfillment is anticipated, and the extent of mutuality or real agreement are not always clear. Obligations occur because people agree in some way to be obligated (e.g., accepting tuition money from one's employer, knowing some form of payback is expected). This book's thesis is that contracts are fundamentally psychological. Agreement exists in the eye of the beholder.

People can think they have agreed to the same terms even when they hold very different beliefs. Many recent college graduates sponsored in evening M.B.A. programs see that company support as part of their current compensation package and have no intention of staying with their current employer or using that education on the job. In some circumstances, their employer

TABLE 1.1 Basic Social Science Findings Relevant to Contracts

- *Voluntariness:* No one can be forced to make a contract. Commitments must be freely made. Voluntariness promotes contract fulfillment.
- *Incompleteness:* Due to bounded rationality, it is virtually impossible to spell out all details at the time a contract is created. People fill in the blanks along the way, and they sometimes do so inconsistently.
- *Reliance losses:* Because contracts are created to benefit their parties, changes can create losses. Contract-related activities focus largely on reducing losses.
- *Automatic processes:* Once contracts are established, they create enduring mental models that resist change. Mental models can actually keep people from noticing changes that do occur.

also sees tuition support as current compensation rather than as a future commitment, but not in other cases. Not until the employee attempts to quit will the degree of agreement be tested. Even agreements in writing are subject to interpretation. The 1985 memorandum of agreement between the Saturn Corporation and its unions specifies: "Individual jobs will be designed with the appropriate resources to develop the optimum balance between people and technology," a statement subject to much interpretation in terms of what is "appropriate" and "optimum."

The old adage "the customer is always right" recognizes the psychological nature of contracts—a service-oriented business gives the customer what he or she believes was promised and not necessarily what the business's manager thought the deal involved. Arguing over whose version of the contract is correct can only cost the organization. In employment, however, different interpretations often receive a less generous response. Managers typically see themselves as less dependent on their employees than on their customers. Nonetheless, how managers and workers each view their contract with the other has a powerful impact on their behavior.

What we speak of as contracts actually covers a wide range of interpersonal arrangements and societal norms. We say, "We've got a contract, let's shake on it," to seal a business deal or agree to give our children a prize (a camera, a car, or a dollar an "A") if they improve their grades. Philosophers speak of social contracts (to obey laws, look out for one another, act responsibly). Newspaper headlines proclaim that Social Security is a unique arrangement with elders ("Social Security," 1993, p. A1), and retirees will add they worked all their lives for their benefits. Organizational researchers have referred to norms in the organization's culture for using ("abusing") sick leave as "absence contracts" (Nicholson & Johns, 1985). Procedures for changing behaviors very often evoke the techniques of contracting, in the case of therapy and discipline. Therapists use contracts to help overweight teenagers curb their eating habits. The progressive discipline system codified in many employee handbooks describes methods for dealing with poor performing employees that would make B. F. Skinner proud, including specification of target behaviors, performance feedback, and escalating consequences (from oral reprimands to termination) for continued poor performance. In short, contracts can promote change or be a source of resistance to it.

All these usages of the term *contract* have relevance for behavior in organizations. "The eye of the beholder" has many vantage points:

1. The *individual contract holder* is an individual employee who gives and receives a promise (and, of course, that person's manager, employer, co-worker, or whoever participates in this contract may well have his or her own individual point of view). Individual contract parties have access to different information than third parties, typically relying on their own direct experience to understand the contract.
2. *A group of contract holders* is an organization or a group of members who see themselves as sharing the same promises with the organization (e.g., GE Aerospace division employees, Northwestern University's tenured faculty). Group members interpret contracts together and often come to share a point of view that becomes reality to new group members.
3. *Outside observers* are third parties (e.g., prospective employees or clients, judges) who interpret the agreements others have made. Third parties often have less detailed information on specific contract terms and interpret a contract in light of other external factors (e.g., industry standards).

In addition, a fourth vantage point is not specifically attached to any particular organization or relationship:

4. *Conditions of membership* are pervasive, widely shared beliefs about collective obligations. These obligations accrue from membership and identification with a society or social role (e.g., how Americans regard seniority or the special rights of elderly people).

Together, these levels and perspectives help us make sense of the many ways in which the term *contract* is used and the different factors shaping each type of contract. These perspectives coincide with the distinct types of contracts (see Figure 1.1).

Promise is most given when least is said.

—George Chapman
(1598, as quoted in
Bartlett's, 1980, p. 177)

	Level Individual	Group
Within	Psychological Beliefs that individuals hold regarding promises made, accepted, and relied on between themselves and another (employee, client, manager, organization) 1	2 Normative The *shared* psychological contract that emerges when members of a social group (e.g., church group), organization (e.g., U.S. Army, Xerox, United Way), or work unit (e.g., the trauma team at a community hospital) hold common beliefs
Perspective Outside	3 Implied Interpretations that third parties (e.g., witnesses, jurists, potential employees) make regarding contractual terms	4 Social Broad beliefs in obligations associated with a society's culture (e.g., reliance on handshakes)

FIGURE 1.1. Types of Contracts

> The deepest truths are best read between the lines.
>
> —*A. B. Alcott*
> *(1872, as quoted in*
> *Carruth & Ehrlich, 1988, p. 557)*

The psychological contract is individual beliefs, shaped by the organization, regarding terms of an exchange agreement between individuals and their organization. Psychological contracts have the power of self-fulfilling prophecies: They can create the future. People who make and keep their commitments can anticipate and plan because their actions are more readily specified and predictable both to others as well as to themselves. A marketing manager hired with the understanding that she is supposed to turn that department around is more likely to initiate a suitable course of action and pursue it than if she had not made that commitment. Psychological contracts function in the broader context of goals and as such, ceteris paribus (all things being equal), make individuals and organizations more productive.

When two people working interdependently, such as a worker and a supervisor, *agree* on the terms of the contract, performance should be satisfactory from both parties' perspectives. As individuals work through their understandings of each other's commitments over time, a degree of mutual predictability becomes possible: "I know what you want from me and you know what I want from you." Commitments understood on both sides may be based on communications, customs, and past practices. Regardless of how it is achieved, mutual predictability is a powerful factor in coordinating efforts and planning.

A key feature of the psychological contract is that the individual voluntarily assents to make and accept certain promises as he or she understands them. It is what the individual believes he or she has agreed to, not what that person intends, that makes the contract. If I contract to deliver a report by Friday knowing it won't be ready until later, the contract is still for Friday and not later. If contracts were defined in terms of what any individual *intended* to do, only honest people would be bound by contracts. However, the terms each party understands and agrees to do not have to be mutual. Typically two people have somewhat different interpretations of terms (e.g., *excellent service* means different things to sellers and customers). Nonetheless, in each individual's psychological contract there is a *perception* of agreement and mutuality, if not agreement in fact.

Imagine two students who agree to meet at the library to study together tomorrow at 8:00. Each can believe the other will "be there at 8:00." But the early riser may think this means 8:00 a.m., and the other 8:00 p.m. Each believes she has made and accepted a promise, and that the agreement is mutual. They each do agree to deliver on their commitments, but there can be no guarantee that what each understands is the same. In actual fact, mutuality is seldom tested directly. People rely on their ability to predict what others will do (e.g., Do they seem to follow through?) as well as apparent good faith efforts and supportiveness (e.g., Do they show interest in the relationship?) and other nondirect indicators of the terms each understands and agrees to. Thus, a psychological contract is potentially idiosyncratic and unique to each person who agrees to it.

> If men define situations as real, they are real in their consequences.
>
> —*W. I. Thomas*
>
> *(1974, as quoted in Goffman, 1974, p. 1)*

Normative contracts exist where the organization has many members who identify themselves in similar ways with it and each other (e.g., part-time employees at McDonald's, retirees from Pacific Telephone, or doctoral students in psychology at Berkeley) and these members believe themselves party to the same contract. For instance, part-timers at McDonald's could believe themselves guaranteed a minimum of 10 hours a week, a uniform allowance, and a meal if they work more than a 3-hour shift. The more these individuals share a common psychological contract, the more likely they will reinforce each other's perceptions of it, rely on it in choosing courses of action, and experience violation and contract changes due to personnel actions encountered by fellow members. IBM employees do not look to Xerox staffers to learn whether their organization is keeping its contract with them, but IBMers in Atlanta may watch carefully what happens to their peers in Chicago. Vicarious learning occurs when people identify others as having the same deal.

Similarly, belief in a shared set of obligations can create social pressures to adhere to those commitments, institutionalizing the contract as part of the shared culture of the organization. The "absence contracts" that groups of coworkers come to share (e.g., that they are entitled to use up their sick leave, regardless of health; Nicholson & Johns, 1985) are beliefs in a contractual exchange that have the power of a social norm. Similarly, many organizations formally offer vacation time, but employees do not believe they can really take all of it. If many employees do not use their vacation time because of concern over appearing to be lazy or less motivated, a norm is created that vacation is *not* part of the employment contract.

Although normative contracts are most common in employment, they can occur anywhere that *insiders* to a contract (clients, customers, parents, and school board members) have sufficient opportunity for interaction with each other to create common beliefs about that contract. The functioning of normative contracts even among nonemployees can be seen in school districts, which vary dramatically in terms of the level of parental involvement in their children's education and beliefs about their roles and that of teachers. The Total Quality Schools program in Chicago is such a program—in part directed at creating a new contract for teamwork between parents and teachers and between families and the school organization. Whenever organizations expand their boundaries to include clients or other "partners," normative contracts can develop in nonemployment relations too.

> The power to guess the unseen from the seen . . . to judge the whole piece by the pattern.
>
> —*Henry James*
> *(1888, as quoted in Bartlett's, 1980, p. 652)*

Implied contracts are the attributions that people not party to the contract (i.e., outsiders) make regarding its terms, acceptance, and mutuality. These interpretations reflect the frame of reference common in research on ethics, that is, the "reasonable third party" who can look past any self-serving bias on the part of the contract's principals in gauging the meaning of the contract's terms. A history of long-term employment may be seen by the general public as a sign of the stability of an organization and its commitment to its workers—historically a common view held of organizations such as IBM, Digital, or even the U.S. Army. In the case of the military, the general public may hold a view of the military's obligation to its people that influences their willingness to support large retirement packages and severance benefits to service personnel. In litigation, judges and juries are in the position of evaluating implied contracts in breach-of-contract suits. Third parties tend to rely on status quo-related benchmarks in forming their judgments: Experienced arbitrators tend to follow an anchored equity norm, adjusting the present wage by the average negotiated increase in the industry (Bazerman, 1985); managers emphasize seniority and previous commitments while evaluating the fairness of another organization's terminations (Rousseau & Anton, 1988).

NCR Japan encountered interesting ramifications from breaching an implied contract. Although American owned, an NCR facility in Japan manufacturing cash registers for the international market had a long history of stable lifetime employment consistent with the practices of large Japanese firms. Also like many traditional Japanese firms, it had a company union with close relations between the union and the facility's management. During the late 1970s, a new plant manager was appointed from the United States. Upon taking over the new post, the new plant manager looked around and saw what he believed was overstaffing in certain positions. He instituted a series of cuts, downsizing the operations area, despite the fact that business was good and the plant profitable. Employee response was intense. Surviving employees organized a second union, this one an aggressive bargaining unit, demanding higher wages and job security. Labor costs at the plant rose to unprecedented levels. At the same time, local suppliers to the plant began refusing to do business with it, deeming the organization untrustworthy. A decade after the American plant manager was removed from his job, both the second union and the boycott persisted.

Implied contracts form part of the organization's reputation and public image. Enforcement can occur both in the court of public opinion as well as in the justice system. Many ways of governing and enforcing contracts involve use of third parties and therefore necessitate the use of implied contracts. The arbitrator called in by disputants after a strike must construct an understanding of a reasonable contract between labor and management. As such, the implied contract in a particular contract dispute can be affected by the climate of the times, pressures to settle, and larger society standards for fairness. In many instances, the frame of reference in gauging the terms of an implied contract are larger societal beliefs regarding equity, job property rights, and understanding of legal precedent.

In an example of the blurring of implied contracts with more general cultural beliefs, Forbes and Jones (1986) conducted a telephone survey of

Omaha residents, inquiring about their beliefs in "at-will employment." As a legal precedent, at-will employment means that employers can terminate people for whatever reason, no justification required, based on a Tennessee Supreme Court ruling in 1888. The survey of Omaha residents asked people if organizations had the right to terminate employees without cause and consistently people responded "no." Despite the prevailing Nebraska law at the time, which supported employment at will, the general public believed in some form of job property rights. Social norms can precede legal trends toward recognizing job property rights and a variety of exceptions to at-will employment practices. Thus, what is understood as an implied contract can be anchored by a societal frame of reference.

> No written law has ever been more binding than unwritten custom supported by popular opinion.
>
> —*C. C. Catt at Senate hearings on women's suffrage (1900, as quoted in Carruth & Ehrlich, 1988, p. 326)*

Social contracts are cultural, based on shared, collective beliefs regarding appropriate behavior in a society. One universal norm is that of reciprocity. This ancient and pervasive cultural belief has two minimal demands: People should help those who have helped them and should not injure those who have helped them (Gouldner, 1960). This norm in effect requires the recipient to be grateful to the giver until repayment is made. Thus, both prosocial activities (giving, helping, supporting) and exchanges can create obligations between work groups or within organizations. Explicit linkage between gifts and returns becomes important for demonstrating that a debt has been retired. People typically report that they would remain at least somewhat indebted if they provided assistance to a benefactor of which that person was unaware (Roloff, 1987). The form that repayment takes varies by circumstances (money for money makes it a loan, money for services creates employment). Repaying a friend who helps with your car can involve timing and resources that are different than those the friend provided to you. Social distance (strangers and corporate employers) usually leads to speedier reciprocity; there is a greater tendency for comparable resources to be exchanged and greater monitoring of the exchange (e.g., counting) in distant relations. Most social exchanges need not be immediate (we wait until our friend needs our help to reciprocate) and parties are less likely to keep count when they are intimates (e.g., happily married spouses). When our intimates start counting what each brings to the relationship, we have some reason to question the shape that relationship is in.

Social contracts in business are evident in pervasive notions regarding what is fair treatment. The term *good faith and fair dealing* can have a variety of meanings, depending on the values of the society in which an organization does business. Treatment the elderly receive in a society may be respectful or neglectful depending on the status associated with age and other communal norms. Appropriate treatment of older workers is shaped by the context in which they work.

Though not promise based, social contracts influence how promises are interpreted. Social contracts derive from the values of the larger society. These values affect how other contract forms operate. No promissory contract occurs in a vacuum. Norms of social contract do affect the nature and, most important, the interpretation of promises. Some societies require promises in writing before they are considered binding (e.g., the former Soviet Union). In others, one's word is one's bond. In the United States, acceptance of payment (a consideration) offered in exchange for promise constitutes a binding contract. Whereas social contracts are largely inherited at birth or acquired by membership, promissory contracts are voluntarily entered. Although one pervades a social unit, the other is person specific. National cultures and legal systems shape the meaning of promises. Social contracts are an interpretative backdrop for promises and account to a great extent for differences in contracting across countries (Atiyah, 1981).

ILLUSTRATING SEVERAL TYPES OF CONTRACTS: THE LETTER

Several types of contracts can operate simultaneously in a given organizational event. A small manufacturing firm with a traditional family-oriented culture met with great resistance when it introduced random drug testing. Although the firm's owners themselves underwent drug testing, many employees were outraged. An anonymous letter[2] found its way to the head office (Figure 1.2).

The quote at the top of the letter from Bill Flynn conveys both a value and a commitment that the owner has publicly expressed. Its inclusion and prominence in the letter suggest that it forms the basis of the writer's own *psychological* contract with the company. Statements such as "I thought I understood our relationship" and "I naturally assumed those rights were reciprocal" underscore how interpretive that contract is. That drug testing violated the contract in the eyes of many employees signifies its widely shared, *normative* nature. At the bottom of the letter, in fine print in fact, the reference to the First Amendment suggests that a broader set of societal principles and values, in our terms the *social* contract, are involved in how both the firm's behavior and its employment contract are interpreted. All that we are missing in the substance of the letter is the third party's view of the

"We must continue to nurture our company with great care. It is in loving hands supported by a devoted workforce."

—*Bill Flynn*

An open letter to Messrs. Michael and Bill Flynn

When I came to work for the company, I thought I understood our relationship. I would give an honest day's work and in return I would receive an honest day's wage. When you asked me to sign a non-disclosure agreement last year, I readily agreed with Flynn's rights to its privacy and protection of its interests. I naturally assumed those rights were reciprocal. I thought Flynn respected the rights of its employees and that corporate policy would insure privacy of the individuals working for it. I was certainly mistaken. The introduction of "random drug testing" throws up an impenetrable wall of mistrust and suspicion between Flynn management and employees.

If employees do their work in a manner consistent with standards of quality and excellence that Flynn Corp. expects, then why the need for a humiliating laboratory examination of their personal lives? The previous policy of testing anyone whose work was poor or questionable, while invasive, should suffice to weed out bad elements in the workplace.

This policy has planted the seeds of a cancer in the Flynn corporate body. Fear and resentment can breed disgruntled employees bent on sabotage.

Sincerely,

Anonymous

NOTE: This letter was produced under the auspices of the First Amendment to the Constitution of the United States of America.

FIGURE 1.2. The Letter

implied contract—a viewpoint that you, the reader, can provide. What are reasonable expectations for employees at Flynn considering the details the letter offers (assuming, of course, that they are factual)? What significance, if any, should be given to Bill Flynn's quote, the company's history, the nondisclosure agreement, and use of drug testing and its style of implementation?

The letter illustrates some of the complexities in contract making and contract keeping. Psychological, normative, and implied contracts are all promissory contracts. That is, all three are based on the offer and acceptance of promises. Organizations, like the Flynn Company, abound with promissory contracts, though mutuality can be more of a perception than a reality. Moreover, social contracts, such as the beliefs reflected in the First Amendment, shape social mores with regard to the meaning of events such as random drug testing. Social contracts and their context also affect mores regarding promise making and keeping—in essence, they shape how promissory contracts are understood.

THE FEATURES THAT MAKE A PROMISSORY CONTRACT

This section will describe key features of promissory contracts: types of promise, frames of reference, forms of agreement, and reliance. Understanding how these features come into play can help people make commitments they can keep and avoid inadvertent or mixed messages.

Promises

There are two kinds of promises: warranties and communications of future intent. Warranties are expressions of fact: "This camera (or car or stereo) is in good working order." Facts can be communicated overtly in statements or implicitly by actions. Pharmaceutical companies who sell drugs without any specific warranties can be construed to warrantee the drug as safe. Warranties in employment convey the nature of work and its conditions (i.e., information regarding the job known to the employer in the present). A recent M.B.A. complains of being hired to do market research only to find himself doing direct phone sales—a plausible case of a false warrantee. Unlike promises of future intent, warranties are less subject to ambiguity and uncertainty.

Promises regarding future courses of action express intent. In both employment and customer service, many of the promises expressed involve future courses of action (e.g., career paths and promotion, product service and maintenance). In promising, it is not what the maker intends but what the receiver believes.

1. An *idle promise* is one that is ignored or not taken seriously by the potential recipient. When we ask for help from a coworker who's in a hurry, she may say, "I'll do it later." Based on our prior knowledge of her and sensitivity to the present situation, we could believe this statement (because she never lets us down) or doubt it even if she seems well intentioned (because it's been a long, trying day or because we suspect she'll tell us anything so she can be left alone). Promises that appear to lack credibility

will be ignored or discounted. Because we do not believe idle promises, they are not contractual. We will neither reciprocate nor rely on them. In effect, then, an idle promise does no harm.

2. A *credible promise* is one the recipient believes. This belief is fundamental to creating a contract. Credible promises yield a sequence of reliance and, typically, reciprocity. A group member promises to prepare part of a document for the next meeting. A coworker who relies on the person to do the work will not prepare that part of the document but will do another section instead as part of their bargain. The important thing to know about a credible promise is whether the *recipient* followed through.

3. *Unattended-to promises* are those promises whose follow-through was obstructed. When circumstances do not permit a party to act on promises and there has been no reliance, no harm is done, in effect, and no contract is violated. If an independent consultant contracts to work with a firm but a week later a change in that firm's top management forces termination of the contract, there is little reliance or harm and in effect no contract. Unless a promise is relied upon in some way, it is not acted upon as a contract.

4. *Relied-upon promises,* in which one person acts based on expressions of commitments by another, are the essence of contracts. Reliance occurs when people forgo other opportunities, such as giving up one job because of another offer (promised job). (These forms of reliance constitute opportunity costs in an economic sense and promissory estoppel in a legal one.) Paid-for promises are evident when an employee accepts a transfer based on the offer of a promotion or a buyer purchases a car based on a salesperson's assurance of reliability and quality service.

A gray area between unattended-to and relied-upon contracts occurs when there has been emotional reliance but behaviors have not yet been affected by a promise. If raises have been promised, but a department's budget is cut, employees suffer disappointment but may not as yet have gone out and spent their promised pay increase. Disappointment is, however, a failed expectation and not a breach of contract. Failed expectations yield dissatisfaction and regret (and, I am tempted to say, nothing more, unless a relationship becomes characterized by these), but broken contracts have more serious consequences because of the behavioral reliance they create.

Another form of relied-upon promise is the exchange of promise for a promise. Such is the case when a manager is hired on the promise of the corporation's support of her efforts to turn around her department, division, or company. Increasingly, employment contracts take this form and involve subjectivity on both sides of the arrangement (What is "support" and what constitutes "turnaround"?).

Are promisors bound to perform a contract? There is no reliance when each person exchanges a promise but neither accepts it. ("Let's do lunch." "Sure.") But even if one acts and the other doesn't, there is not necessarily a requirement to perform the contract. If you promise to sell me your car and I give you a check for the asking price, are you bound to sell me your car if you change your mind? In the United States, protections are typically limited to making good any "reliance losses," which may be less than the full promise. So if you refund my money in full, you have made good on our contract. If people are not required to perform the contract, but only to avoid harming the other party, this opens up the possibility of remedies for nonperformance. By substituting a remedy, such as severance bonuses for "lifetime employment," or money-back guarantees instead of customer satisfaction with a product, some flexibility is introduced into the process of making and keeping contracts.

Sanctions for contract breaking in many ways seem mild compared with what might be enforced. This suggest lots of toleration for contract breaking. The opportunity to choose between performing a contract or compensating for damages makes it possible to adapt a variety of relationships to changing circumstances. Because this flexibility in the face of change is probably more valuable in a modern society than in a traditional one, it gives us an idea of perhaps why voluntary contracts have come about in the first place. Contracts permit both cooperation and flexibility.

In summary, turning a promise into a contract means that the promise is to be believed, accepted, and relied upon. But despite the importance of promises to contracts, promise keeping is not the essential theme of contracting. Reducing *reliance losses* is. But the major concern here is how difficult it can be to determine what the actual reliance losses were. You can refund my money if I offer to buy your car and you later change your mind. But I still may resent the loss of my chance to buy another car, which someone else bought instead. Buying people out of their employment contracts is made complex by the fact that jobs are symbolic as well as economic in nature. Work has emotional and social significance, not easily substitutable even with money. We will deal with reliance losses when we discuss remedies for contract violation in Chapter 5.

Limited Frames of Reference

Contracts, despite the trust and interdependence they foster, suffer from the limitations of their makers. The major limitation is not a moral or ethical problem but a cognitive one. People have limited cognitive capacities. The well-known 7 ± 2 rule is the classic example of our limited information processing potential (Miller, 1956). At any one time, a person can consider on average about seven bits of information, down to five in some cases or as great as nine bits in others. This means it is difficult for us to rank order more than seven things (favorite restaurants or high-performing employees) without resorting to some sort of maneuvering (grouping the restaurants by price or type and then ranking, or alternating best with worst employees to make the contrasts greater). The notion of comprehensive contracts, assuming perfect rationality with knowledge of each party's needs and competencies, is inconsistent with what we know to be real-life cognitive limits of individuals. We can't think of everything! Add to this problem the incomplete amount of available information (about each party's skills and capabilities as well as the uncertain future) and the idea of a contract covering all contingencies in detail becomes virtually an impossibility.

These cognitive limits lead to two parties to the same interaction focusing on different bits of information in creating their understanding of the contract. Contracts are "constructions," an image or idea created by interpreting what a promise or commitment means. These constructions emerge from the information each party focuses on. Consider the typical new-car warrantee, which might specifically guarantee only against mechanical defects. A warrantee is a statement of fact that someone has promised to be true (i.e., that this car has no mechanical defects). Customers might assume that the dealer will also warrantee exterior trim and postsale work commissioned through the dealership, though the dealer may explicitly promise no such thing. Most dealerships seeking to retain customer business will honor the customer's interpretation of the contract (service being defined by what the customer believes it should be and less by what the dealer actually warranties or promises). The statement "the customer is always right" honors the power of that psychological contract. Because people have cognitive limits (no one can think of all contingencies when a formal deal is made) and different frames of reference (so service means different things to dealers and customers), we expect that different interpretations can be held by parties who believe that their promises are mutually agreed on. Not only can people only know so much—but there is only so much to know. Contracts are about the future: present intent and future behavior. Yet the future cannot be accurately predicted. The longer the contract's duration, the more incomplete it will have to be.

Completeness is not a fact of contracts. But it can be a goal if parties are willing to keep updating their arrangements as circumstances change. In socializing new recruits, firms such as Teletronix have found it helpful to develop programs such as Fast Start in which recruits and their new managers independently rate their job priorities and expected results to clarify the newcomer's role as well as foster a working relationship between newcomer and manager. In this way, the initial employment contract can continue to be clarified. Moreover, periodic updates of these perceptions allow employees and their managers to reality-test their current understandings against each other's points of view and changing circumstances.

Mutuality and Acceptance

Creation of a contract hinges on the belief that an agreement exists. How do we judge whether this is true? Communication is the essence of promise. If one makes a promise in a letter and then puts the letter in a drawer, there is no contract. In studies of cooperation behavior in groups (when there is some incentive not to), promises to cooperate substantially increase cooperation rates, but only when everyone in the group makes an overt promise (Orbell, van de Kraft, & Dawes, 1988). Such studies suggest that both public affirmation of a promise and trust that the other is acting in good faith are required to create a credible promise. Public assent by each partner promotes belief in agreement by both parties and provides evidence to third parties of a deal's existence. Filling out an application form, showing up at the office, and endorsing the back of a paycheck are expressions of some form of promise and acceptance in employment.

Although mutuality is largely tested indirectly (i.e., observation of the other party for good faith efforts), testing declines markedly once promises are accepted. Because trust and reliance are a result of contracting and reduce the need for monitoring and control, we would expect that testing for mutuality is event related (initially and when violations occur) rather than ongoing. Often, when the consequences of not keeping contracts are greatest, we may actually seek fewer efforts to test for mutuality or agreement. Veteran employees who make more critical decisions for their company often are subject to far less scrutiny than newer members. In longer term alliances, performance monitoring may be less and trust higher. Contract acceptance can increase trust and reduce tests of mutuality or agreement.

The fact of hiring or being hired makes public some form of promise. Payment (referred to in law as a "consideration") makes it clear that circumstances were conceived to render a promise morally binding and deserving of legal protection. There is, in fact, some debate as to whether promises have to be paid for to be contractual or whether acceptance of payment merely makes more tangible the fact of a promise. But payment does tend to change a promise's meaning. Payment shows that someone is relying on a promise and promotes that promise from an idle statement to a credible commitment. In a sense, an individual who receives a promise doesn't have to pay for it to know that a promise was made. The payment serves to convey to *others* that a promise was offered.

Underscoring the voluntary nature of contracts, acceptance is critical to motivate individuals to acknowledge and comply with them. A sense of choice (e.g., between taking this job or refusing it) underlies willingness to be bound to a contract. As researchers of goal setting (Latham & Saari, 1979) have found, people perform highly when they accept the goals assigned to them. As the rate of organizational change escalates (through downsizing, restructurings, mergers, and acquisitions), people often find themselves members of organizations whose conditions of employment are no longer what they agreed to when hired. It is risky to assume acceptance of contracts by employees (e.g., commitment to conditions of employment) if significant changes have occurred since the individual was hired. Unless individuals perceive alternatives (i.e., some form of choice such as jobs elsewhere), the existence of a psychological contract can be questioned due to the absence of real acceptance. Not surprisingly, veteran employees from one organization may continue to play by the rules they learned from the organization that hired them, resulting in lower performance on any newly introduced standard. Lower performance, resistance to change, and unwillingness to assimilate to a new culture and ways of doing business are symptomatic of a contract that is not accepted.

Contract acceptance requires active expression of willingness to commit oneself. Some of the difficulties organizations face following mergers and acquisitions can stem from the failure to foster new contract acceptance when new owners or new strategies come into play. When acquiring another company, it may be necessary to create a sense of joining up on the part of employees. In the case of RR Donnelly, a commercial publisher (e.g., phone books and catalogues) moving increasingly into the electronic (and nongraphic) information business, employees moved from traditional Donnelly publishing businesses into acquired businesses are often asked to actually recruit into the new company. Recruitment entails all the trappings of a new hire: Donnelly veterans complete an application form and interview with potential managers and coworkers. This process facilitates acceptance of a new work role in the more competitive and changing information side of Donnelly businesses. Signaling acceptance is key to creating a viable contract.

IMPLICATIONS

We need a new lexicon for contracts to understand the many forms they take in organizations. The three basic promise-based contracts are the individual's psychological contract, the normative contract shared by members of a social group, and the implied contract understood by third parties. Because *promise* has different meanings across situations and cultures, cultural values affect the meaning of promissory contracts. The basic building block of contracts in organizations is the individual employee's, employer's, or customer's psychological contract. Contracts are created by promises, reliance, acceptance, and a *perception* of mutuality. How much people agree on contract terms is a major factor in shaping the operation of the contract. Cognitive limits, limited information, and different frames of reference make it likely that people will hold different views regarding the existence and meaning of contracts. Contracts based on some degree of mutuality are the basis of flexibility in emerging organizations and enterprises.

There is something basic and essential about agreements between people on future courses of action. They make possible planning, mutual cooperation, delayed gratification, and effective deployment of resources. In a real sense, contracts *create* resources. Because we trust in reciprocity, we can ask another for help knowing that we can eventually repay it (and what we do for that person tomorrow will be more valuable than what we have to offer them today). Contracts make possible many new organizational alliances, ventures, and forms.

In their book *The Virtual Corporation,* Davidow and Malone (1992) describe LSI Logic's development of a contractual relationship with customers and underscore its psychological quality. As a chip maker, LSI Logic was engaged in rigid contractual procedures with the customers it supplied—until it discovered that it could manufacture and deliver new products faster than customers could move the contracts through their legal departments. LSI chose to ship products on telephone orders and let the paperwork follow weeks or sometimes months later. The tight time frames of high-tech manufacturing mean that parties need to be protected against bad faith by means other than formal documents. At LSI Logic, trust between the parties created an interdependence that protects against bad faith and results in greater efficiency. For organizations and workers to function successfully, an understanding of how contracts work is critical.

NOTE

1. Taken from a *Dear Abby* column by Abigail Van Buren, August 1, 1988. Dist. by *Universal Press Syndicate*. Reprinted with permission. All rights reserved.
2. The letter has been slightly edited for reasons of confidentiality and brevity.

2 Contract Making

In Shakespeare's *Richard II,* the Duchess of York seeks mercy for her son from Henry IV. Not satisfied with the royal pardon, she demands, "Speak it again. . . . Twice saying 'pardon' doth not pardon twain, But makes one pardon strong" (4.3).

People think contractually. When we believe a person *intends* to *keep* a commitment he or she has made, we rely on it. Similarly, knowing someone relies on us pressures us to keep our commitments. This chapter describes why people keep promises, and how promises turn into contracts. It will also detail how the three forms of promissory contracts (psychological, normative, and implied) come about.

Thinking contractually means

1. believing one has made a commitment and is therefore bound to some future action,
2. relying on the understandings one has regarding commitments received from others,
3. when faced with competing alternatives, making choices based on the relative harm involved in honoring and not honoring those commitments.

Commitments, like all promises, are subjective. Any promise has two sides: the promisor's and the promisee's. Both our own interpretations and situational factors influence how promises are understood and kept. An engineer accepted a job with one employer and was offered "the job of a lifetime" by another firm the next week. He came to my office and asked, "Is it right for me to tell the first company I've changed my mind after they flew me out to meet with them and I accepted their offer?" Before choosing a course of action, the engineer considers what he has committed to by accepting that job offer, the cost to the first employer if he doesn't take the job, and the costs to himself of forgoing the "dream job." Is he bound to accept it? The first employer's losses are weighed if the engineer reneges, including its recruiting costs such as travel for him and his spouse, and the opportunity costs of giving up job offers to other qualified candidates. Although the relative harm to himself and the first employer is weighed by the engineer, contractual thinking is not a simple calculus of losses and gains. It is also an interpretation and reconstruction of commitments.

WHY DO PEOPLE KEEP PROMISES?

From the promisor's point of view, there are many reasons to keep a promise:

Acceptance. Making a commitment to do something in the future is a form of goal setting. All these statements are goals: "I will pay you X." "I will help you learn the skills required to advance in this organization." "I will deliver it to you on Monday." A stated goal, if made willingly, is one the maker is likely to agree with and accept. Goals people commit to are a major determinant of performance (Locke, Shaw, Saari, & Latham, 1981). But the key feature in the relationship of goals to performance is whether the goal is *accepted.* Promisors who intend to meet their commitments have, in a sense, set and accepted a goal for themselves.

Self-Image and Esteem. People act in ways that promote consistency in how they see themselves. To those individuals valuing consistency in word and deed, there is considerable self-generated pressure to follow through on commitments made both publicly and privately. This follow-through is greatest when individuals believe they have a high degree of control over circumstances and cannot easily attribute contract violation to situational factors. Experiments attempting to induce contract breaking have found individuals highly reluctant to violate a contract, unless the incentives for doing so are made highly salient (e.g., greatly increasing the amount of money offered by another employer; Shanteau & Harrison, 1991).

Imagery Formed by the Act of Promising. People who make an overt statement of promise may have, in effect, exercised the fact of that promise in their minds. To make a promise about a future course of action can cause one to imagine oneself engaging in that action, itself a form of activity. When people visualize themselves engaging in an activity, the chances that they will actually perform that activity are increased. For this reason, therapists often use imagery to overcome client resistance to certain activities such as public speaking or confronting one's boss. Vivid acts of promise (e.g., convincing a potential employer that we know precisely how to deal with a given situation) are more likely to be acted on.

Reliance Losses. Despite the tolerance for contract violation described in Chapter 1, contract makers are typically reluctant to violate agreements in ways that they believe would create losses for another party. We call a friend to say we'll be late to a scheduled lunch, but if we can't reach him or her, we try harder to get to the lunch on time. A good deal of adjustments made in contracting are attempts to reduce reliance losses.

Social Pressure and Concern for Reputation. Where promise keeping is a social norm, social pressure is a factor in enforcing contracts. In industries and occupations where individual behavior is often visible to a wide public (e.g., academia), reputation promotes promise keeping: "It's a small field and a long life." In a famous media event from the 1970s, Lee Iacocca, chief executive officer of Chrysler Corporation, repaid a government loan made to keep Chrysler in business—several years before the note was due. When reputation is important, contract completion may go beyond mere compliance.

Incentives. Because contracts are voluntary, there must be some benefit to each party for making the contract in the first place—promises of future benefit for present efforts or rewarding people for entering into an agreement. But rewards play a complex role in contract keeping. There is a difference between rewards for making the contract and rewards for keeping it. The incentives attached to accepting a job offer (e.g., opportunity for steady income) are often different than the rewards for doing the work itself (e.g., pay for performance versus pay for membership). The value of incentives may change once the contract is made and performance begins. Shanteau and Harrison (1991) experimented with incentives for contract violation by increasing the financial rewards to subjects for quitting the employer for whom they had promised to work. Not until the rewards were made high and very salient did a plurality of subjects show willingness to break the contract. Thus, even when the incentives for contract keeping decline, the contract still may be executed.

Promise keeping is a major feature of maintaining contractual agreements. It is likely to be greatest in the following situations:

1. People are conscious of making a promise and are committed to keeping it.
2. People perceive high degrees of personal control. Individuals are likely to keep promises when they feel capable of doing so and break them when they feel powerless to do otherwise. Situational factors, such as economic problems, can compromise promise keeping.

3. Individuals have personality types with a high internal locus of control or strong ethical or moral standards affecting their behavior, making them resistant to situational pressures and constraints.
4. Knowledge is easily available regarding the effect of breach on others (when the other parties to the contract are highly visible to the promisor, such as one's coworkers or immediate staff). When the promisee is relatively distant from the promisor (employees at lower levels in a large firm) or when one party is relatively invisible to the other (e.g., individual stockholders), breach of promise is more likely.
5. Social norms support promise keeping as appropriate behavior. Stable work groups, whose norms are intact, will demonstrate more promise keeping than unstable ones. When there is a long history of contract breach (e.g., repeated downsizing), such changes erode promise-keeping norms.

use in motivation paragraph

HOW ORGANIZATIONS USE PROMISE-KEEPING MECHANISMS: AN EXAMPLE FROM GENERAL ELECTRIC

Organizations actively express promises and make use of vivid imagery, social norms, and consequences of violation in creating commitments with employees. Mutually binding promises or contracts can be expressed explicitly to motivate people and focus their efforts in support of business goals and strategy. In a 1992 annual report to GE shareholders, Jack Welch conveyed four types of contract terms for GE managers/leaders:

1. "One who delivers on commitments—financial or otherwise—and shares the values of our Company. His or her future is an easy call. Onward and upward."
2. "One who does not meet commitments and does not share our values. Not as pleasant a call, but equally easy."
3. "One who misses commitments but shares the values. He or she usually gets a second chance, preferably in a different environment."
4. "The fourth type—the most difficult for many of us to deal with. That leader delivers on commitments, makes all the numbers, but doesn't share the values we must have. This is the individual who typically forces performance out of people rather than inspires it: the autocrat, the big shot, the tyrant . . . whether we can convince and help these managers to change . . . or part company with them . . . will determine the future of the mutual trust and respect we are building" (Welch & Hood, 1992, unpaginated).

This public statement serves several purposes. It communicates what GE promises to do in response to its managers' efforts and spells out what managers need to do to realize that promise. It creates social pressure to support contract keeping, evoking negative images of those who would breach the contract ("big shot," "tyrant"), and appeals to a larger sense of belonging, trust, and respect. This text also expresses a number of related messages to shareholders and employees: that culture change is a major component of GE's business strategy, that members will receive support in this change, that good faith efforts to change will be rewarded, and that if there are trade-offs between short-term performance and long-term development they will be at the expense of the short term. It provides us with an example of several drivers supporting promise keeping: goal acceptance, self-esteem, imagery, and social pressure.

This kind of statement both articulates a contract and signals developments in GE's culture. Often efforts to change a culture signify changes in the psychological contract, possibly one of the most difficult features of culture change. Contracts can become deeply rooted mind-sets intertwined with past commitments and visions of the future.

THE CONTRACT AS A "MENTAL MODEL"

Promise-based contracts, as we have seen, exist in three forms: the individual's psychological contract, the social group's normative contract, and the third party's implied contract. Each has its own interpretative framework, but all three involve a mental model or image.

A contract is a mental model that people use to frame events such as promises, acceptance, and reliance. The promises that make up contracts have no objective meaning. Promises ultimately are perceptions of what was sent and what was meant. Perceptions are not simply passive interpretations of reality; people create their meaning for many events. The close supervision one person sees as controlling may seem supportive and helpful to her coworker. Two siblings close in age still may not recollect similarly the events of their childhood. Similarly, two people in the same setting can have different psychological contracts.

Yet reality is not constructed wholly in the minds of individuals. Groups sometimes do agree on events and their meaning. A sheet metal plant's production workers might agree that their organization supports teamwork or punishes poor performance. Investment bankers may share a belief that their firm rewards those who make profitable deals. These examples suggest that members have some common interpretation or social construction of organizational events and their meaning. Agreement between ourselves and others helps foster the view that a promise is real and can be relied on. Such agreement helps create normative contracts.

Social psychologists Uriel Foa and Edna Foa (1974) argue that our knowledge of the world enters the mind not as raw data but in an already interpreted form called "structures." Structures can change but resist doing so. Borrowing an example from Foa and Foa, consider our coworker Joe and the clothes he wears. When Joe wears a new suit, what this means to us depends on what we know of Joe and our work setting. If we know Joe to be disinterested in fashion, we are more likely to actively interpret this behavior. If Joe were known as a "clotheshorse," we might ignore him and his new suit. But if we know Joe has a big presentation, we might think that he is trying to impress a client or the boss. We could infer that Joe is willing to alter his appearance for social reasons, thus creating a new structure in our thinking about him ("ambitious" or perhaps "insecure"). Because we would ignore Joe's clothes if he wore the same old thing, cognitive structures can be seen to provide continuity. Our mental models change only when new information is discrepant and not readily interpretable using the old model. For structures to be created or patterns recognized, some information must be ignored while other information is emphasized. Because events are categorized into classes, being aware of the classes people employ makes it possible to understand the meaning they give to events.

Knowing the model people use helps us to understand how they come to understand their employment contract. Consider Sheet Metal Company (SMC), a leader in its markets but undergoing tough times due to a dependency on the automobile industry as its major customer. In a survey of this organization, lower level managers in one division provided answers to several questions regarding their psychological contract:

1. What did your organization promise you 5 years ago? What do they promise you today?
2. What did you owe in return 5 years ago? What do you owe them today?

As a group, SMC managers reported that 5 years ago SMC offered them job security and good salaries in exchange for their loyalty and hard work (Table 2.1). But greater competitive pressures, combined with cuts in the number of suppliers used by the automobile industry and other manufacturing firms, have created a push within SMC to meet short-term sales goals while trying to change their relationship with the market and support the business's growth. The majority of these managers see *today's* contract as working to help the business grow and to develop their staff's technical and marketing skills. Generous salaries were still the most salient reported return to these managers. Both change and stability are evident—though today's contract appears to be a somewhat more demanding version of its predecessor.

TABLE 2.1 Sheet Metal Company

Employees With More Than 5 Years With Firm	
What did SMC promise you 5 years ago?	What did you owe in return 5 years ago?
■ job security and stable environment ■ future growth and challenges	■ loyalty ■ honest day's work ■ "doing my best"
What do they promise you today?	What do you owe in return today?
■ future growth and challenges	■ investment in time and ideas, willingness to grow "to be the best"
Manager	
What did you promise?	What did they owe you?
■ job latitude ■ recognition ■ generous compensation	■ hard work and creativity to improve results of existing businesses
What do you promise now?	What do they owe you now?
■ very generous compensation ■ dismissal if failure occurs	■ above average results ■ development of subordinate skills ■ loyalty to owners
Newer Employees	
Company promises me:	I promise in return:
■ fair compensation for goal success ■ growth potential	■ performance that attains goals

The division manager in this largely decentralized firm has a different view. When he was asked to describe the contract made 5 years ago and then asked what he was conveying today, the division manager indicated a push to meet goals and produce results. He went on to stress the threat of job loss for those managers whose goals were not met. Why don't these reports match? Self-serving biases are clearly a factor. Employees may think they are doing a fine job by responding with extra efforts over and above what they used to give, and therefore feel they deserve high salaries. Their manager, in control of their compensation, may play up in his own mind, or in his reports to the researcher, the importance of that control and his willingness to be tough. Moreover, because the manager is less likely to be hurt by these changes (e.g., his performance may not be threatened by the new goals), he may be more willing to change.

Another factor is evident in the contrasting viewpoints of SMC newcomers and veterans. Newcomers (those with less than 5 years' SMC experience) described a contract that coincided much more closely with that of the division manager. Both newcomers and the division manager emphasize the importance of accomplishing performance goals and achieving financial growth in obtaining high levels of compensation. Why would newcomers report a deal more closely in line with their manager? Recall that the psychological contract people use to think about their jobs and guide their actions is one they have accepted. For many people, the only operative contract is the one *they were hired under.* Newcomers brought in during a different economic situation, and after the firm changed its business strategy, are likely to be party to a deal closer to their manager's current understanding of the business and its needs. Veterans may gauge compensation practices and statements of their manager in terms of their previously established contract. If old contracts persist until new ones are accepted, effective changes in existing contracts must focus on generating acceptance of new ones. Veterans are aware of the different performance standards of then and now but underestimate the organization's commitment to aggressively pursue a new strategy. Unless their models change, veterans are at risk of underperforming by the new rules. In the case of SMC, the contract of 5 years ago remains the "mental model" for most of its current employees.

Mental models cue people to what events they should expect and how they should interpret them. These models play a role in all three forms of contract: psychological, normative, and implied. The differences in the models reflect the distinct *information* available to the interpreter.

Our understanding of contracts as mental models is based on the fact that individuals are discontinuous processors of information. Discontinuous information processing means the following:

- Contract-related information is *sought* only at certain times.
- Contract-related information is actively *processed* at certain times.
- Contracts tend to endure until a noticeable signal conveys a break or interruption (i.e., punctuation).

People process information in two ways: (a) systematic-controlled and (b) automatic. Controlled information processing is used in novel situations where there is little prior experience to fall back on. Here information is actively sought and carefully processed to make a high-quality decision. This type of decision making is often characterized as "rational" (Sims & Gioia, 1986). Models of rational decision making such as expectancy theory (Vroom, 1964) tend to work well in accounting for behavior in nonroutine situations (e.g., choosing a career) but do less well in trying to explain routine behaviors such as sustained levels of performance (Wanous, Keon, & Latack, 1983). Once experience accumulates with a particular decision or task, systematic decision processes give way to reliance on automatic processes using established mental models and routines. The first time a chef prepares a dish involves very different information processing than the hundredth time. Mental models that organize knowledge in a systematic way are schemas. Schemas organize experience in meaningful ways and make it possible for people to deal with ambiguity in well-practiced ways and predict what should happen next. If people have experience with travel, marketing, or damage control, there are schemas for planning a trip, introducing a new product, or breaking bad news. Once a schema is formed, there is less review of current facts and circumstances and more reliance on what is already known.

A contract is one type of schema developed through experience. It may be created by controlled, rational processes (e.g., what's in it for me, what evidence is there that I can trust the other party), but once created, contracts become more automatic. The newcomers and veterans in Sheet Metal Company display two different sets of schemas (contracts) existing side by side based on whether people were hired in the 1970s or the 1990s. As there is a great tendency to continue a contract, the schemas people form are stable and predictive of future behavior. People do not necessarily work hard on changing schemas. People work hard on fitting experiences into them. Changes at SMC are seen through the lens of the contract each member holds.

Because of discontinuous information processing, people often see what they expect to see, gather information only when they think they need it, and ignore a lot. Several years into a major reorientation focusing on customers, teamwork, and quality, a Xerox executive encountered a manager who mentioned that he had taken his team with him to go through a refresher training course. The executive asked why the course was needed given the company's sustained change efforts. Kearns and Nadler (1992) provide the manager's response:

> "Because I never paid much attention the first time through, since I thought this thing would be gone by now. I thought it was just another ice cream flavor. But I got scared when I saw that [the new CEO] had picked it up with vigor. So we know we can't hide in the weeds anymore." (p. 236)

Because schemas are stable and events are viewed in preconceived ways, a lot of external change is unnoticed or ignored. People do not continuously seek and scan for information, nor do the groups or organizations they create. Recruits ask a lot of questions while they are newcomers and, once they start getting the answers they expect, they stop asking. Veterans may do little inquiring at all. Organizations tell things to newcomers that they would never bother mentioning to a longtimer (e.g., how to do his or her job better).

Active information gathering tends to be triggered by events. Triggers evoke information-gathering schemas—signaling "this is the time to ask questions" (e.g., recruiting for a job in a new firm, introducing a new CEO for a family business who is not one of the family). Information is processed when there is a felt need for it (e.g., old information doesn't seem to work) and otherwise pretty well ignored. Events will punctuate the contract when they signal or are interpreted to mean (a) an existing contract is completed, (b) a new contract is being created, or (c) both.

In contract making, we expect that the broadest search for information is early on in the initial phases of establishing a relationship. Organizations usually make active efforts to socialize newcomers (and try to socialize veterans only in times of change) when individuals are actively seeking information (what to do, what to expect, the "ropes to skip and the ropes to know"). Moreover, there is a sort of contract-making schema for new hires; people believe it is both necessary and appropriate to give and receive commitments at this time.

Part of the reason people keep the contract they were hired with is that they may only look for contract-related information *when they join* the organization. The more general point here is that contract-related information is likely to be recognized, gathered, or sought when people believe it is either necessary or appropriate to do so. New hires or transferees or members of newly acquired organizations, unlike veterans, are more likely to notice, seek out, and observe information related to the conditions of their employment (e.g., job demands or requirements, inducements and rewards). Otherwise, people may not get the message when it is sent or seek one out when understandings don't mesh.

In a study of how engineers learn the cultures of their company, information gathering practices were found to change dramatically from the first year to the third year with the company (Gundry & Rousseau, 1994). Engineers were asked to describe how they learned about what the organization expected from them. Each indicated "critical incidents" in which they came to understand the company's expectations. The engineers reported events and indicated how they interpreted what they meant:

> 95% of the people here are more than willing to answer technical questions. One senior engineer took a whole hour of his personal time to answer . . . my questions. . . . He said, "In order to make an omelette, you have to break a few eggs. The same applies to electronics." Meaning you have to make a few mistakes in order to learn.

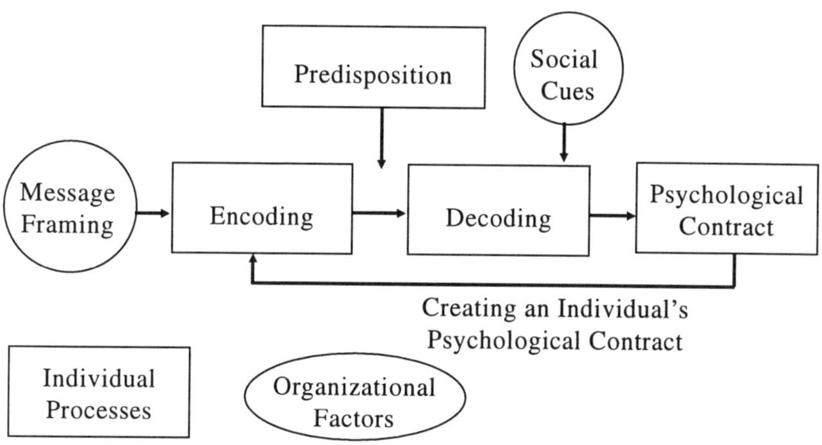

FIGURE 2.1. Creating an Individual's Psychological Contract

> During the first three or four weeks of my employment, I was given little or no guidance by my boss in regard to the job I was performing and how it would benefit me in future assignments. The tasks I was performing were remedial at best . . . all [my boss] could say was that there was nothing else for me to work on . . . [meaning] this organization does not really emphasize performance or accountability. (Gundry & Rousseau, 1994, p. 1075)

Supervisor-related incidents are the most frequent with both supportiveness of supervisor and supervisor-subordinate conflict reported frequently. Controlling for the length of time these engineers were members of the organization, the rate of critical incidents reported declined over time. Not only are there fewer surprises for engineers to encounter, but also they cease to observe events around them in the same way once a pattern or schema is established. Information gathering behavior shifts with time and familiarity with the setting. Ashford (1986) explored the use of two feedback-seeking strategies: monitoring (observation) and inquiry (direct requests for information). She found that the perceived value of information is the major determinant of both forms of feedback seeking. Moreover, it is organizational tenure and not job tenure that best predicts information gathering. Changing jobs within the same firm does not necessarily signal to people the need for or value of new information regarding performance expectations and organizational rewards. Organization changes do cue the need for more information when they signal legitimate or inevitable change. Ease of information availability coupled with its perceived benefits shape the contract-relevant information obtained by organization members at all stages of their careers.

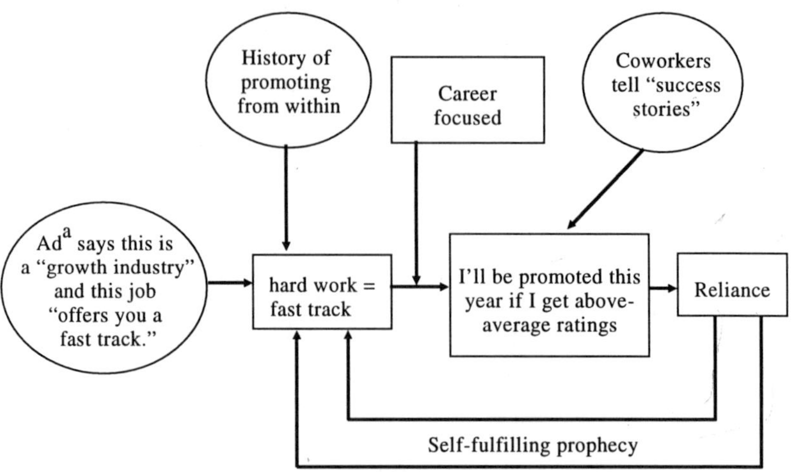

FIGURE 2.2. Illustration of a Psychological Contract
NOTE: a. Top 2% of performers are promoted within a year.

A THEORY OF PSYCHOLOGICAL CONTRACTING

We now turn to describing how the mental model of a contract is created, and to considerations of how an individual's psychological contract is formed. The two individual parties whose psychological contracts we focus on here will be the employee and the employer/organization. (These could also be a client, customer, supplier, or any other interdependent party.) A series of organizational and individual processes affect the creation of a psychological contract (Figures 2.1 and 2.2).

Two sets of factors operate in forming the psychological contract: external messages and social cues from the organization or social setting and the individual's internal interpretations, predispositions, and constructions. Consider the scenario that creates the psychological contract of a bank's newly hired loan officer, Anne Lee. Anne applies for a job with the bank after reading an ad and several informational brochures saying, "This is a growth industry." The interviewer, eager to recruit a competent young woman, indicates that the job offers "fast track" advancement to those who commit themselves to the organization. An ambitious person, Anne takes the job. Her new coworkers talk about the bank's history of promoting from within. They explain that most senior managers started at the bank's entry levels and that the current president, a member of the bank's founding family, is committed to growth and has targeted several areas for expansion. The message received by Anne Lee is that "hard work puts you on the fast track here." In her day-to-day decisions, Anne concentrates on achieving growth targets and learning the business, and as a career-oriented individual looks forward to her first annual performance review. The message that "hard work puts you on the fast track" elevates her efforts in the course of her first year at the bank, and she anticipates what her next assignment will be. When her colleagues tell her "success stories" of previous loan officers' advancement, specific features of her contract take shape: Anne expects to be promoted this year if she gets high ratings. Relying on that belief, she prepares to sacrifice her social life to attain the promised fast track. She also begins to anticipate how much she'll gain from the next job (challenge, a sense of accomplishment, more status), vicariously enjoying her next achievement. She relies on her contract both behaviorally and emotionally.

Walking through this scenario again, as described in Figure 2.2, we can highlight the processes involved in the creation of a psychological contract. Anne applied for a job with the bank after reading an ad and several informational brochures saying, "This is a growth industry" (organizational messages). The interviewer, eager to recruit competent young women, indicates that the job can offer "fast track" advancement to those who really commit themselves to the organization (organizational message). An ambitious person, Anne takes the job. Coworkers she meets talk about the history in the bank, as in many other banks, of promoting from within (social cues). Most senior managers started at the bank's entry levels and the current president, a member of the founding family, is committed to growing the organization and has targeted several areas for expansion (organizational messages). The message received by Anne Lee is that "hard work puts you on the fast track here" (encoding the message). In her day-to-day decisions, Anne concentrates on achieving growth targets and learning the business, and as a career-oriented individual (her individual predisposition) looks forward to her upcoming (annual) performance review. The message she heard, "Hard work puts you on the fast track," elevates her efforts on the job in the course of her first year at the bank as she anticipates what her next assignment there will be (reliance). When her colleagues tell her "success stories" of how several of the previous loan officers advanced (social cues), specific features of her contract take shape: Anne expects to be promoted this year if she gets high-level ratings (decoding of the messages). Relying on that belief, she'll forgo other things she enjoys doing, including time with friends, to attain the promised fast track. She also starts anticipating how much she'll gain from the next job (challenge, a sense of accomplishment, more status), a sort of vicarious enjoyment of her next achievement. She relies on that contract both behaviorally and emotionally (reliance on the contract).

The Anne Lee scenario contains the elements essential to psychological contract creation: external messages and social cues (offering expressions and interpretation of the firm's future intent) and individual cognitions and predispositions (what messages she receives, her interpretations, and her own personal style of processing this information). Figure 2.1 outlines the basic framework and Figure 2.2 depicts the features of Anne Lee's specific experience. The following are the basic elements in psychological contract creation, both external and internal to the individual contract holder.

EXTERNAL FACTORS

Messages organizations send, and social cues coworkers and work groups provide, are the basic external contributors to psychological contracts.

Messages

Organizations convey commitments through events signaling intentions for the future. Whether organizations actually have intentions is arguable, but clearly their agents (managers, recruiters, and coworkers) do. Events that convey future plans (to grow the business), proposed actions (introducing a compensation system), or even references to past company actions or practices (a tradition of stable employment), all imply some anticipated future. Events expressing plans for the future, of course, signal commitments. Such events often occur during personnel actions (hiring, socialization, promotion, developmental activities) or during organizational changes (e.g., announcement of restructurings, strategic shifts).

Organizations express various forms of commitment in an ongoing and relatively continuous fashion. Behavioral events involving communication of promises include the following:

- *Overt statements:* "People with the right values will get a second chance" (Jack Welch, GE).
- *Observation* of treatment of others perceived as party to the same deal. Cutbacks at one General Dynamics defense plant can influence its employees elsewhere regarding the firm's intentions toward them.
- *Expression of organizational policy,* including manuals, handbooks, compensation systems, and other personnel/human resource-related structures.
- *Social constructions*—references to history or reputation: "Remember the last recession, they cut the workweek but everybody kept their jobs."

Overt statements are perhaps the most powerful, because they have the potential to actively manage the meaning people ascribe to an organization's actions and expressed intentions. Following Jack Welch's statement to shareholders, it is likely that terminations of veteran members who managed by the numbers would be seen as commitment to change rather than insensitive treatment of employees.

Actions may speak louder than words, but action without words leads to misinterpretation. A bank president interested in supporting his managers took a longtime veteran who had made a number of blunders and gave him a less demanding assignment. Feeling pleased with his positive and supportive management style, the president was surprised to learn a few months later that people were upset that such a respected veteran employee had been "sent to Lower Slobovia for no good reason." Not communicating the purpose of the action was a failure to manage its meaning. In contrast, Jack Welch of GE appears to be managing the meaning observers and participants associate with future promotions and terminations.

Observations of how others are treated are a readily available source of information regarding one's own relationship with the organization. Observations send messages in two ways: proactively, when the organization initiates some action (e.g., promotion, layoff) that individuals must react to and interpret, and passively, when organizational actions are monitored by individual employees needing further information about their status and relationship to the organization. In essence, organizations are always sending messages—intentionally or otherwise. This is consistent with the saying, "Half the promises never kept were never made." On the other hand, even when messages are deliberately conveyed, members pay attention to them only when motivated to do so. People are not always actively seeking information. They do so when they feel a need for it, or when the situation signals the importance of doing so. Because information is processed episodically rather than continuously, some observations will have more impact than others.

Vicarious learning is a large part of how organizations socialize members. Joel Brockner (1988) has identified "survivor effects" whereby what happens to peers affects one's beliefs regarding one's employer's future behavior. Because most organizational actions toward members have witnesses, there are any number of critical incidents that can occur to signal promise or its absence to those who believe themselves party to the same employment deal. In a recent study of newly recruited engineers, the most common critical incidents reported were conflicts between one's boss and other subordinates—most of these incidents were seen as negatives, indicating the boss could not be trusted or did not treat the subordinate fairly (Gundry & Rousseau, 1994). How coworkers are treated can shape people's beliefs about their own entitlements (or lack of them). Along these lines, people often rely on *referent others,* or people we use when we need some point of comparison, who also provide observations conveying contract terms. How much support can one reasonably expect from the boss, the company, or one's coworkers? Individuals who feel the need to obtain such information typically look toward people of similar background, job function, and demographic charcteristics—age, education, year hired—to observe how those people are treated and what experiences the individual is likely to have in turn. Beliefs individuals hold about their own contract are likely to be more greatly affected by observations of people who are believed to be party to the same contract. People who work for Xerox don't look to those who work at IBM to understand their own employment relationship. But newcomer Xerox sales representatives in Chicago may look to Xerox sales representatives in Hartford and other newcomers locally in forming their own contractual beliefs.

Expressions of policy include the organization's documents (e.g., faculty handbooks), compensation systems (as formally conveyed or informally understood), titles, and promotion practices. Although seemingly objective, these are subject to interpretations as well.

Messages abound in corporate personnel practices. Basing a compensation system on seniority can convey the organization's intention to reward employees who loyally remain with the firm, earning less now but anticipating salary raises in future. Other employers may base compensation on seniority in the hope of creating a general sense of internal equity and fairness, without intending any future commitments to individuals. The terms the organization and its members use to describe senior employees and newcomers also send messages subject to interpretation. The virtual abandonment of the term *permanent employee* in the United States (used to distinguish probationary employees from those past that stage) has come about as an attempt to avoid signaling a commitment to long-term employment.

Pay levels and how they are interpreted provide another example of a policy-based expression of the contract. High-wage organizations tend to have better quality employees (Brown & Medoff, 1989). In the absence of complete and accurate information, job applicants make inferences about nonpecuniary job attributes based on what they know about relative pay levels. (High pay may signal a successful organization or generosity to employees.) Applicants for exempt positions often have an opportunity to gather information on other job attributes through plant visits or other means. Nevertheless, pay is always one of the more visible and probably one of the most important attributes in such decisions (to the extent that organizations monitor it closely so as not to get out of line with other firms; Gerhart & Milkovich, 1990). Although pay level is only one attribute among many, evidence suggests it is critical to being considered an "employer of choice" (Milkovich & Newman, 1990, p. 198). Pay levels convey a commitment to sustain that level of pay, because wages tend not to decline and differences in pay across levels and length of service signal what is rewarded.

Personnel arrangements such as compensation and benefits are also subject to interpretation, and yet the organization is likely to do little to manage the meaning members ascribe to them. Employees often underestimate their employer's benefit contributions, sometimes believing that employers contribute nothing at all toward their health care benefits. This need to educate employees regarding benefits has recently been recognized by Northwestern University, which sent around a letter summarizing the annual contributions that Northwestern and the employee make toward that employee's benefit package.

Although organizational policy, as conveyed in personnel manuals and handbooks, seems in one sense to be objective and fact based, most people do not read such documents until they have a good reason to. Employees go looking for a copy of the handbook when they feel mistreated or have a question regarding the appropriateness of some policy or action. Manuals are not contract making but in fact convey a discrepancy between expectations and experiences when perused only when a problem occurs. (Use of policy manuals as contract makers is confounded by a tendency in the United States for written policy to be rights based; that is, a high value is placed on constitutional guarantees and legal protections, which are sought out and reviewed as a precursor to litigation.) In contrast to observed events and overt communication, many policy statements also lack vividness or ready availability. *Fortune* 1,000 organizations generally devote few resources to evaluating personnel procedures, recruiting activities, or compensation decisions (Rynes & Boudreau, 1986). In contrast, in a manufacturing firm committed to teamwork and equitable treatment, all newly hired employees receive a copy of the firm's personnel manual along with a copy of Peter Scholtes's *The Team Handbook* (1988), a combination signaling the firm's code of conduct for itself, individual employees, and their work groups.

Social Cues

Social cues are information acquired from one's coworkers or work group. They play three roles in the contracting process: providing messages for contract creation, conveying social pressure to conform to the group's understanding of terms, and shaping how individuals will interpret the organization's actions. Social cues appear twice in our model, as part of both the organization's message and the message's context.

Information that is vivid and easily available often provides the most salient messages in contract creation. In most firms, the most frequent source of organization-related information is coworkers. They communicate norms and standards, provide impressions about the workplace, and often help each other understand what is going on at work. A coworker who is upbeat engenders a more positive view of the organization than a negative coworker. As described by Salancik and Pfeffer (1978), such social information has powerful effects on perceptions of the job and the organization. Overt statements can provide descriptive information ("the job is great," "management can't be trusted"), focus attention by making certain aspects of the work setting more or less salient (talking about working conditions makes them more important), and help members interpret environmental cues. People can figure out on their own whether the workplace is hot, cold, or dirty. But more ambiguous, or less obvious, features are understood through easily available and salient information provided by coworkers. The absence culture, described earlier, was created by social cues interpreting sick leave as an entitlement. Messages individuals receive informally from coworkers deal with topics including what qualities the organization has (supportive, safe, rigid), what the organization has promised them and others (historically or in the present), and what constitute appropriate levels of performance (the minimum or something higher).

Internal Processes. Messages individuals actually receive and the way individuals interpret this information influence the contract they create more than the messages that were sent.

ENCODING

Encoding the message signifies the process individuals use to interpret organizational actions as promises. There are two basic questions here: What leads employees to interpret organizational actions as promissory? How can organizations frame their actions so that employees will understand what is intended or promised? These questions need to be answered from the perspective of the recipient of the promise.

A basic concern with encoding events as promissory is whether the individual receives and recognizes a message. For individuals to attribute a credible or intended promise requires that the contract maker

1. be perceived as having power, authority, or capacity to make that commitment,
2. operate in a context where promise making is deemed appropriate,
3. behave in ways consistent with the commitment made.

The Power and Authority to Make Commitments. The legitimacy of the promise maker in conveying commitments affects his or her credibility. An influential superior is likely to make commitments that are more readily relied on than those made by a boss who we believe has little clout.

Organizations undergoing frequent changes in top management may find that senior executives no longer have the ability to make credible commitments to the workforce because people do not believe the executives will be there long enough to enforce their commitments. Similarly, when one's manager has low status (a newcomer himself, or not well connected politically), commitments made may not be believed. Subordinates tend to be more satisfied with their managers when those managers have clout and influence. Weak managers are not empowered to make or create contracts they can keep.

Appropriate Situations for Making Commitments. Messages organizations express regarding commitments are likely to be viewed as promissory when conditions signal to individuals the need for future commitments and planning. Promises made at the time one is hired, or before one accepts an assignment overseas, are more likely to be acted on and remembered than ones made in a situation where promises are less appropriate or not required. It is socially appropriate to make a promise when asking someone to do something in return, in part because people do not tend to believe gratuitous promises and feel uncomfortable receiving something they cannot otherwise reciprocate. Circumstances typically signaling the organization's future intent include

1. personnel actions involving changes in status (hiring, transfer, promotion, new assignments),
2. communication of performance standards (adding new ones or clarifying existing ones), or
3. changes in organizational direction or structuring (new titles, mission statements, and so on).

The key feature of a commitment-signaling event is *change or transition.* Commitment-signaling events involve some sort of punctuation or break between what was and what is to come. When a person is hired, there is a change in status from outsider to employee. Many organizations reinforce this change by permitting a person to wear the organization's uniform only after he or she is promoted from trainee to member. Personnel actions and organizational changes signal some transition between what was and what will be. Given our limited information processing capacities, it is unlikely that messages are interpreted continuously. But when some change is conveyed, messages receive more active interpretation. Discrepancies become signals. In situations where there is an obvious (or apparent) change in status, new job, new economic circumstances, or job transfer (especially drastic changes such as an overseas assignment), individuals are likely to look for cues regarding the organization's future intentions. Note that this event-related processing of organizational messages occurs at a different rate and pattern from the organization's actual sending of messages. Messages consistent (or that appear to be consistent) with previous expressions of commitments receive little processing because they conform to the expected pattern or structure. Discrepant messages are interpreted more complexly.

Organizations may find it easier to create consistently understood contracts regarding certain aspects of employment than others. In research on expatriates, Guzzo, Noonan, and Elron (1994) observe that employees often feel shortchanged on the organization's commitments to help out their families (with expenses, child care, and schooling) while assigned abroad, possibly because this is an arena that would be irrelevant or at least not typically considered while at home. Due to prior experience, organizations may have an easier time fulfilling contract terms involving pay and career opportunities than they do meeting family and personal needs. With the growth of global companies with overseas assignments and employees with increasingly complex family situations, effective contracting in these areas may lag behind other areas.

When organizations undergo change, events are likely to be construed as signals. The uncertainty accompanying change creates the need to make sense of events and rely on interpretations in choosing future behaviors. An example is RR Donnelly, which attempted to convey a new contract to veteran employees by moving them to new assignments where they must be recruited to obtain the post. For change to promote encoding of new promises and ultimate acceptance of a contract, that change must be recognized, be accepted as legitimate, and convey some set of new expectations regarding the organization's contributions to the individual as well as the person's to the organization. Vivid, active events involving promises convey commitments that are credible and relied on. As a recently promoted bank manager reports:

> They flew me out to California [headquarters] for three days. I met with the new CEO and his staff. After he described his plans for the bank, I was excited to accept the new assignment even though the demands it put on me were enormous.

Attention-getting promises influence how people view their contracts, especially when the new promise is at odds with the old.

Message Consistency. Consistency of messages received makes the promisor's intentions easier to understand. As in the quotation from *Richard II* opening this chapter, saying something consistently several times conveys that we meant it. Message consistency is important to its credibility for two reasons. First, because people tend to accept messages tracking with their existing beliefs, messages sent consistently over time (of job security or career opportunities) become internalized to the point that they are simply assumed. When contract terms become fundamental assumptions, they function almost unconsciously, as part of the person's basic worldview. Second, although discrepancy is key to getting a message noticed, messages regarding new contract terms may not be truly believed until the organization has taken enough action to convey that they truly intend to create a new set of terms. In the case of the Sheet Metal Company described earlier, absence of training coupled with poorly understood changes in compensation made it difficult for veterans to hear the division manager's new message and believe it. Changes in performance requirements may need to be coupled with consistent reinforcement from the compensation system as well as with performance reviews before people assimilate the new standards.

INDIVIDUAL PREDISPOSITIONS

The characteristics of the individual affect how encoded information is used. Two important personal factors are cognitive biases, which appear to be generalizable information processing styles, and career motives that are person specific.

Cognitive Biases. Many biases have been identified in the processing of information directly relevant to one's own interests. Those biases reported consistently in self-relevant cognitions include unrealistically positive views of the self, exaggerated perceptions of personal control, and unrealistic optimism (Taylor & Brown, 1988). The traditional view of mental health asserts that well-adjusted people have a view of the self that includes an awareness and acceptance of both positive and negative aspects. In contrast, evidence indicates that most (normal) individuals possess a very positive view of self, to the point that most people dismiss negative aspects of self as inconsequential. For example, tasks we are not proficient at are seen as less important than those we are competent in. Most people believe themselves to be "above average"—to have more skills, to be luckier, and to work harder than others. In effect, the Lake Wobegon phenomenon of Garrison Keillor fame—where the men are handsome, the women strong, and the children above average—is the norm. These illusions are perpetuated by recall: People can remember information that fits their self-concept better than information that contradicts it. This cognitive style characterizes much of the normal population and contributes to a number of contracting features:

- The tendency to believe that one has fulfilled one's part of the deal
- The tendency to recall making those commitments one is most successful at or feels competent performing (this tendency toward what Taylor and Brown term "positive illusions" exists for both employee and employer or customer and vendor)

Motives. What people look for in a job—whether it is a stepping stone to another job somewhere else or part of a long-term career in the organization—affects their interpretation of what they owe and are owed in turn. Motives can act as filters to information received. These motives can also affect recall of commitments over time. In a study of business school graduates, alumni were found to vary considerably in terms of their orientation toward their first job after graduation (Rousseau, 1990b). Individuals scoring high on "careerism" described themselves as planning to leapfrog from organization to organization in pursuit of fast track advancement. Careerists expected to stay with the organization for less than three years on average. Individuals low on careerism sought commitment to a firm and had relatively long anticipated stays in that first job, five years or more. These groups differed in the kind of contracts they reported being party to in the first job. High careerists had contracts stressing high salary in exchange for hard work, but those low on careerism reported that job security had been offered in exchange for firm loyalty. The type of career aspirations one has can affect both the actual and the perceived contract one makes.

DECODING

Decoding reflects the judgments people make regarding the standards of behavior that must be met to fulfill commitments made by themselves and by the organization. "To give one's best efforts," "be loyal," or "offer excellent training" all require some interpretation of what actually has been promised. Because words and observations are the primary sources of contract terms, interpretation must occur to turn promises into behavioral standards. Does loyalty mean saying nice things about the company to outsiders, supporting the firm through adversities, or criticizing the firm to help it be more effective? Until a behavioral standard is formulated, there is no way for individuals to monitor compliance with the contract. Social cues and organizational norms may be relied on to help interpret what performance means.

Because contracts are a form of self-control—encouraging people to keep their commitments—both parties must create and adhere to a behavioral standard for compliance to occur. Frederick Kanfer and his colleagues

(Kanfer & Karoly, 1972a, 1972b), early researchers on contracts, began with the question: "What is self-control?" Interested in therapeutic and behavior modification programs designed to help people change their own behavior, Kanfer investigated the use of contracts that lead to people avoiding behaviors that may be reinforcing for them but not necessarily functional (e.g., poor study habits, overeating, or substance abuse). He hit on the role of contracts as a method for promoting self-discipline. In a series of studies, people were asked to make a commitment to keep their hand in a container of ice water (1 degree centigrade). A standard instruction given to subjects stated:

> I would like for you to keep your hand in the ice water as long as you can. The longer you keep your hand in water, the more data we can collect . . . you can decide for yourself how long you can manage to keep your hand submerged. (Kanfer & Karoly, 1972a)

A more explicit contract instructed them: "Keep your hand in the ice water for 5 minutes." Subjects were asked to read and sign the latter agreement. Making the terms explicit created longer endurance of the painful experience than the more general guideline "as long as you can."

The layperson often thinks of self-control as a personal characteristic similar to willpower or self-discipline. Too, those who keep contracts are good (trustworthy and so on) while those who do not are bad (weak and so on). However, situational factors shape the willingness to perform despite temptation and interference. The trustworthiness and attentiveness of the experimenter and the clarity and specificity of the contract proved to be powerful predictors of whether people adhered to the task. If the experimenter started talking on the phone during the experiment, subjects were more likely to break their contract and take their hand out of the icy water before the 5 minutes were up. Kanfer, Cox, Griner, and Karoly (1974) argue that "more attention [should] be given to [how] . . . promises, intentions or performance criteria are developed, since these events may determine later execution of self-control" (pp. 605-606). Keeping commitments despite discomfort or attractive alternatives is driven by social cues and expectations the person is exposed to (from manager, coworkers, therapists, and other contract makers) as well as by the individual's resulting internalized standards of performance (what I think I can or should do). These influences lead people to make intention statements ("I will . . ."), commitments (" . . . do X . . ."), or contracts with themselves or others. Once made, the contract serves as a self-generated, internal, personal standard that determines the behavior required to keep a commitment. This standard becomes a goal a person is committed to accomplishing.

Contracts appear to be processed in ways similar to those observed in research on goal setting. Ed Locke (1978) and others have found that acceptance of specific goals is a major driver of individual performance. When goals are specific, challenging, personally endorsed, or assigned by someone (e.g., manager) who is liked and trusted by the performer, motivation and resulting performance will be high. Contracting occurs in goal setting when an effort is made to promote acceptance of the standard or target to be attained; classic management-by-objectives—MBO—approaches to managing performance are forms of contracts. Some of the failure of MBO in many organizations has been linked to weak goal acceptance and poor management follow-through when goals are achieved.

Psychological contracts are based on information available to individuals regarding their organization, their work groups, and their own motives. Such contracts are composites of individual and organizational factors, as interpreted by the individual contract holder. Individual factors make each psychological contract potentially unique. However, when a contract is shared, its nature and meaning may shift.

CREATING A NORMATIVE CONTRACT

Normative contracts occur when several people (e.g., colleagues or coworkers) agree on terms in their individual psychological contracts (Figures 2.3 and 2.4). Organizational factors, such as messages, social cues, and their interpretation by work groups, dominate the normative contract; individual characteristics are less important than situational ones. For employee and employer to share a psychological contract, the critical concern is not whether they agree on what happened (an objective event) but whether they make the same interpretations of events (a subjective cognition). When employees in a department or members of a church congregation interpret their commitments and obligations similarly, they are likely to share the same psychological contract. This "cognitive matching" is a central issue in the creation and maintenance of contracts and is largely a function of situational factors that shape the interactions between organization members, including socialization and frequency of interaction. For example, in a work group where mentored support and teamwork are part of the contract, the organization's message that teamwork was valued was reinforced both by the practice of sending people to training and by observation that group members actually did support each other. A normative contract becomes one where cooperation is an actual condition of working in the troop.

When coworkers agree among themselves on the terms of their individual psychological contract (PC) with the employer, that agreement becomes a

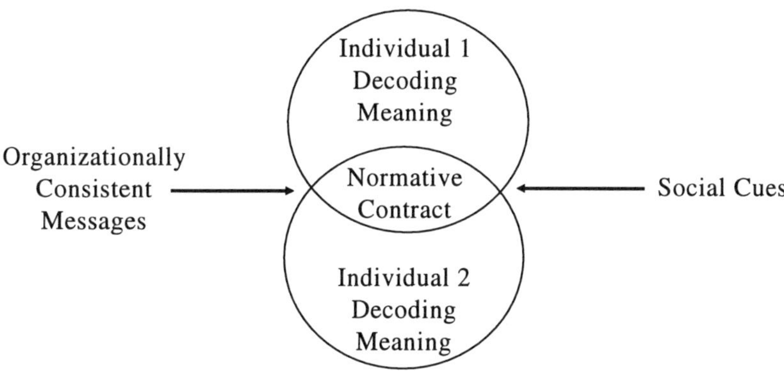

FIGURE 2.3. Creating a Normative Contract

normative contract. A normative contract is a sort of PC^2; as in the case of "saying pardon twice," the sharing of a contract makes that contract even stronger. For contract terms to overlap in some way, individuals need to interact, share information, and have a common social environment. At the previously described Sheet Metal Company, there were two groups of normative contracts: one for veterans and the other for newcomers. Normative contracts are products of social interaction, discussion, comment, and interpretation, creating similarity in the way people see their organization and their relationship to it. Benjamin Schneider (1987) argues that "the people make the place." Using a model of Selection-Adaptation-Attrition, Schneider details how people in organizations become similar in their beliefs, values, and behaviors. When organizations recruit, they often seek a person who fits the culture (Selection). People who don't fit that mold initially can be socialized to change their behavior through training and performance management (Adaptation). Those failing to assimilate over time will leave because they are uncomfortable behaving in another way or because the organization forces them to (Attrition). The Selection-Adaptation-Attrition cycle creates a certain degree of homogeneity in member values and behavior. This similarity creates a shared view of the organization and people's role in it.

It also can give rise to attraction and retention of those whose ideal or preferred contract with an employer fits what the employer offers. Lakeside, a business publisher in its second century (founded before the Civil War), had a tradition of recruiting people at entry level and keeping them throughout their careers as they advanced. This developmental human resource strategy meant that people stayed in entry jobs for several years learning the ropes, which included norms of high quality, attention to detail, and meeting

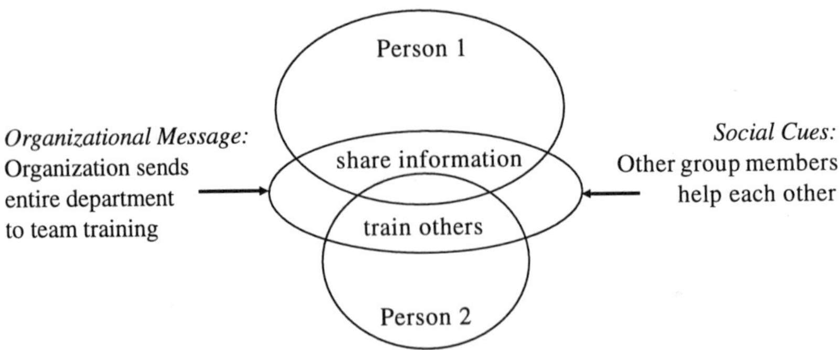

FIGURE 2.4. Creating a Normative Contract for Teamwork

deadlines. A bindery employee at Lakeside who does not complete work in a timely manner would not be popular among his more diligent coworkers and is also likely to feel personally frustrated by his poor performance. In thinking about how normative contracts affect behavior, we need to consider their cultural context. In the 1980s at Lakeside, people unwilling to wait for advancement dropped out at high rates in the first years on the job. But through Selection-Adaptation-Attrition cycles, Lakeside was for many years able to create both strong production norms and a normative contract by retaining those people comfortable with its developmental approach to human resources.

Once people hold common beliefs about what they owe their employer and what they are owed in turn, these normative contracts become part of the social norms of the workplace. If work group members agree that it is appropriate to finish one's work for the day and leave whenever it's done (regardless of scheduled quitting time), people who finish at 3 p.m. will go home before the office closes at 5 p.m. If people get used to leaving when work is done and if their organization accepts this behavior, leaving early becomes a contract, relied on to guide future behavior. In effect, the normative contract becomes part of the organization's or work group's culture.

Culture is the shared set of values, beliefs, and behaviors found in a social group. Creating a normative contract is part of developing a stable culture. People who share beliefs about the behaviors they are committed to demonstrate are in a sense doubly bound to those behaviors, both by their personal commitments as well as by social pressure to fit in and be accepted.

Characterizing an organization's culture often seems comparable to trying to nail Jell-O to the wall. Researchers struggle with finding ways of describing culture, an amorphous and fluid concept, and frequently dispute exactly

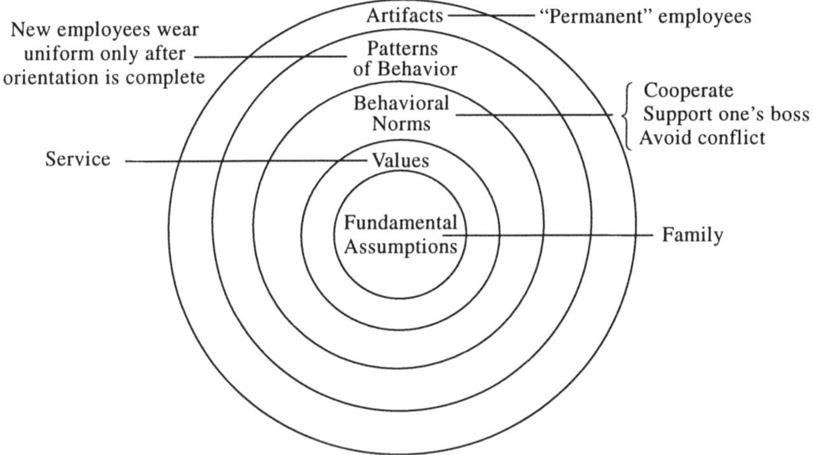

FIGURE 2.5. Layers of Culture and Normative Contract

how this should be done. Integrating the different approaches, we have proposed that culture be thought of as a system of interconnected layers of social experiences (Figure 2.5; Rousseau, 1990a). Culture has five layers, varying from subjective to objective. This "onion model of culture" can represent contributions each element of organizational culture makes to the normative contract:

1. *Fundamental assumptions* are the often unconscious beliefs that members share about their organization and its relationship to them. Like the lens of your eye, you can't see fundamental assumptions, yet they affect everything you see. Because fundamental assumptions reflect taken-for-granted aspects of organizations, they typically are long standing and unquestioned. Employees, managers, and owners may share very similar beliefs about the employment relationship, as is often the case in family businesses. These shared beliefs are mutually reinforcing over time—part of the constant backdrop of being in the organization. Beliefs such as "this organization takes care of its own" may be unconsciously held and more closely linked to members' beliefs about "family" than to their beliefs about "corporations." Challenges to these assumptions engender anxiety, which can be a major factor in resistance to change. When a contract is long standing, as in the case of organizations such as the military and IBM, with a substantial history of valuing membership and rewarding loyalty, it is likely that the contract is passed down from generation to generation. When cultural forces underpin

normative contracts, key aspects of the contract are likely to be unconscious, taken for granted, and subject to tremendous upheaval when violated.

2. *Values* are goals, priorities, or preferred results. What organizations prize as most important in terms of their accomplishments and performance is what they value. Values are organized in a hierarchy, with some ranked as more important than others. Perhaps the best indicator of what is truly valued in an organization's culture are the trade-offs it is willing to make. Given a choice, does the organization prize profit over innovation or innovation over profit? Organizations make their true preferences known when trade-offs and tough choices are made. The choice reflects priorities placed on economic factors and employee well-being. Fundamental assumptions are manifested in organizational values. Seeing the organization as a family can lead to values emphasizing relationships, but seeing the organization as unsafe and threatening can lead to values stressing self-aggrandizement and political protectionism. Values reveal themselves in the trade-offs people make between various ways of behaving in specific situations. During a busy morning, does the secretary respond quickly to a customer request or put that person off while completing other work for the boss? Values determine *which* norms are followed *when.*

3. *Behavioral norms* are beliefs about appropriate and inappropriate ways to do work and relate to other people, or what it takes to fit in and be accepted by members. Behavioral norms are often performance terms in a work group's normative contract. To be a "good employee" or "citizen," certain behaviors must be demonstrated (cooperation, attention to detail, working through channels, or going straight to the top).

4. *Behavioral patterns* are observable and repeated practices (e.g., quarterly reports). These more objective features of the organization's culture manifest themselves in the human resource practices (compensation systems, promotion requirements, performance criteria) that can be primary contract makers for organization members.

5. *Artifacts* are the physical and symbolic ways in which culture is communicated (company slogans and logos). Artifacts in themselves have no meaning. Take, for instance, this logo:

It is the symbol of the Square D company. Show it to an outsider, and he or she responds with some hemming and hawing and a few guesses ("square deal"?). Show it to a Square D employee and that person is likely to give a

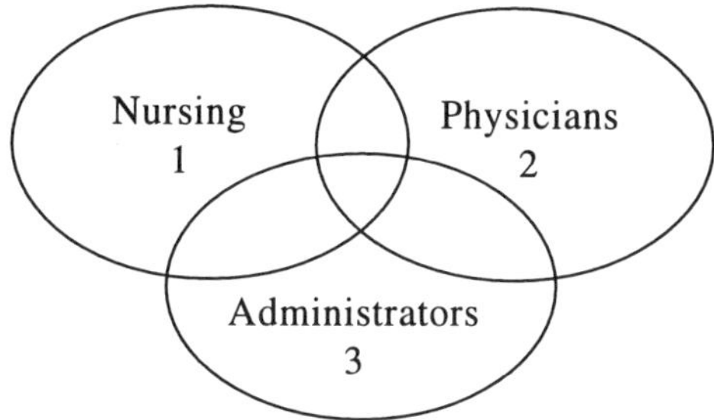

FIGURE 2.6. Normative Contracts in Subcultures: The Case of Hospitals

5-minute description of its varied meanings (ranging from the company's history in Detroit to more recent practices regarding teamwork, quality, and innovation). The point is that artifacts get their meaning from all the other levels of culture that the member understands, the layers being something the nonmember has no access to. When organizations actively attempt to change the culture, including normative contracts, they frequently alter artifacts to signal commitment to a change (e.g., eliminating the term *permanent employee* or changing the company logo).

Normative contracts reflect a social consensus and reinforcement of specific behaviors and exchange patterns. Such contracts occur where there are other culture-creating forces: stable workforce, history or tradition, and opportunities for people to interact with each other. Organizations with high turnover, many recent restructurings or new leadership, and a workforce that is widely scattered are less likely to have normative contracts. Small group research demonstrates that, when people have incentives to benefit themselves at the expense of the group, they will honor promises to help the group, but only when all other group members promise as well. The power of the normative contract lies in members who trust that others will play by the same rules. Normative contracts can create trust and predictability among the people party to that contract.

Cultures and Subcultures. Because normative contracts are part of cultural beliefs regarding what members assume to be conditions of membership, there can be as many normative contracts in an organization as the organization has subcultures (Figure 2.6). Subcultures are groups of people who share common values and beliefs that are in some fashion distinct from those held by other organization members. The doctors and nurses in an intensive care unit (ICU) may share some common values, such as supporting teamwork or catering to hospital administrators. However, the nature of their positions is such that nurses often have less job security and fewer organiza-

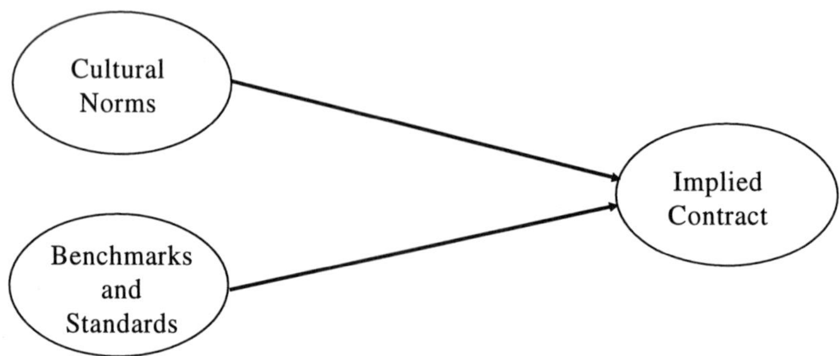

FIGURE 2.7. Creating an Implied Contract

tional entitlements than physicians, despite the fact that nurses are employed by the hospital and physicians often are not employees at all but have admitting privileges. Status differences can create differences in behavior between these two groups as well two distinct sets of normative contracts. Physicians may seldom be terminated, but nurses might lose their jobs for displeasing physicians.

> Nursing is a job to them. Being a physician is, I think, more than a job.
>
> —*ICU attending physician*

> Face it, we can't have a hospital without doctors. If a doctor is angry with a nurse about how a nurse does her job, she's got to go.
>
> —*Hospital administrator*

Subcultural differences in status and conditions of membership are associated with distinct normative contracts regarding job security among physicians and nurses. This normative contract reflects that "social fact."

CREATING AN IMPLIED CONTRACT

Implied contracts are external judgments made by courts, the public, and other outsiders about the relationship in which a contract is created (Figure 2.7). Outsiders act as "reasonable third parties" in gauging (a) whether a contract exists, (b) what its terms are, and (c) whether it has been maintained or violated. When judging fairness, third parties use different information than insiders and operate under different rules.

Ethicists evoke the judgments of "reasonable third parties" in advising decision makers (managers, policymakers, and arbitrators) on how to make tough ethical choices (Bok, 1978). As outsiders, third parties

1. evoke more universalistic standards than might a contract's principals, who focus on specifics in the relationship,
2. adhere more closely to standard procedures and norms of procedural justice,
3. employ legalistic criteria,
4. "benchmark" against past practices and the status quo.

Because their frame of reference is outside the relationship, third parties pay more attention to widely held beliefs regarding terms of employment than to specific features of the relationship. Seniority, for instance, is associated with strong societal norms; the general public in the United States believes that employers have special obligations to veteran employees (Forbes & Jones, 1986). Thus, when judging termination fairness, third parties rely heavily on time with the company when weighing the fairness of a particular employee's termination. Rousseau and Anton (1991) found, however, that a two-way street exists: Senior employees have special rights *if* they have continued to perform well for the organization. Substantial economic troubles for a firm may not reduce its responsibilities to those senior members who continue to perform well, regardless of the firm's obligations to others.

Procedural justice refers to whether the processes used to implement decisions, allocate rewards, or otherwise affect employees are themselves fair. The components of fair processes include participation of affected people in the decision, impartial decision makers, and warning or advance notice when actions will hurt others (e.g., plant closings, cutbacks). The "hot stove rule" frequently employed in organizational discipline cases is an example of procedural justice. The rule holds that discipline should be given much in the same manner as we react to a hot stove: immediate (quick reaction following wrongdoing), impersonal (same response to everyone regardless of their status or background), and consistent (every time you touch the hot stove you risk getting burned—the same infractions are always sanctioned). Employee handbooks and the due process procedures they set down are often employed by third parties as setting a standard for procedural justice.

Law is a primary determinant of the universal standards adopted by third parties. Especially if it is reasonable to expect that contract parties knew the law or had access to legal counsel, legal criteria such as precedent, consideration (payment in exchange for a promise), and other criteria outside of the courts themselves may be invoked by third parties.

Because third parties seek external standards by which to gauge the nature of contracts in employment and elsewhere, they look to established practices in the industry as a benchmark. Bazerman (1985) observed that arbitrators in labor disputes looked to existing wage levels and added some constant increment in determining a fair wage—a status quo-oriented view of fairness that would keep their decision from being "out of line" in the industry. Similarly, although employees at Apple are unlikely to look to IBM to understand their employment contract, third parties may compare practices in one firm with another in the same industry to determine the "realistic" commitments that exist between employee and employer.

"Facts" available to third parties are different than those known to contract insiders. Third parties are more likely to focus on explicit commitments of long-term employment by either employee or employer. Insiders to the contract are likely to focus on additional information more readily available to them, including specific past contributions and sunk costs. Different vantage points bring not only the distinct information to which participants and observers have access but also different ways of evaluating the facts.

CONCLUSION

People think contractually, interpreting statements and behaviors as promises and commitments to be relied on. But what they understand these commitments to be is shaped by both personal beliefs and social processes. Just as the concept of a goal in hockey can be defined only against the background of the rules of the game, so the concept of a contract can be understood only when viewed in the context of the organization's setting and specifics of the situation (Atiyah, 1981). Because people are discontinuous information processors, understanding contracts requires attention both to the information provided and to the information interpreted by contract parties. Contracts are not continuously made or revised. Distinguishing features in the three forms of promissory contracts derive from different vantage points and the information available. Psychological contracts develop from a complex blend of individual characteristics and cognition, social cues, and organizational messages. Normative contracts are products of social information processing and organizational socialization, but implied contracts rely on external standards and points of comparison. Insiders and outsiders, individuals and groups, view contracts somewhat differently because neither their information nor their frames of reference are the same.

3 The Contract Makers

My deal changed when my boss left. Since then my treatment has been less special.

—*Assistant brand manager*

Organizations have many "contract makers." As customers and employees encounter an organization, opportunities arise for conveying commitments and future intentions. Sales representatives and advertisements make promises to customers about product performance and service quality. Recruiters who describe the firm's past practices, current employees who share information about their jobs and experiences, organizational literature (from brochures targeted to recruits to laminated mission statements carried in the pockets of veteran employees), tales of company history, and managers who cue, advise, support, criticize, and appraise their employees—all convey commitments that can be understood as the *organization's* promise.

Employees report:

Sales training was promised as an integral part of marketing training.

The company promised that no one would be fired out of the training program—that all of us were safe until placement (in return for this security, we accepted lower pay).

I was promised a dynamic and challenging environment . . . rubbing elbows with some of the brightest people in the business.

I came because they offered me the chance to learn the latest techniques.

Who is making these promises? This chapter identifies who the contract makers are, the ways in which contracts are conveyed, and how individuals react to different contract makers. We will begin with an example of contract making in an innovative academic program to illustrate how a wide array of contract makers came to create "the deal that wasn't" and then, later, "the deal that came to be."

WHO MADE THE CONTRACT?

"The Deal That Wasn't"

A major university created an innovative advanced degree program to train experienced engineers to become manufacturing managers, specifically to help rebuild the hard-pressed American manufacturing base. A joint venture between its business and engineering schools, the university's fledgling program offered an education in manufacturing management to promote both technical excellence as well as leadership development. Manufacturing had been declining in the United States since the 1970s. Erosion from foreign competition and lagging technological development, especially in the area of information systems, had taken a toll on both the productivity of American manufacturing as well as on the esteem that industry once held. The program's goal to attract the best and the brightest engineers to U.S. manufacturing management underscored the need for interdisciplinary (management and technology) education.

The schools' two deans, both leaders in their own right, formulated a program, solicited faculty involvement in curriculum development, and organized school administrators to begin a plan for recruiting and admissions. To attract a first class (with 60 admissions targeted), advertisements were sent, articles published in *Industry Week,* brochures distributed, and an advisory board with representatives from leading manufacturing firms created to help design the program and spread the word of its inception. After a year and half of planning, the first class arrived in the fall. Knowing they were to some extent guinea pigs in an innovative collaboration between schools of business and engineering, lots of tinkering with curriculum and layout of the program was expected. As many of the students had enrolled because of the business school's reputation, they wanted their mailboxes at the business school rather than at the engineering school. To accommodate their desire to be more a part of the business school community, mailboxes were moved. Business school classes start on the hour, engineering courses at ten minutes after the hour. Class starting times had to be lined up to permit students to travel from the engineering school to the business school and back again for courses in the joint program. Many adjustments, large and small, were made in the spirit of continuous improvement. No one seemed particularly surprised at the need for them.

Despite ongoing efforts to develop a well-integrated joint program, discontent surfaced over issues much more intractable than scheduling and program integration. Listening to the first-year class's complaints revealed an array of mixed messages.

> I applied to the business school. I was contacted by [the program's] admissions directors and arm-twisted into the program. My understanding was that this . . . degree would be the best of both schools. . . . I was so sold on [the business school]. I would have done anything to be accepted.
>
> I thought it would be a lot more organized than it was.
>
> I came knowing I'd be a guinea pig . . . with a chance to participate in a new way of doing things.

Some students reported being told that the program was clearly targeted to return them to manufacturing as plant managers. Others recounted conversations where they were promised help in making career choices, including the possibility of a career in the highly paid consulting field. Who had made these promises? The list was broad and included recruiting interviews with the admissions director, conversations with students in the regular business school program, brochures and advertisements, and meetings with the deans held during the first few weeks of fall classes. More to the point, these different sources said *different* things. The deans shared their vision for the program (including a focus on rebuilding U.S. manufacturing), but the business school's admissions personnel described the program based on their previous experiences in the regular business program. Moreover, the recruiting brochures offered very general statements: "[A] program . . . providing interdisciplinary education that integrates required management and engineering skills . . . the main thread of the . . . program is customer satisfaction and total quality management."

Although this theme was picked up in descriptions of course content, many students came expecting that total quality management was part of the program's governance. Participative decision making involving students and faculty was assumed by many to be an integral part of the program, including participation in its design and development. "I assumed that to be a responsible citizen I would need to go to class, complete coursework, and help shape the program." In fact, faculty and administration continued to play traditional roles in designing the curriculum.

Although some recruiters visited the campus, many students discovered they had to find summer placement through their own initiative and personal networking. As one recruiting brochure described it: "The career development office . . . [offers] extensive counsel and assistance in identifying summer internships and full-time career opportunities." Feeling pressured to obtain summer internships, many students were surprised to learn that there were no *guaranteed* internships; in many cases, they had to initiate their own contacts with industry. The placement office actually had little experience with manufacturing internships and job searches. Although most students obtained internships, and placement was high at the end of the program's two years, anxiety over the job market and dissatisfaction with placement were apparent.

Recruits had formed a mental model of what they could expect from the program based on whatever sources were available to them during recruiting and the first week's orientation. In reviewing experiences with the first class, particularly statements made by students regarding what promises had been made by whom, the program committee members' reactions included the following: "They shouldn't have listened to [so and so]" and "Those students can't speak for the program."

The fact of the matter is that many people spoke for the program. It is difficult for programs to begin with internal consistency, especially as they continue to go through a "shakedown phase."

In the program's second year, new incoming students were asked to describe how they determined what the program had promised them and what they owed in turn for these commitments (Table 3.1). Again, the number and variety of contract makers became apparent. The list included recruiting officers from the university, deans, other administrative personnel, teachers, and current participants in the program. New recruits provided detailed descriptions of the conversations during which these commitments were conveyed. Recruiting documents, including brochures, also expressed future goals, program intentions, and allusions to benefits to be reaped by enrollment in this program of study. Another frequent source of new commitments were second-year students, as well as administrators and staff—many of whom had, at the suggestion of the administration, actively marketed the program to applicants and provided orientations for newly admitted students after arrival on campus. Program participants reported that promises made by these individuals led them to incur substantial opportunity costs (lost wages and employer-sponsored tuition elsewhere) to obtain the promised cutting edge, experimental education offered (typically without any employer sponsorship). Administrators of the program were quite surprised to learn that incoming students received messages about their commitments from a broad array of people who acted as the program's "agents."

Three Years Later: "The Deal That Came About"

The program recognized a need to coordinate the messages sent to potential recruits as well as to students enrolled in the program. In wrestling with

TABLE 3.1 Multiple Contract Makers in the Manufacturing Management Program

Contract Makers	*Promises*	*Obligations*
Brochures	"Build industry leaders"	"Save U.S. industry" "Participate in new way of doing things"
Deans	"Terrific placement rate"	—
Administration (includes recruiting and placement)	"Chance to shape a new program"	"Pay tuition/work hard" "Get good job, not necessarily in manufacturing"
Program Directors	"State-of-the-art facilities"	"Get job in manufacturing"
News articles	"Highest quality professors"	—

how to do so, it became apparent that faculty, administrators, and staff had some very different ideas regarding the program's goals and how to implement them. Recognizing the need to create a coherent statement of the program's mission for all its constituencies, including faculty and staff as well as students, the process of creating a program mission statement was begun by a joint committee of students, faculty, and administration.

The most important aspects of creating a public statement of purpose occur *before* and *after* the statement is written. In an existing program or organization, generating a viable mission statement requires consensus building. A committee of students, faculty, and administrative staff worked for several months identifying the program's goals, its constituents, and ultimately a list of pledges regarding the program's values and its focus of attention. Teamwork (joint participation of students and faculty), continuous improvement, and closer ties to the manufacturing community were among the values emphasized in the statement.

Once created and endorsed by the larger program community (students, faculty, and administration), the new mission statement was used as a focus in meetings with admissions, placement, and orientation with incoming students to help program members "stay on the same page." In effect, messages the program members now were sending to recruits were more consistent with its manufacturing orientation and emphasis on student involvement in program development. Articulating the program's contract more clearly required significant organization building and integration on the part of its members. It also helped identify the array of constituents and contract makers the program actually possessed.

As graduating students report:

> The contract is now . . . you are supposed to go into manufacturing and help save companies. Going into consulting is bad. (I don't mind this obligation.)
>
> How can I complain? I got a great education in two top ten schools, made an impact on a new program and had more job opportunities than I dreamed possible. No one promised that the journey would be easy. They only promised that the end result would be a great education and plenty of opportunities.

TYPES OF CONTRACT MAKERS: PRINCIPALS AND AGENTS

Who can create a contract with another? From the vantage point of a psychological contract, any person who conveys some form of future commitment to another person is potentially a contract maker. Organizations become party to psychological contracts as principals who directly express their own terms or through agents who represent them. Although owner/employers create their own contracts with individual employees, most contract makers are individuals acting as the organization's agents, who communicate demands and expectations upon which employment, advancement, remuneration, and retention are predicated. In organizations with strong cultures, coworkers who actively play a role in socializing newcomers may also become contract makers. Such members are assumed to be integrated into and empowered by the organization. Decentralized organizations tend to have more contract makers than centralized ones.

There are two basic types of contract makers:

1. *Principals:* individuals or organizations making contracts for themselves (e.g., proprietors who hire an employee or sell a product personally)
2. *Agents:* individuals acting for another (e.g., recruiters who convey commitments in the name of the organization)

Contracts vary in terms of the parties' status as principals or as agents (Table 3.2). Principal-to-principal contracts are most characteristic of private employment arrangements (such as home child care workers and domestic help) but also include owners of firms who directly hire employees. Contracts between principals have fewer filters and a clearer attribution of responsibility in cases of breach or contract change. Principal-to-principal

TABLE 3.2 Types of Contracting

Principal-to-principal:	
	Employment contract between employee and owner/employer (e.g., hiring a worker to landscape your house)
Agent-to-principal:	
	Organization's representative (e.g., recruiter, trainer, manager, coworker) conveys and agrees to commitments with employee
Principal-to-agent:	
	Employer/owner contracts with representatives of workers (e.g., agency employment)
Agent-to-agent:	
	Organization's representative (e.g., management) and employee's representative (e.g., union leaders) construct an agreement

contracts have the broadest array of forms, ranging from very close relationships, such as partnerships, to more arm's-length transactions, for example, hiring a college student to paint one's house. Principal-to-agent contracts characterize the agency model of employment (e.g., owner and job boss, labor hall, outsourcing). In agency arrangements, there is an arm's-length relationship between employees and principal that limits the scope of contract terms and reduces the level of involvement between employer and employee. (A concept with both positive and negative connotations, "arm's length" has several meanings: interaction in a way that maintains one's objectivity by avoiding familiarity, as in fiduciary or trustee relations, or interaction signifying awkwardness or an imbalance of power.) Agent-to-agent contracts are the classic union-management agreement, filtered and interpreted on both sides, typically characterized by social distance between the parties, which often connotes mutual mistrust. Agent-to-principal contracts cover the majority of employment contracts. Recruiters and supervisors express commitments in the name of the organization ("fast track advancement," "top pay"), as do impersonal sources such as advertisements, brochures, and mission statements. Agent-to-principal contracts can take an array of forms, as in the case of principal to principal, ranging from hiring a temporary employee to recruiting a new hire into a management trainee job. Because there are potentially more agents than organization-principals, agents are often more available to convey contract-related information to employees.

One important feature of principal/agent contracting concerns the filtered communications agents offer. As the stand-in for another, agents may make commitments that are inconsistent with the principal's true intent. Moreover, agents may send mixed messages regarding the actual parties to the contract. Is a manager who promises career development to a recruit speaking for himself or for the organization? It appears that recruits tend to believe that the organization has made a commitment regardless of whether a recruiter or the owner made a specific promise. In a study of newly recruited M.B.A.s, the majority reported that the organization had violated promises made at hire. Closer examination of these instances revealed that a common explanation for this "violation" had been that the recruit's boss had quit or been fired or promoted. In effect, recruits often blamed the organization for not keeping commitments their erstwhile bosses had made. Employees may not know at the time a deal is created whether the contract maker is acting as a principal or as the company's agent: "After working hard all year on the performance goals I negotiated with my boss, she was transferred and the new guy had a different agenda."

As the manager in the opening quote of this chapter indicates, when a manager with whom an employee has a good relationship leaves, the way the employee is treated can change radically, and preexisting commitments may cease to exist.

The following are basic features of principal/agent roles in contracting:

- Agent-created contracts tend to involve distortion of the principal's intent.
- Use of employee-agents reduces the scope of the contract, including levels of involvement and commitment. Employee-principals have greater flexibility than agents regarding the kinds of contracts they can create.
- Use of agents can create confusion in terms of whether the agent is contracting for him- or herself or for the organization.

Use of agents in contracting increases the likelihood of mixed messages and signals unintended by the principal(s) to the contract. This ambiguity is over and above that which we normally expect due to the inherent subjectivity of contract making.

A variety of contract makers often exist. As we saw in the academic program described above, some contract makers actually play a dual role, acting as both principal and agent. For example, both managers and coworkers can speak for themselves ("I will help you meet the deadline if you will

TABLE 3.3 Contract Makers

Human contract makers:
- through interaction
  - recruiters
  - managers
  - coworkers
  - mentors
- through observation
  - managers
  - coworkers
  - top management

Administrative contract makers:
- structural signals
  - compensation
  - benefits
  - career path
  - performance review
  - training
  - personnel manuals

do this for me now") as well as acting as the larger organization's agents ("If you work on solving this problem, you'll have a good shot at the next promotion"). Contract makers can influence people through a variety of mechanisms (Table 3.3):

- *Interaction* is direct oral or written communication in the form of directives, advice, or actual statements of promise, from managers, coworkers, recruiters, and so on.
- *Observation* can be used by the individual employee to monitor the behaviors of coworkers, managers, and other members, thus to collect social cues.
- *Structural signals* convey information through human resource practices including benefits, compensation, and performance criteria; *documentation* is formal written expression of commitments, made through ads, mission statements, and other organizational documents.

People: Primary Contract Makers

Managers. By far the most complex agents in employment, managers make contracts both for the organization and for themselves. Acting as both principal and agent, managers play a special role in making or breaking the psychological contracts of their employees. Managers can mitigate effects of unmet expectations on the part of their employees by cutting special deals, creating opportunities, and providing emotional support and confidence building (Major, Kozlowski, Chao, & Gardner, 1992).

A basic building block in the employment relationship is the interaction between manager and employee. Current research on leadership (Graen & Scandura, 1987) provides evidence that managers interact very differently with individual employees depending on the following:

- *The competence and maturity of the subordinate:* Less competent or mature individuals receive closer supervision.
- *The routineness or structure of the task:* The more unstructured and uncertain the work, the more likely it is that individuals are managed differently, with some given more flexibility than others.
- *The quality of communication between manager and subordinate:* Trust and flexibility characterize relations with good communication.

Viewing manager-subordinate interactions in terms of "leader-member exchanges," Graen and colleagues argue that when work is unstructured there will be a complex set of arrangements differing across the subordinates of a given manager. The interpersonal relationship between employee and manager shapes the type of role the subordinate will play within a particular work group or department. Because managers do not have a lot of time, they can only develop close relationships with a few key subordinates while managing the rest of their work group through formal authority, rules, and policies. This line of reasoning suggests that in-groups and out-groups are formed within work units such that those subordinates close to the manager experience high trust, support, and formal and informal rewards, but the out-group encounters low trust, little direct interaction and support, and fewer rewards. In-group members offer and receive contributions valued by both parties and display more loyalty (expressions of public support). A logical result would be different contracts for in-group and out-group members.

Consistent with this differential treatment, recruits who have high-quality relations with supervisors (called "dyadic relations") demonstrate faster and higher career progression (Wakbayashi & Graen, 1984). Subordinates with good-quality relations with their bosses spend more time on less routine activities and do more challenging work than their less favored peers. Significantly, good dyadic relationships can be learned. Training programs that develop manager skills in creating focused and supportive relations with their subordinates produce more productive subordinates than found with managers who were not trained. Such findings suggest that high-quality manager-subordinate relations are related to the processes used to foster communication, mutual expectations, and support. Leader-member relations are often described as a negotiation, where roles are construed based on interaction and agreement. Yet many forms of supervisor-subordinate relations show little evidence of bargaining and flexibility. Relations that take the form of overseer-peon have a very different construction than the mentor-protégé model. Whether or not managers negotiate roles with subordinates or simply assign them, within-supervisor variation exists in subordinate treatment, suggesting that separate contracts exist between employee and manager as principal, as well as between employee and manager in the role of organizational agent.

There is some dispute about the characteristics of leader-member relations. Do they have to be equitable? Do the parties have to like each other? (See Dienschen & Liden, 1986.) However, a basic driver of this relationship is the degree of *mutuality* that exists between the parties. Mutuality has three primary components:

- *Predictability:* Can the parties effectively anticipate what the other will do, to coordinate work and behave in ways consistent with each other's expectations?
- *Enablement:* Do the actions of manager and subordinate help each other achieve goals?
- *Clarity of the effort:* Are performance expectations well understood?

In effect, a workable contract between manager and subordinate is characterized by mutuality, which exists regardless of whether the individuals liked each other or had anything in common personally aside from their interdependence.

Mentors. Both formally and informally, mentors provide newcomers and other junior organization members with opportunities not readily available otherwise. Mentors can act as sensors, helping others discern what is not obvious—the fundamental assumptions and basic workings of the organization. Two decades ago, Goodman and Salipante (1976) observed that hard-core unemployed people adjusted to organizational life better when they had buddies who acted as mentors as opposed to relying on therapy and support groups as a means of adjustment. *Mentor* is the Greek name of the trustee Odysseus left behind to watch his wife and son when he departed for the Trojan wars, and thus conveys an image of a sort of tribal elder (Wilson & Elman, 1990) who provides insights and access not readily available otherwise. Mentoring is useful at all levels, not only in assimilating newcomers. Transitions such as grooming a senior executive to be the next CEO or helping members to accept and adopt a new or redefined culture can be facilitated by mentoring. When changes occur and current employees cannot easily understand them, mentors can help them adopt new ways to adjust. Newcomers with mentors rely on observations of others as well as input from their mentors to learn about their jobs, relations with others, and organizational norms (Ostroff & Kozlowski, 1993)—and they learn significantly more in terms of quality and quantity of information than do nonmentored newcomers.

There is a supportive quality to mentoring that often makes it unlikely that a mentor and a hierarchical superior could be one and the same. Mentors may be peers slightly more senior than the employee or they may be other well-informed people. The support works two ways. Formally appointed mentors are often two or three levels apart from the mentee, with no direct chain of command to undercut the mentee's boss. Moreover, mentoring can allow senior members to accept the entrée of junior people to the organization by creating a bond of support, akin to parenting, that prevents older employees from being jealous of younger ones (Wilson & Elman, 1990).

Mentors can help members, both newcomer and veteran, to adapt to the organization's culture. Because organizations often have very different subcultures across each level, mentors make it possible for newcomers to learn the different deals that exist. Given the support mentors offer, training insiders to mentor may prove more useful than organizational practices simply emphasizing training and socializing newcomers.

Coworkers. Coworkers and other informed members close in status (e.g., supervisors in accounting firms near in age to their subordinates) are often the subject of direct questioning and inquiry as newcomers seek to learn the ropes. There is less social cost to asking a peer when an individual is anxious not to expose his or her ignorance or inexperience to a superior. Especially in organizations where there is little formal socialization and training for incoming employees, coworkers are likely to be a frequent source of information on the organization, its management style, treatment of employees, and past practices regarding personnel actions (e.g., promotions, suspensions, performance criteria).

Probably no contract maker is more easily accessed than a coworker. Future colleagues who go to lunch with a candidate can share a variety of norms, advice, experiences, and beliefs that newcomers frequently construe as being directives from the organization. A young Ph.D.'s first job interview involved a position partially supported by "soft money," that is, outside research funding. She asked a future coworker (at breakfast before her first job talk) how long a grace period she could have before she needed to get her own outside funding. His unhesitating answer was "3 years, no problem." After 3 years of pursuing her own research interests (and writing a few outside funding proposals here and there), the scholar left for a better job elsewhere. In conversations with her soon-to-be former colleagues, she thanked them, saying how much she had appreciated the three-year grace period, only to be told there was no such thing. They had been wondering why she never had produced in the way they had expected her to. Though they appear to know the ropes, coworkers offer a variety of perspectives that may or may not speak for the organization.

Top Management. Because of their visibility and influence, top management actions receive a special form of scrutiny. Because fewer people have direct access to them, they are not easily available for direct inquiry, and their behavior and communications are subject to monitoring and evaluation. The concept of walking the talk (i.e., signaling through their own actions what types of changes executives desire in their organizations) is based on the insight that top management's behavior is highly monitored and has tremendous signal value.

Prosecutors in an office of the state's attorney, when asked to describe their contract with the state agency they served, frequently mentioned the state's attorney himself as a source of their contract:

> He promised me the opportunity to lead a bureau and expand the scope of law enforcement against more criminals.
>
> —*Special prosecutor*

> He said there would be latitude and resources to do the job . . . been the same since I took the job.
>
> —*Attorney*

> The State's Attorney hired me. He said I would never be bored. I [would have] a chance to assist in office operation and develop policy to use the office for public good.
>
> —*Executive secretary*

What is their obligation in this contract?

> "Loyalty."
>
> "Willingness to teach, willingness to learn, willingness to self-sacrifice."

These messages are backed by the visible presence of top management (the state's attorney himself) at staff meetings, including off-site training and development sessions. Those activities that top management pays attention to, follows through with, and rewards are contract affirming.

The types of contractual arrangements senior managers themselves have with the organization both create the basis of their individual motivation as well as signal to employees the nature of top management's commitment to the organization. Recent outcry over the disparity between executive pay and that of "shop floor" workers conveys messages of both inequity as well as instrumental motives on the part of executives. Top management's ability to create contracts with employees that engender some levels of commitment may be directly related to the senior manager's own contract with the organization, owner, or board.

Recruiters. During recruitment, interviewers, potential supervisors, and coworkers all provide information regarding the nature of the job, the organization, and its management practices. Some organizations focus on selling the organization to the applicant. The more selling is done, the more likely it is that the expectations created will go unmet. In the words of a first-year recruit to the academic program described above: "I believe the program was oversold [via the business school image] initially in order to attract talented students." Realistic recruiting, advocated by personnel psychologists such as John Wanous (1980, 1992), presents outsiders with pertinent information about the job and the organization without distortion. Organizational entry is viewed as a two-way process—organizations choose people, and people choose organizations. Thus realistic recruitment involves an attempt to match the person to the organization, in addition to identifying whether applicant skills fit the specific job. Lower expectations about the job are a form of inoculation against negative aspects of organizational life. The best sources of referral for new employees are often those from which the recruit is likely to obtain the most realistic expectations, such as former or present employees. Among the best source of recruits in terms of attendance, performance, and retention are actually *rehires,* those who have quit and come back, perhaps because of their more realistic appraisal of what the organization offers. Given that individuals have greater knowledge about themselves, their skills, and their motives than any recruiting process is likely to reveal, self-selection into appropriate work settings is a product of realistic job previews. Discussions of likely job duties (varied schedules, demands), career paths (if any), and management styles (close supervision, reliance on personal initiative) produce an accurate picture of the new hire's job and role.

Realistic recruitment can also involve the use of screening devices such as work samples. By giving a piece of the job to the candidate to do, the interviewer discovers if the candidate possesses the requisite skills, and also conveys what the job is really like. Work samples such as programming tests for programmers, in-basket tests for managers, and oral presentations for salespeople predict job success. They typically are used to select employees rather than to recruit them. However, exposing individuals to job demands before hiring creates a more realistic sense of working conditions, and as such offers clearer specification of the terms of the employee's part of the contract.

Realistic recruiting is associated with reduced turnover and higher member commitment to the organization. In contractual terms, it conveys a contract that the organization is more likely to keep. Elements of realistic recruitment (Table 3.4) entail three major activities:

- *Realistic preview:* Acquaint candidate with specific job responsibilities and likely career developments.
- *Work samples:* Screen and recruit with specific tasks used on the job or by simulating representative situations by framing these as problem-solving questions in interviews.
- *Managing the psychological contract:* Specify performance expectations and personnel practices while exploring the candidate's own expectations and preferences.

STRUCTURAL SIGNALS: SECONDARY CONTRACT MAKERS

Structural signals are organizational processes and procedures that convey future intent in the name of the organization (e.g., handbooks, deferred compensation systems, mission statements, and job titles). In one sense, structural signals are secondary contract makers, vehicles people use to convey commitments and offer inducements for present and future behavior. Organizations frequently rely on documents, memos, and systems to convey their intent and to manage and motivate people. By doing so, systems emerge that themselves become contract makers. In some organizations, these systems are more salient and visible than are managers or executives in the contract-making process. Organizations with strong cultures, such as IBM or General Motors, have a substantial infrastructure of mechanisms for promoting the culture and conveying the contract. A bonus plan tied to next year's sales targets creates a contract that rewards growth. A compensation plan weighing seniority heavily signals deferred compensation and rewards for tenure.

Many members, as we have seen, act as the organization's agents in contract making. As a result, any artifacts that recruiters, managers, coworkers, or top managers use to reinforce their message, such as memos, stories,

TABLE 3.4 Realistic Recruiting

Realistic preview:

- Acquaint candidate with specific job responsibilities.
- Realistically describe career opportunities (e.g., likely next job) and "drawbacks."

Work sample:

- Identify types of situations/problems handled differently by good and poor employees.
- Use these to frame questions. ("What would you do in a situation like this?")
- Identify aspects of the job that can be simulated (e.g., presentation/sales approach/report writing).
- Establish criteria for good and poor performance on these before obtaining this "work sample."

Managing the psychological contract:

- Specify expectations regarding performance (examples of good performance).
- Specify review process and time frame.
- Describe training if any (use example).
- Describe expected length of employment (e.g., how long in first job, typical length of employment).
- Explore candidate expectations, preferences (reality check).
- Check with candidate how accurately you have understood what he or she expects.
- Convey behavioral expectations (e.g., interpersonal and task norms such as individual initiative or teamwork).

and practices, can themselves become contract-making mechanisms. A powerful source of relied-upon promises are the features of the human resource management system. As detailed by Miles and Snow (1984), human resource practices in recruiting (making talent versus buying it), performance appraisal (focusing on short- or long-term results), and compensation (rewarding membership or merit) are implicitly linked to the organization's business strategy. Many structural signals are actually artifacts of the organization's culture (titles, promotion paths, and so on). However, in a broader sense, these signals are a way to "manufacture consent" (Buroway, 1979) or systematize elements in a manner that supports the prevailing contract of the organization. Individual employees commonly view bonus plans, performance appraisals, and training programs as forms of contracts (promises to be relied upon) and act according to the commitments conveyed and behaviors cued.

The contract-making role is, however, sometimes ambiguous with regard to structural signals. Greenberg (1992) reports that when employees feel fairly paid, they attribute the equitable compensation to the organization's fair practices. However, when perceiving pay as unfair, they are more likely to attribute this inequity to a failure on the part of their manager. Part of a manager's role may in fact be to buffer employees from inconsistencies in structural signals. Although they may get less credit for this task, managers are likely to be blamed when this job is not accomplished.

Appearances are a major issue in procedural fairness. A manager who makes tough decisions by drawing lots, but does so in private, is likely to cast doubt on his or her impartiality. Demands for procedural fairness have increased in recent years (Greenberg, Bies, & Eskew, 1991). Thus the interpretation people make of structural signals may be related to process consistency as well as to outcome fairness.

Personnel actions such as recruiting and performance reviews are interactions that shape employee perceptions of contracts. If people are open to contract-communicating information only at particular points in time, episodes signaling change (e.g., recruitment) or periodic reviews (e.g., performance appraisal) take on a special meaning. Some events are merely illustrative, confirming previous beliefs, but others may signal a turning point. From a psychological contracts perspective, commitments regarding future benefits and opportunities in exchange for membership and performance frequently shape contracts made during interviews and performance feedback, in specification of pay systems and associated benefits, and in other stipulations regarding the conditions of employment.

By looking at human resource practices contractually, we can examine the messages conveyed by various personnel activities. Contract features associated with personnel practices include the following (Rousseau & Greller, 1994; Table 3.5).

Future promises involve the extent to which actions are based on an anticipated future as opposed to contemporaneous actions. Deferred compensation, seniority, career paths, and retirement benefits convey future commitments, but their absence signals the lack of such commitments.

The issue of *multiple contract makers* concerns how many actors (individuals, organizational entities) are involved in negotiating and certifying the contract. The organization may have a single personnel manual but as many ways of reviewing performance as it has managers.

Performance standards indicate the explicitness of employee contributions in exchange for inducements the organization offers. Contingencies may be spelled out thoroughly in some performance reviews but poorly articulated in either the recruitment or the compensation systems.

The issue of *different contracts with different employees* involves the extent to which the individual's contract is specific or unique. The generality of the contract may be a defining feature of the company culture (e.g., IBM's traditional employment relationship) and as such functions to attract and

TABLE 3.5 Human Resource Practices and Contract Features

	Recruiting	*Performance Review*	*Compensation*	*Training*	*Personnel Manuals*	*Benefits*
Future promises	yes	sometimes	yes	yes	sometimes	yes
Performance standards	sometimes	yes	sometimes	yes	sometimes	broad terms
Multiple contract makers	sometimes	sometimes	no	yes	no	generic
Different contracts across employees	yes	yes	sometimes	yes	no[a]	no[a]
Interpretation	personal	personal	social	typically personal	social	social
Dynamic/fixed	dynamic	dynamic	dynamic or fixed based on system	dynamic	relatively fixed	fixed

a. Unless there are employee classifications (e.g., exempt and nonexempt) with different employment arrangements.

hold members. To the extent that managers can "cut" different deals for their subordinates, the organization may be party to a variety of distinct contracts with its members.

Interpretation is how one makes sense of what entitlements and obligations are, personally or through social information processing. Some benefits, such as sick leave, may be subject to social interpretation (entitlement to use it all even if the employee is not ill), but others may be more person specific and idiosyncratic.

Dynamic/fixed describes the malleability of the contracts as conveyed through a specific practice over time. Benefits relied upon by generations of employees may be more difficult to change than compensation systems, especially performance contingencies.

PERSONNEL HANDBOOKS AND MANUALS

Personnel manuals vary in the range of behaviors and human resource activities they address. Some commit the organization to grievance mechanisms, some to career paths, and others to specific performance requirements (or at least definitions of substandard performance). Far more unequivocal than recruiting activities, such documents outline general conditions of employment for broad classes of organization members. Employees are likely to perceive themselves as party to the same contract terms as coworkers with respect to handbooks. Manuals and handbooks are less salient and attention getting than compensation or interaction with people. Personnel manuals often are not used until a problem that requires adjudication has arisen. Then the reader peruses the manual looking for information supportive of her sense of grievance or justification for actions already taken.

As contracting mechanisms, manuals do convey some future promises. Handbooks specifying the status of probationary employees, for instance, indicate that point (usually from three months to a year) after which the member attains status in the organization, which makes termination more difficult. Handbooks and manuals often are written for legal reasons. Frequently used to strengthen American firms' claims of "at-will employment status," such documents contain disclaimers for obligation or commitment. Disclaimers or "weasel clauses" maintain an organization's flexibilities or justify inconsistent application of procedures. The strength of the language used and the absence of disclaimers are important in determining perceived obligations (McLean Parks & Schmedemann, 1994). Often, however, the function handbooks and manuals perform is to spell out the requirements of procedural justice in case of dismissals or discipline situations.

Performance standards are spelled out in some documents, including rules governing attendance, substance abuse, and requirements for progressive discipline in the case of substandard performance. Personnel manuals tend to be unilateral, reflecting the organization as principal contract maker. Status differences may be spelled out, conveying different entitlements across *types* of employees. However, idiosyncratic deals are not the subject of handbooks, which give rise to more universalistic contract terms. Consistent with Parks and Schmedemann's findings that handbooks use commonly understood language, a social consensus exists regarding the meaning of handbook terms. As a relatively stable source of employment conditions, handbooks and manuals change infrequently. Revisions can signal significant broad-based change in the organization.

INTERNAL CAREER LADDERS AND TITLES

Hierarchy is a culturally loaded phenomenon. Norms of status or equality can vary across organizations as well as nations. Research on Japanese firms transplanted to the United States indicates that American workers require more job classifications than the Japanese to provide the appearance of an internal career ladder (Florida & Kenney, 1991). Differentiation of jobs signals both personnel movement as well as possible rewards in the form of status and increased responsibility, and is associated typically with increased pay.

The changes to internal career ladders that are often most resisted are those involving status rather than pay. In a manufacturing firm where the role of "engineer" required a minimum of 7 years of training and line-work experience, the engineers themselves were the major source of resistance to self-regulated teamwork. Their major objection revolved around the loss of status achieved by years of training. Even though pay would initially remain the same, the status loss appeared to be a violation of an agreement made as they began their apprenticeship.

Career ladders are laden with promises regarding rewards for training or for rotation through a certain set of assignments ("ticket punches"). Performance standards are often articulated in career progression, especially with regard to the types and length of experience required for advancement. Multiple contract makers do exist in internal labor markets, where rate of advancement can depend on the type of assignments available to the employee and the supportiveness of bosses, especially earlier in one's career. Though there are general features to career ladders, the manager-subordinate interaction can create different contract terms across employees. As visible signs of status and achievement, career ladders become associated with social esteem, which gives them strong culturally supported meanings. The title of professor might not readily be shared in a university, even with an adjunct instructor who has taught there for years and for all intents and purposes has "moral tenure." Similarly, titles have special significance when associated with distinct career paths, as in the case of technical hierarchies. Career ladders have historically been relatively stable and resistant to change. However, the emerging notions of boundaryless careers and lateral moves suggest that in the future our models of career may become quite dynamic and fluid. In the study of Japanese firms transplanted to the United States (e.g., Nissan and Honda), it is interesting to note that, although U.S. workers preferred more levels in the internal career ladder, transplants were characterized by greater status equality than in Japan. Managers and workers had fewer distinctions in terms of dress. For example, all employees wore uniforms, rather than workers wearing uniforms and managers wearing suits. Perhaps cultural notions about what makes a job good—many promotion opportunities but few status differences due to rank—affect the meaning of career ladders in the employees' psychological contract.

COMPENSATION PRACTICES

At the heart of the employment relationship are decisions employees and employers make about compensation. Typically the single largest cost incurred by the organization, compensation is also critical to being an "employer of choice" in the labor market (Gerhart & Milkovich, 1992). Compensation has direct effects on job satisfaction, attraction, retention, performance, cooperation, flexibility, skill development, risk taking, and a host of key outcomes. It also facilitates and constrains the effects of human resources activities, from recruitment to retention. Compensation decisions have important consequences for individuals, not only in terms of income but also as indicators of social status and success in life (Gerhart & Milkovich, 1992).

As a contract-making mechanism, compensation is a visible, salient, personally and socially significant signal of the nature of the employment relationship. Messages conveyed by compensation include

- *Values:* objectives achieved by the system varying from productivity to parity to cost containment
- *Performance standards:* what is rewarded, such as membership or risk taking
- *Time frames:* short-term returns versus long-term growth
- *Equity:* how much disparity exists between employees doing essentially the same work, between senior management and workers, and between the organization and the external labor market

Employer surveys conducted by the Conference Board show that the relative importance of factors used to set corporate wage objectives changed from the 1970s to the 1980s (Belous, 1989). In the 1970s, building a loyal, stable workforce was the foremost value, and pay parity was viewed as a means to that end. Concerns over productivity and labor force trends finished fourth on the list. By the 1980s, this pattern had reversed. Increased competition and a tighter job market altered the objectives pursued in corporate pay systems. By the 1980s, pay systems focused on pay-for-performance and reduced labor costs.

Despite extensive research indicating the motivational value of pay, especially of performance-contingent or incentive pay, historically managers have resisted strict payout formulas. Supervisors can feel that incentive systems undermine their power to reward individuals and groups informally. Moreover, some managers oppose incentives for paying people to do "what they are already supposed to do." If performance standards are viewed as a condition of employment, managers can view merit pay as an incentive only for exceptional or superlative performance, and not as pay for performance per se.

From a contracts perspective, compensation clearly has a promissory quality. Labor economists speak of "sticky wages"—wages may rise with the value of labor in the external market, but they are less likely to go down. Reliance losses by employees who have formed a lifestyle around their income level impede wage cutting. Seniority systems create rewards for membership and offer a promise of higher pay tomorrow if junior people accept less money today. Compensation packages that include stock options promote an interest in the long-term viability of the organization and also signal a higher level of involvement and inclusion for individuals in the organization. From the CEO ranks to the shop floor, stock options signal a commitment—enhancing identification with the organization and motivating actions in the best interest of the organization. Thus stock options alter the nature of the employment relationship. They also permit labor costs to vary with organizational performance, adding a clear performance term to the employee's psychological contract.

Parity with the market has traditionally been a compensation objective. Equity, the perceived fairness of the pay system, is one reason for parity's importance. By creating comparisons, the concept of parity produces yet another pay feature: gift giving. Organizations paying higher than market wages, especially without a performance contingency, can be viewed as giving their employees something extra, in other words, a gift. Gift giving connotes expectations of reciprocity, often in terms of greater loyalty to the giver, support and accommodation in the relationship, and the potential for extra forms of contributions over time. Employee citizenship behavior (desirable behaviors that one does not *have* to do) occurs where people feel not just fairly treated but also extremely well treated by their employer. Citizenship, customer service, and internal support to coworkers are linked to employment arrangements that go beyond transactional exchanges to emphasize membership and involvement.

Performance standards are conveyed by compensation systems. Employees are more willing to take risks when variable compensation exists (Gomez-Meijia & Balkin, 1989), for example, when employee entrepreneurial activities are rewarded. High performers are also more likely to remain in organizations where pay is contingent on performance, affecting both actual performance levels as well as expected ones (norms).

PERFORMANCE REVIEWS

What the organization measures, monitors, and controls are major signals regarding the nature of the contract. Performance appraisal processes are central to contract making. Messages are sent in three ways through the appraisal process: by what is measured, by who measures it, and by how the information is used.

What Is Measured? Two basic types of information are gathered in performance reviews: *results,* or the goals and objectives achieved, and *behaviors,* or how people go about doing their jobs.

A results-oriented performance review focuses on measurable outcomes (e.g., sales, profits, errors), often using goal setting and accomplishments as found in Management by Objectives (MBO)-type appraisals. A key performance term in the employee's contract is the extent to which the goals are individual or group level, thus signaling the importance of being an individual contributor or an interdependent team member. Results-oriented assessments reflect the degree of external competitiveness recognized by the organization, and can be measured in the short or long term. Short-term measures reflect immediately demonstrable outcomes, such as monthly sales figures. Long-term measures include both growth and innovation-related indicators, for example, market share and rate of change, as well as intervening indicators of long-term trends, such as percentage of sales from products developed in the past three years, new programs initiated, or number of staff developed.

A behaviorally oriented assessment focuses on how people do their jobs. Information gathered can be related to employee traits (e.g., dependability), skills (e.g., written communication, presentation style), or specific demonstrable behaviors (e.g., filing reports on time, responding quickly to customer requests). In general, organizations with a strong culture emphasizing long-term membership largely focus on behaviorally oriented assessments. By telling people what behaviors are expected, the organization creates norms and shared roles.

Who Measures Performance? Obtaining performance information from peers, coworkers, and customers signals whose perspective is valued by the organization. Traditional managerial performance reviews are being supplemented by other constituencies interdependent with the employee. If information is not obtained from any group with whom the employee is interdependent, this omission indicates a lower priority for servicing the needs of that group.

How Is Performance Information Used? Performance information might be used to make decisions about the employee, or it might be fed back to the employee, or it might just sit in a file folder. How it is used affects its potential to reward behavior and focus employee attention and efforts on specific results or activities. Uses of performance information include motivation and feedback; remediation, training, and development; organizational planning; and legal actions. Performance appraisals can bring organizational expectations of both the employer and the employee to the surface. Role clarity and goal setting also improve motivation. Reviews foster development when they identify areas for improvement or strengths to be capitalized on. Performance appraisals can be used in individual career planning as well as in documenting capabilities available for organizational use. In this manner, they contribute to overall organization planning, for example, through the use of integrated databases or human resource information systems. Finally, performance appraisals are also useful in defending or protecting an organization that is attempting to dismiss an employee "for cause" (substandard performance or inappropriate conduct). Because courts in the United States frequently require a "paper trail" of two or more substandard reviews before justifying a dismissal "for cause," performance reviews document organizational adherence to due process.

Contractually, performance reviews are replete with future-oriented language specifying both performance and promised benefits. They set both psychological and legal standards for the employee's part of the contract. Increasingly, there are multiple contract makers in the performance appraisal process. Team-oriented, networked, and matrixed organizations may have many different raters expressing their definitions of the "performance standards" required of a particular employee. Unless wholly archival (e.g., based on sales records), performance standards generate a diversity of contracts across employees. This divergence escalates when managers handle the feedback process differently among themselves as well as across their own employees. Performance reviews create contracts that are interpreted at the individual level and are thus subject to the employee's recall and experiences in the feedback process. As a contract communicator, performance reviews provide relative flexibility for conveying new contract terms.

Training. Typically the focus of training is to benefit the individual rather than the firm. Hussey (1985) argues that it may be better to design training to implement the firm's strategy, thus indirectly benefiting the individual through the firm's growth. In this manner, training creates promises that are more likely to be kept. Training viewed as an investment signals a desire to retain and deploy the individual and his or her skills over time. Some forms of training, for example, sponsoring bank employees to obtain their M.B.A. degrees at night, may be viewed as perks. However, for an ambitious employee who expects to change employers eventually, training can be considered a long-term investment. Firms often require "golden handcuffs" by having sponsored employees sign a payback agreement promising enough service to return this investment.

It is more likely that training that focuses explicitly on strategic organizational objectives, such as GE's investment in team-building training as part of a shift toward self-managed work groups, will be *understood* as conveying a statement of future intent. Given the mutual investment such strategically focused training entails (both employee and employer spend time, effort, and resources), it becomes a strong structural signal. The potency of such an investment for the contract maker is underscored by the case of organizations that have attempted to promote team building through extensive training investments, only to terminate employees and restructure the organization during lean times. Orsburn, Moran, Musselwhite, and Berger (1990) relay the outrage of employees who believe the organization betrayed the trust implicit in both teamwork and extensive investments in *organization-specific* developments. It may be better to put training and teamwork on hold until the organization can honor the promises that development makes.

Training does convey future promises, especially when the training focuses explicitly on strategic organizational concerns. Performance standards can be conveyed in terms of accepting training, developing mastery, and transferring learning back to the organization. Training can have multiple contract makers, especially because much of its success depends on the support received from immediate supervisors. If training is contingent on individual performance, different deals often exist for different employees. Training, especially when focused on individual skills and learning, is subject to personal interpretations of commitments made, but the increasing popularity of group-focused training facilitates development of social constructions. Because training is undertaken for both personal and organizational reasons, it is subject to change and thus becomes a dynamic element of contracting.

Benefits. Benefits are becoming increasingly important in bringing potential employees to the job market and in retaining current employees. Rising health care costs and an aging workforce concerned about pensions are drivers in the pursuit of benefits. Meanwhile, dramatic increases in the cost of benefits have spurred containment efforts aimed at improving corporate profits (Lucero & Allen, 1994). Changing economic conditions have made it difficult for organizations to sustain attractive benefits packages, let alone respond to demands for their expansion, especially in the area of health care. Reviewing the history of employee benefits in the United States, Lucero and Allen begin by describing the emergence of contemporary benefits issues in the workplaces of the 1940s. The relatively homogeneous workforce of this era, backed by the support of organized labor, led organizations to create "one size fits all" benefits packages. Under this model, benefits and costs borne by employers increased over time due to growing workforce needs, union pressure, and favorable tax considerations. In recent history, competitive pressures and rising costs have fostered a reexamination of employee benefits, especially the composition of the "package." Cost reduction has been a factor in the move toward independent contracting and part-time employment as a means of reducing the benefits burden to employers. In the 1980s, 29% of the U.S. workforce was contingent—made up of part-timers, temporaries, subcontractors, consultants, and "life of the project" and leased workers. Contingents have a lesser chance of obtaining various employee benefits, including health care and pension coverage, making them economically less secure than traditional employees. More than three quarters of individuals who work full-time receive health insurance coverage from their employers, in contrast to less than one third of part-time employees (Levitan & Conway, 1988). The contingent growth rate is twice as fast as the civilian labor force as a whole (Belous, 1989).

Benefits as contract-conveying devices are rich in promises with regard to the future. As I read over my annual benefits description from my university, sent to remind employees of the large investment the university makes in us and our families, I was struck by its breadth: Social Security and Medicare (matching payments); several forms of life, medical, dental, and disability insurance; retirement; and reduced tuition plans for spouses and children. Reliance on this package arises because of its costliness and also because of its impact on the wide scope of one's life.

Performance standards are notably missing from descriptions of benefits, because they are more directly related to conditions of employment (having benefits-entitled status as opposed to a contingent or peripheral role). In the future, benefits may become a better indicator of status than the title one holds. Though multiple contract makers are rare in benefits negotiations, different contracts do exist across employees by rank, and among smaller employers there may be many idiosyncratic deals. Interpretation is largely social, given the general nature of benefits. And despite much pressure to reduce costs, benefits packages remain relatively stable features of employment.

Mission Statements. Proclamations of an organization's goals can act as artifacts that transmit the deeper values and tacit knowledge that characterize membership in the larger group. In his early seminal work on psychological contracts, Levinson (1962) offered the basic missions of several organizations in depicting their psychological contracts with members. He argued that people seek out organizations whose basic missions and values are consistent with their own. Although Levinson was a clinician and inclined to view many aspects of contracting as unconscious, he identified a host of patterns that characterized the different contracts associated with diverse organizational missions. Some aspects are conscious, such as return of loyalty and service for guaranteed employment; others are unconscious, for example, the assumption that today's core business (product or service) will continue to be *the* viable core business in the future.

Midland Utilities, an organization described by Levinson (1962), had a mission to generate electrical current, to return a profit to its stockholders, and to serve its customers. In its contract, it promised to be a "good company" to each of its constituencies. In return, its management "wanted to be liked. Nothing pleases its management more than to be recognized as a responsible management that provides good return on investment and good service" (p. 291). Like many utilities, Midland preferred to be invisible and taken for granted, providing a service so stable and profits so steady that people relied on it without question. This mission generates a risk-averse culture valuing reliability and continuity. It also has a public side—stability and favorable stockholder ratings—and a private side—rule oriented, failure avoiding, with both conflict and change suppressed. Mission statements in reliability-oriented organizations convey continuity and stability as well as promoting confidence and discouraging disagreement.

In contrast, organizations in the midst of change in strategy and culture often go through the process of creating a mission statement (or rewriting an existing one) to signal a commitment to change. Mission statements cannot change culture by themselves, but they are capable of indicating that deeper changes are planned. The processes used to create a mission statement can be culture-changing events that signal new expectations and commitments. A drug abuse counseling organization seeking to become more responsive to its community goes off site to a retreat and begins questioning its identity, role, and mission. This self-study can open up the organization to problem solving; writing a mission statement is a tangible task in the deeper process of change.

Contractually, mission statements frequently rely on future promises ("employer of choice," "continuous growth and development") and express performance standards such as "teamwork" and "risk taking." Mission statements convey broad terms to all organization members and as such send a global message. Social interpretation, or signaling values and change to promote general discussion, is the basic purpose of a mission statement. Organizations that get to the point of laminating mission statements for people to carry in their pockets are creating an artifact that is not readily changed without breaking with the past. Mission statements cannot be effective if revised from year to year.

Other "Artifacts": Brochures and Advertisements. Selling is a central purpose of corporate recruiting literature. As illustrated in the previously described academic program, recruits form impressions of the organization's values and management style based on its brochures and descriptions provided to the media in the form of news items and industry features.

Unrealistic, global, and vague overpromises abound in brochures. Typically, little is conveyed regarding expectations for employee performance, because such brochures are more concerned with marketing the organization than with educating the applicant. Brochures present extremely general contract terms for the organization at large and for all new incoming employees. However, their interpretation tends to be personal rather than social, because their target audience is individuals who are not yet part of an intact social group. Because of their external nature, advertisements and brochures are perhaps more readily changed than other documents.

DISCONNECTION: WHEN HUMAN AND ADMINISTRATIVE CONTRACT MAKERS DISAGREE

The systems organizations use to recruit people, assess their performance, and compensate and manage relationships with them are the essential human resource practices in organizations. Each system, though in theory interrelated (Miles & Snow, 1984), typically functions distinctly in organizations. Recruitment may be handled by part of the organization and compensation and benefits by yet another. This disconnection reflects the specialization and distinct expertise contemporary organizations employ in the management of human resource functions. Lack of integration, however, sends mixed signals to contract parties and can hamper ability to make a contract that can be kept. Misaligned messages confuse employees about appropriate ways to fulfill their end of the contract and may commit the organization to terms that are difficult to keep or even mutually exclusive.

Contract makers are most likely to be aligned when the organization's culture is itself coherent and consistent. Martin (1992) observes that cultures can promote integration (when values and norms are consistent and widely shared) or conflict (when there is no consensus). Going back to the onion model of culture (Chapter 2), we argue that when basic assumptions, values, norms, behavior patterns, and artifacts affirm a common belief system, the organization is more likely to create both well-articulated contracts with individuals as well as shared normative contracts across members.

Take, for example, an intensive care unit (ICU) where both nursing and physician leadership stress the importance of teamwork and cooperation among caregivers (Figure 3.1). Physicians and nurses have different contract makers due to their professions and the roles they play. Physicians may or may not be full-time employees (e.g., private admitters have their own practices; physicians employed by the hospital may work elsewhere) but nurses usually are. Similar culture elements will sometimes need to be created by different means for the two groups (e.g., nurses receive formal performance reviews annually but physicians often receive none). The jobs that nurses and physicians do clearly are different, because only physicians can authorize medical care. Nonetheless, a teamwork culture requires that the two groups share behavioral norms (e.g., cooperation), values (e.g., quality care matters more than status), and behavior patterns (e.g., joint meetings). Such a sharing occurs when they also share a normative contract whose performance terms are comparable. The fact that both are influenced by both the nurse and the physician managers of the unit gives them some contract makers in common. On the other hand, when ICUs have hierarchical cultures with limited cooperation between nurses and physicians, the performance terms for each will differ with the distinct roles they play. Contract makers will send different messages to each.

EMPLOYEES AS CONTRACT MAKERS

There remains one other critical contract maker in the employment relationship: the employee. In recruitment and socialization as well as in interactions with managers and coworkers, individual employees are actively involved in information gathering and communicating. These behaviors shape the specificity and focus of the contracts that evolve.

Both as newcomer and as veteran, employees create contracts. This process has received attention in research and in organizational efforts to socialize newcomers. What has been neglected in both research and practice is a recognition that newcomers often take a proactive role in initiating and managing various aspects of their own socialization. Anticipating new information, newcomers actively observe and monitor. Little wonder that in the case of the academic program described in the opening of this chapter, first-year students had no trouble reporting a long list of contract makers, from deans to fellow students to assorted brochures and documents. Moreover, cognizant of their need to learn, newcomers are often assertive in gathering information through inquiry, scanning, and search. Researchers on socialization report that newcomers who actively seek information adjust better, assess the organization's culture more accurately, and understand their own jobs better.

Wolfe Morrison (1991) argues that newcomers seek three types of information about their job: technical (how to perform required tasks), referent (role demands and expectations), and normative (the organization's culture), thus obtaining both performance and social feedback. Monitoring entails

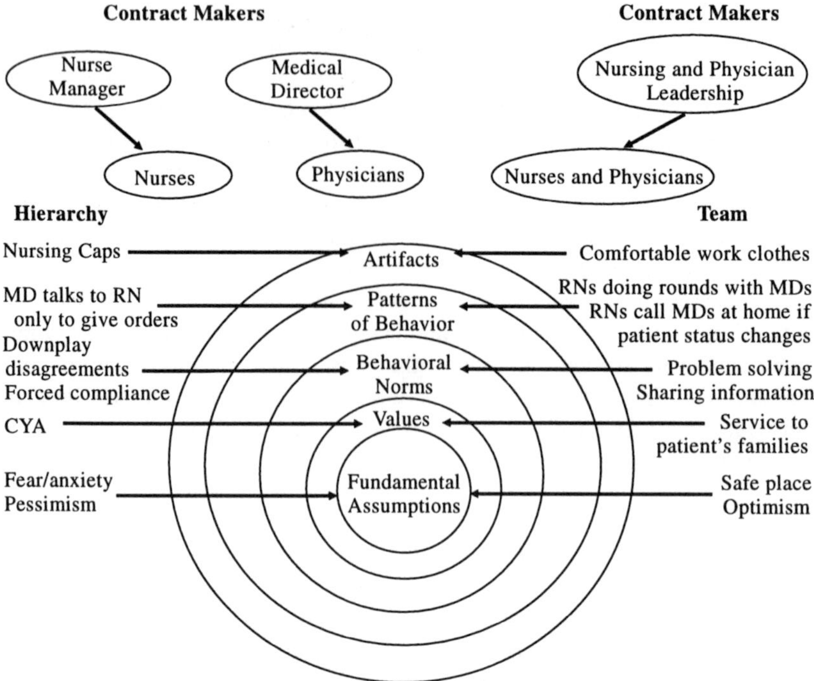

FIGURE 3.1. Contract Makers and Culture in ICUs

attending to information cues obtained from watching the behavior of others. It requires construction of meaning, which potentially leads to misinterpretation (Ashford & Cummings, 1983). Inquiry involves active solicitation of information, which might cause the seeker to appear insecure, incompetent, or ignorant (Ashford & Cummings, 1983). Direct information seeking also can reveal deficiencies in the seeker's interpersonal skills or draw attention to performance failures (Wolfe Morrison & Bies, 1991). As such, individuals may avoid direct inquiry to protect their image. All things being equal, individuals may be more likely to engage in monitoring (Ashford, 1986), except when in need of technical information, which is often obtained more accurately through inquiry.

Newcomers do tend to rely more on monitoring than inquiry, unless they have a readily available mentor. A supervisor or a peer close in age and status might make them feel comfortable enough to actively ask questions. An array of means are available for information seeking: overt and indirect questions, use of third parties, testing limits, disguised conversations, observing, and surveillance (Miller & Jablin, 1991).

Rates of information acquisition decline over time as members accommodate to the organization and rely on the information they have stored and processed. Over time, feedback seeking is more likely to occur when people expect the information to be positive, for example, when they expect to receive praise for a job well done (Wolfe Morrison & Cummings, 1992). Given our view of contract creation as intermittent and episodic, it is no surprise that employees do not seek information continuously. The longer the members are in the organization, the less they inquire or monitor. Significant changes, including both normal transitions (e.g., promotion or transfer) as well as unexpected ones (e.g., downsizing, culture change), cue employees to seek new information, to make sense of new information, and to interpret it in light of existing models.

THE "REAL" CONTRACT

What is the "real" contract? Probably nowhere do we observe more disagreement regarding the creation of contracts than when there are multiple contract makers. Legally there is much contention regarding what constitutes a reasonable employer commitment. As a recent court case has argued: "A causal remark made at a meeting, a phrase plucked out of context, is too fragile a base on which to rest such a heavy obligation inherent in . . . a contract" (*Brown v. Safeway Stores, Inc.* 1960, pp. 299-300).

Nonetheless, all sorts of commitments are in fact being made all the time in organizations. We often encounter the belief that "if it is not legally binding it is not a contract." How can an organization be held accountable for commitments made by someone else in its employ? A better question, however, might be, When should an organization hold *itself* accountable for commitments made by its agents and relied on by its members?

Recall the adage "the customer is always right." Despite warranties to the contrary, service-minded organizations find themselves bound to honor the customer's point of view regarding service quality or else forgo their future business. It is often not the legal deal but the perceived contract that drives the response of organizations to a customer complaint. Similarly, in the case of employment contracts, when employees are valued, valuable, and difficult to replace, it likely that responses to complaints of violation will take the employee's point of view into account, regardless of any legal standing they might have.

We are approaching the danger point of arguing that perhaps it doesn't matter what employer and employee or buyer and seller actually committed to, only what they think they agreed on, or perhaps even only what one or the other can convince the courts was the basic nature of the agreement. However, contracts are not an exercise in manipulation or distortion of reality. Rather, they are attempts at the creation of mutuality—where an exchange occurs that both parties desire and value. Mutuality means that each party benefits, obtains some capacity to predict what the other will do, and is enabled to improve his or her ability to yield desired results. Neither 100% agreement on the facts of the situation nor a total convergence of values is required for each party to benefit. In organizations, the multiple perspectives possible mean there need be no single "real" contract. It is what organizations and their members hold themselves accountable for that matters.

HOW TO MAKE OR NOT MAKE A CONTRACT: ILLUSTRATION

Aligning the messages contract makers send is a large part of making a contract that the organization can keep. Consider the case of two corporate education programs (Table 3.6). Two firms sponsor selected employees in a full-time M.B.A. degree program at major universities. Both companies refer to these full-time students as Fellows. The stated goal for each is to groom future middle- and upper-level managers. With this goal, in effect, the contract might be expressed as "successfully complete the M.B.A. degree and the organization will utilize your training and create career opportunities for you."

Commutech selects older (30+) employees who have a successful track record with the company. During their two-year graduate school studies, Commutech Fellows remain on company records as full-time employees assigned to the same division where they worked before graduate school. Salary and benefits continue as before and time in school counts toward seniority. Company newsletters continue to be mailed out to Commutech Fellows, who speak regularly by phone with their boss and other work group members. Commutech Fellows make regular reports to their division regarding how their school experience applies to problems they have worked on within the company. In effect, Commutech Fellows are still on the job.

Domestic Enterprises recruits younger (in their twenties) employees into their program. Employees are placed on leave from the company and lose seniority while away. A stipend and tuition is offered for Fellows, administered out of a special Benefits department. Their contact with the company is an executive-level mentor. Fellows usually initiate contact with the men-

TABLE 3.6 How to Make a Contract (or Not): The Case of Two Continuing Education Programs

	Commutech	*Domestic Enterprises*
Program	Two-year M.B.A. program paid for by employer	Two-year M.B.A. program paid for by employer
Status	Employed	On leave
Implementation	Graduate school seen as valuable developmental assignment; akin to a regular work assignment	Graduate school seen as a "ticket punch"; akin to taking time off where students are "slackers"
	Select older, loyal employees	Select younger, less experienced employees
	Company and work group communicate frequently with student	Executive-level mentor communicates infrequently with student
Reentry	Assignment builds on experience at school	Former department still owns students; little use of new skills
	Student keeps seniority while at school	Student loses seniority while at school

tor, who may not know the Fellow personally. Although Fellows are still technically tied to their original department, mentors are usually from other areas and are usually more senior than the Fellow's original boss. Mentors have little interaction with the Fellow.

In the culture of Commutech, going to graduate school is seen as a valuable assignment. Indeed, it is a regular work assignment. At Domestic, going to graduate school is seen as a "ticket punch," a lucky break for the fortunate Fellow who is chosen. Being at school is seen as being away from the company and students are viewed as slackers, enjoying a good time at company expense. After obtaining the degree, Commutech Fellows receive assignments that build on their education. Marketing majors might be reassigned to an area requiring that expertise with similar use of other specialties. At Domestic, Fellows return to their previous jobs and hope for promotion. Turnover among Fellows at Domestic is 35% after 2 years (the minimum payback time required) and substantially higher for those who received no promotion within that time. Turnover among Fellows is virtually nonexistent at Commutech. Recently, Domestic cut back substantially on the Fellowship program because of the limited benefits it appears to offer. Commutech's program continues.

Critical differences between these programs involve the clarity of expectations and consistency in messages they create. There are no clear performance terms for Domestic Fellows or for their mentors. Fellows treat the program as a personal benefit not tied to any payback or contribution to the company other than a 2-year minimum stay. Commutech Fellows are performing company-related duties while at school. Commutech managers make specific requests of their Fellows and tie them back to the organization and their work group. Domestic mentors, typically unavailable to the Fellow, convey no particular performance expectations. Fellows at Domestic have little idea how their schooling might be used by the organization later. They view the M.B.A. education in terms of their own interests and concerns rather than the company's. On the other hand, the contract between Commutech and its Fellows is one of ongoing participation, idea exchange, and involvement.

Key differences between making and not making a workable contract include whether

performance terms are specified during the fellowship;

long-term planning uses acquired skills;

ongoing contact between organization and Fellow maintains relationship, loyalty, and identification;

consistent messages are sent by various human resources functions regarding Fellow's membership and status in the organization;

cultural support exists for the kind of contract the program claims to offer.

In effect, the difference between the two programs and the results they achieve are tied to the alignment of contract makers, the messages they send, and the actions they take.

CONCLUSIONS

Employers have multiple contract makers who act for themselves as principals and as agents for the organization. Many disconnections can occur between commitments made by managers, expectations shared by coworkers, and the human resource practices through which the organization rewards, retains, and motivates people. Several "disconnections" must be overcome in the process of creating effective contracts:

- Discrepancies among contract makers
- Discrepancies between the organization's agents and the organization itself

Contract violation occurs at least as commonly as contract completion. In a recent study, 54% of new hires reported some contract breach in the first 2 years of employment (Robinson & Rousseau, 1994). It is likely that a good deal of this breach arises from different interpretations of the deal and changes among contract makers. Understanding how managers, coworkers, human resource practices, and organizational culture shape individual psychological contracts can lead us toward more consistent communication and management of the psychological contract.

Contemporary Contracts

Three pieces of advice to would-be contract makers:

Today's shocks are tomorrow's conventions.

—*Carolyn Heilbrun*
(1973, as quoted in Partnow, 1993, p. 409)

I like to deliver more than I promise instead of the other way around. It's one of my many trade secrets.

—*Dorothy Uhnak*
(1977, as quoted in Partnow, 1993, p. 445)

Always be smarter than the people who hire you.

—*Lena Horne*
(attributed, in Partnow, 1993, p. 381)

"The old psychological contract is dead," proclaims Hal (1993) and many other contemporary writers (e.g., Hirsch, 1987; Hirschhorr & Gilmore, 1992). This statement can be interpreted in a number of ways:

1. An established employment practice (or contract term, such as that higl performers have job security) has changed.
2. Some form of widespread social contract such as steady employment has bee: eroded.
3. Organizational changes have reduced trust between employees and employ ers, making contracting difficult.

Pervasive organizational and workforce changes have disrupted any nur ber of contracts at several levels. Because individual contracts can poter tially take an infinite number of forms, changing business practices (Davi:

1987) and economic pressures (Bettis, Bradley, & Hamel, 1992) can easily erode many traditional employment features if not abrogate entire contracts. To provide a basis for understanding contemporary contracts, this chapter addresses the patterns in which discrete promises or contract terms are typically arrayed. It outlines historical developments in employment contracts along with current trends in employment and worker-organization attachments, and their implications for successful contracting.

FEATURES OF CONTRACTS

Although contracts can take an infinite number of forms, certain types of contact terms tend to cluster together. For instance, terms such as *incentive pay* and *well-specified performance levels* tend to go together as do *loyalty* and *concern for employee well-being.* Although each organization and each worker has his or her own idiosyncratic ways of expressing contract terms, these terms do tend to fit into certain general categories. The general terms that researchers have focused on in the study of psychological contracts have been referred to as *transactional* and *relational.* These terms can be thought of as being at two ends of a contractual continuum (Macneil, 1985; Rousseau, 1989; Figure 4.1).

Transactional terms are exemplified by *a fair day's work for a fair day's pay*—focusing on short-term and monetizable exchanges. Employment agencies such as Manpower, Kelly, Nursetemps, Accountemps, and other temporary employment services offer organizations the opportunity to create purely transactional agreements with workers.

Typical transactional contract terms include the following:

- Specific economic conditions (e.g., wage rate) as primary incentive
- Limited personal involvement in the job (e.g., working relatively few hours, low emotional investment)
- Closed-ended time frame (e.g., seasonal employment, 2 to 3 years on the job at most)
- Commitments limited to well-specified conditions (e.g., union contract)
- Little flexibility (change requires renegotiation of contract)
- Use of existing skills (no development)
- Unambiguous terms readily understood by outsiders

At the other end of the continuum is the relational contract, which focuses on open-ended relationships involving considerable investments by both employees (company-specific skills, long-term career development) and

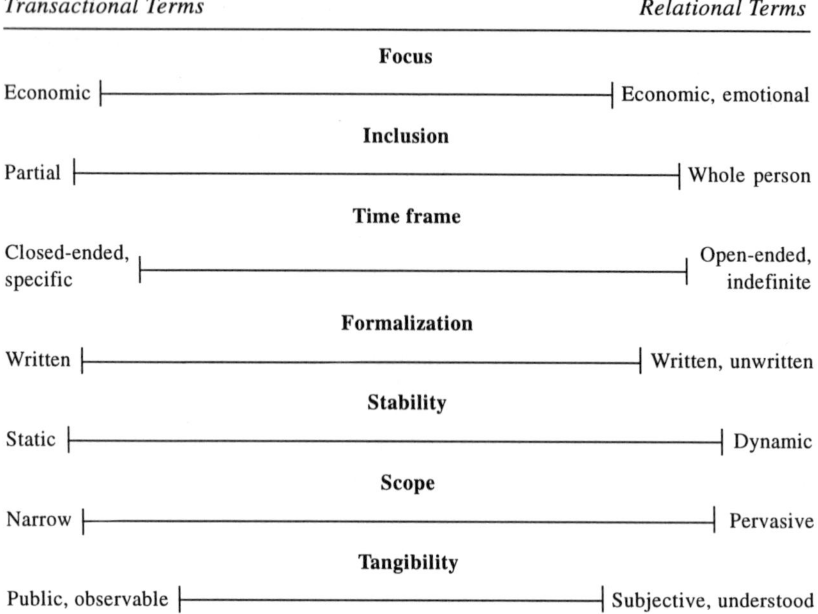

FIGURE 4.1. A Continuum of Contract Terms

employers (extensive training). Such investments involve a high degree of mutual interdependence and barriers to exit. The clustering of contract terms into relational and transactional patterns is consistent with various areas of contract law, including laws governing agency, employment, incorporation, and marriage.

Typical relational terms include the following:

- Emotional involvement as well as economic exchange (e.g., personal support, concern for family well-being)
- Whole person relations (e.g., growth, development)
- Open-ended time frames (i.e., indefinitely)
- Both written and unwritten terms (e.g., some terms emerge over time)
- Dynamic and subject to change during the life of the contract
- Pervasive conditions (e.g., affects personal and family life)
- Subjective and implicitly understood (i.e., conditions difficult for third party to understand)

Contracts in organizations weave these terms in various ways, with some arrangements being almost fully transactional while others are highly relational in nature. Recently, many organizations, especially those with high-involvement work teams, have blended the two sets together. To understand how these terms have come to characterize contemporary contracts in organizations, we need to consider historical trends in employment.

> Ideas move fast when their time comes.
>
> —*Carolyn Heilbrun*
> *(1973, as quoted in Partnow,*
> *1993, p. 409)*

A BRIEF HISTORY OF EMPLOYMENT RELATIONS AND CONTRACT FORMS

Employment relations in modern organizations have undergone transformation in the course of three major historical phases: emergent, bureaucratic, and adhocratic. These phases have given rise to diverse forms of employment relations and contracts.

Emergent. In the late eighteenth century, modern industrial production organizations began. Basic industries such as textiles and ceramics traditionally were a cottage industry where farmer-craftspersons worked at home. Urban merchants traveled the countryside trying to purchase enough goods to satisfy the growing demand in town. Many goods were produced by people who farmed in good weather and produced handiwork in bad weather or when they felt inclined to do so. Although merchants often provided equipment and material to craftspersons (e.g., looms and yarn), these middlemen had little control over such workers and, despite increases in demand, the merchants' means of increasing productivity were limited (Dickson, 1974). Factories were created to make supplies more regular.

Historically, industrial organizations were a means of control, factories bringing weavers under one roof making it possible to monitor their work and ensure a steady supply of cloth. Predictability was a major driver. Factories concentrating labor and production in one spot *preceded* development of sophisticated technology such as power machinery. Thus technological breakthroughs such as turbines and steam engines were not the cause of modern organizations but the result. Concentration of work was a managerial, not a technological, necessity (Dickson, 1974). Early factories had potters working at individual wheels and weavers at their individual looms.

Working in one place permitted production to be overseen by a foreman, changing the looser standards by which rural people often worked from what Wedgwood called "dilatory, drunken, worthless workmen" to "a very good set of hands." Early factories provided consistency in output not available from individual craftspersons. Following creation of factories, it became possible to develop and use power machinery (e.g., water-powered looms) and redesign work to improve the speed of production. Consistency in work was thus augmented by efficiency.

Efficiency developed from concentration of production in one place coupled with new technology, making it difficult for those craftspersons working at home to still compete. In a few decades, many industries changed from home-based crafts to centralized factory work. Merchants had become factory owners, and managerial work emerged in the form of foremen and overseer jobs. Evolution in employment relationships and in contracts had begun (Table 4.1).

Key features of employment relations in the emergent phase were

1. A centralized workplace
2. Worker/manager/owner distinction
3. Managerial control over time and rate of production
4. Organizational ownership over means of production
5. Development of hierarchical controls enforcing regular hours and supervisor-subordinate relations
6. Development of transactional contracts with employees having few alternatives

Bureaucratic. The next phase responded to forces for predictability and efficiency, taking them to elaborate conclusions in the form of complex hierarchical organizations with internal labor markets (Hirsch, 1994). It is this bureaucratic phase from which modern organizational theory derives (e.g., Barnard, 1938; Thompson, 1967). The traditional view of work in organizational theory is embedded in three fundamental notions: administrative control over employee wielded by the organization, development of long-term relationships between organization and employee, and physical proximity between organization and worker (Pfeffer & Baron, 1988).

This is the era portrayed by William Whyte's *Organization Man* (1956) and Rosabeth Moss Kanter's *Men and Women of the Corporation* (1977). Successful employees were those who developed organization-specific skills for working with both the technology and the social system that constituted the organization. Successful managers at the most widely admired firms entered early, climbed the rungs of the company ladder, and fulfilled the role of "company men" (Hirsch, 1994). The organization's memory and distinc-

TABLE 4.1 History and Attachment

Phase	*Contract*
Emergent	Transactional
Bureaucratic	Relational
Adhocratic	Varies with type of relationship

tive competencies typically rested in the minds and skills of its employees and managers. Consistency, efficiency, and refinement of technology were facilitated by creation of internal labor markets (ILMs) in which members who remain with the organization for indefinite periods of time develop norms for dealing with each other, as well as norms for how they go about their work, and where managers had once done the job they now oversee. ILMs create not only predictable behaviors among workers but also a predictable supply of future talent, including the organization's managers. ILMs also create career paths that offer a promise of long-term employment as organization-specific skills are acquired. Such workers became a core part of the organization, intrinsically a part of it because of the codes of behavior they had learned through socialization as well as the specific skills and technologies in which they had become proficient.

Key features of employment relations in the bureaucratic era include the following:

1. Internal labor markets involving
   - early career entry into organization
   - long-term retention
   - development of organization-specific skills
   - assimilation into an organization's culture to promote efficiency
   - delayed rewards for contributions (seniority system)
2. Organizational hierarchies facilitating
   - control over behavior
   - career opportunities
3. Slack resources seen as source of competitive advantage
   - workers paid more than market wage to foster commitment and retention
   - expansion of hierarchical levels to reward retention of managers
4. Development of relational contracts with employees, including managers,
   - and expansion of employee commitment to the organization, including identification with its goals and values, and personal sacrifice to fulfill organizational objectives

- escalation of organizational investment in individuals creating organizational commitment to members (e.g., desire to retain)

Adhocratic. Present and future employment relationships derive from a fundamental shift in the nature of work. Breakthroughs in information systems, global competition, and escalating interdependence between organizations and among people have created some new fundamentals: rapid change and tight time frames, interdependence within and between organizations, and multiple constituencies and decision makers. Speed of change makes consistency less valuable than adaptability. Diverse and segmented global markets make responsiveness critical. Flexibility is a major driver.

Established bureaucracies are slowly being replaced by adhocracies whose flexibility comes from looser structures and more individual autonomy. There are many labels for this "postbureaucratic" phase—"adhocracies," "high tech," "postindustrial," "networks" (Kanter, 1989; Venkatesh & Vitalari, 1992). Because these adaptations involve changes in the structure of occupations and the nature of work, organizational changes wrought by current technological, social, and economic forces are likely to be fundamental, not merely incremental (Venkatesh & Vitalari, 1992). By definition, fundamental changes conflict with structures created in an earlier time. Organizational research has not yet fully come to grips with this postbureaucratic form; changes in administrative control/hierarchy, relationships, and location of work have not yet shaped how organizational attachment is studied (Rousseau & Wade-Benzoni, 1994a). However, some key features of employment relations in postbureaucratic adhocracies have been identified by Handy (1989) and Hall (1993):

1. Development of differentiated employment relations within the same organization
   - core employees, essential to organizational memory and continuity, with long-term relationships to the organization
   - peripheral employees, providing flexibility as demand fluctuates or new opportunities emerge, who have limited relationships to the organization
2. Altered forms of careers (less upward mobility but more alternative career paths including midcareer shifts, phased retirement, and the option of high- and low-involvement work roles)
3. Emphasis on continuous skill development
4. Boundaryless employment relations where work may be performed in the context of several organizations simultaneously (e.g., customers serving on supplier design teams)
5. Proliferation of contract forms and varying degrees of commitment between labor and the organization

These historical trends indicate that a number of strategic organizational issues shape employment contracts. We now move to a description of the forms contemporary and emerging contracts are taking and some new "classic" contract forms.

A 2 × 2 MODEL OF CONTEMPORARY CONTRACTS

Transactional and relational terms are basic elements in most employment contracts. However, to adequately describe modern employment contracts, we must take into account two key contract features closely intertwined with transactional and relational terms (time frame and performance requirements). *Time frame* refers to the duration of the employment relationship (limited/short term or open ended/long term), but *performance requirements* involve the specification of performance as a condition of employment (well specified or weakly specified). How long the relationship is meant to last typically differentiates contracts that are largely transactional from more relational ones. However, there are relationships that though intense are meant to end (e.g., professor-student mentoring). Nonetheless, the longer a relationship endures, the more the interaction fosters the development of trust and subjective contract terms. Performance requirements are another dimension that often differentiates relationships from transactions. Well-specified performance demands characterize temporary employment (e.g., in the gift wrapping department at a department store during the Christmas rush). Veteran employees often have very loosely specified job requirements. In fact, as job tenure increases, the more likely it is that occupants will define their own jobs (Miner, 1987)—a pattern that can make it difficult to conduct job analyses in firms with veteran employees. However, performance requirements can be used as a condition of continued membership even for a veteran, especially when competitive pressures necessitate changes in the performance (standards and types of effort) organizations demand of members. More organizations are interjecting (new) specific performance demands into performance appraisals, incentive systems, and training programs. Thus it is likely that well-specified performance terms will be found in otherwise relational employment. These trends make the traditional transactional/relational distinction in contracting too simplistic.

Time frame and performance requirements have emerged as important contemporary contract features. When these two contract features are arranged in a 2 × 2 framework, four types of contracts emerge with distinct behavioral implications for workers (Figure 4.2):

Duration	*Performance Terms*: Specified	*Performance Terms*: Not Specified
Short Term	Transactional (e.g., retail clerks hired during Christmas shopping season) ■ Low ambiguity ■ Easy exit/high turnover ■ Low member commitment ■ Freedom to enter new contracts ■ Little learning ■ Weak integration/ identification	Transitional (e.g., employee experiences during organizational retrenchment or following merger or acquisition) ■ Ambiguity/uncertainty ■ High turnover/ termination ■ Instability
Long Term	Balanced (e.g., high-involvement team) ■ High member commitment ■ High integration/ identification ■ Ongoing development ■ Mutual support ■ Dynamic	Relational (e.g., family business members) ■ High member commitment ■ High affective commitment ■ High integration/ identification ■ Stability

FIGURE 4.2. Types of Psychological Contracts

- Transactional contracts—of limited duration with well-specified performance terms
- Transitional or "no guarantees" condition—essentially a breakdown in contracts, reflecting the absence of commitments regarding future employment as well as little or no explicit performance demands or contingent incentives
- Relational contracts—open-ended membership but with incomplete or ambiguous performance requirements attached to continued membership
- Balanced contracts—open-ended and relationship-oriented employment with well-specified performance terms subject to change over time

Transactional and relational terms are not mutually exclusive. Although firms employing temporary workers are likely to have pure transactional contracts (with limited commitments on both sides), and family businesses may hold to highly relational arrangements with employees, who often are also family members, two other forms also occur. Balanced contracts, which blend transactional and relational terms, occur when relationships are desired but the organization is able to specify performance demands as a condition of membership. Moreover, contemporary organizations, due to changes past and present, may manifest no clear contract terms (neither relational nor transactional), giving rise to an unstable, transitory situation referred to here as a "transitional" contract.

The following examples found in actual organizations illustrate these four distinct forms of contracting in employment.

Public Accounting's Transactional Contract

The largest public accounting firms (currently known as the Big 6 or "six-pack") are highly interdependent although they compete with each other. Because large clients tend to rotate among the firms every few years, a certain degree of standardization has arisen in the way services are provided, particularly audit and tax preparation. Although in the 1980s the growth of revenue in the Big 6 came largely from management consulting fees, the highly structured cultures of tax and audit tended to dominate most firms. To remain competitive, firms kept employment costs down by creating a pass-through system employing new college graduates willing to work public accounting's long hours at low-level jobs for the experience offered them. Typical 22-year-old entrants to public accounting spend most of the workweek on out-of-town assignments, work for low pay, and have little expectation of making partner in the firm (a realistic perspective). Regular ratings of the new recruits' project performance both promote predictable levels of performance and provide clearly defined criteria for job retention. By the time the typical entrant has left (within 3 to 5 years), he or she has sat for the CPA exam, been exposed to an array of clients, and has a job offer from another firm in a track for a position such as that organization's chief financial officer. Continual recruiting of ambitious college graduates looking for a "ticket punch" keeps labor costs down and creates a well-defined employment relationship allowing both the firm and the employee an easy exit.

Inland Oil's Era of "No Guarantees"

In the late 1980s the glut of oil on the market, fed by Saudi Arabia's push to reduce the influence (and wealth) of renegade oil producing states, coupled with worldwide recession, led to plummeting oil prices. Inland Oil, which recently had acquired a foreign petroleum producer, had extensive holdings in equipment, oil drilling facilities, and manpower (including petroleum engineers). Driven to keep its stockholders' dividend up while repositioning its organization to be more exploration (and less production) oriented, the firm initiated a series of deep cuts, which included terminating substantial numbers of staff. Because other oil companies experienced the same tough marketplace and initiated similar cuts, job prospects for terminated petroleum engineers were few and far between in their chosen field. Inland's remaining employees often worked arduously long hours under increased pressure to cut costs and improve operating efficiency. Continuing terminations had a demoralizing effect on its workforce, especially overseas, where survivors of Inland's acquisition of another petroleum producer were themselves a glut on the market. As part of an ongoing study of psychological contracts among managers, Inland Oil members were asked to describe what their organization owed them and what they owed their organization in turn. When Inland employees were asked, "What was the contract five years ago?" typical of their answers are the following:

> "A reasonable chance of promotion [in return for] hard work."
>
> "Loyalty."

When asked, "What is the contract today?" replies included the following:

> "Ability to add skills to improve your internal/external marketability. Stay where you are . . . justify your continued existence."

Inland Oil employees also expressed what they anticipated 5 years in the future:

> "Few opportunities anywhere for Americans. Most services provided by contractors."
>
> "Employment only at foreign locations. Will be separated by age 50 regardless of performance. [I owe in return] outstanding, highest level, performance."
>
> "Nothing."

Typical candidates for this "no guarantees" scenario are organizations, like Inland Oil, in the midst of major transition away from a known strategy toward one that has not yet been formulated or put in place. Typically, there is not yet an articulated plan to retain current employees, yet the organization seeks to maintain certain functions during the transition. From the employees' perspective, a "no guarantees" contract may often exist following major downsizing (as was also the case when thousands of employees were terminated, often with generous severance packages, following the merger of

Baxter Travenol and American Hospital Supply). Terminations at Inland Oil and Baxter created tremendous anxiety for surviving employees, who reported not knowing whether the changes were over yet.

An organization clearly cannot maintain this unstable climate indefinitely. The "no guarantees" scenario is a transition, in most cases, toward the transactional contract described above. The upheavals associated with this scenario make it difficult to adopt a longer term view, hence organizations seek the flexibility associated with the transactional contract. Moreover, survivors of the "no guarantees" era are reluctant to trust the organization again, demanding higher pay and more immediate benefits if they are to stay. A workable transactional contract following the turbulence of "no guarantees" may be necessary to restore a modicum of trust between employees and employer.

Lakeside Company's Relational Contract

Traditions and long history are characteristic of organizations with relational contracts. The Lakeside Company, in the commercial publishing business since before the Civil War, has had a long history of stable employment. With an emphasis on high-quality production processes, technical mastery of skills to produce high-quality graphic products (including retail catalogues and local telephone books), Lakeside traditionally had a functionally oriented organization in which individuals spent a long time in lower level positions before advancing up the hierarchy. People who left the company did so at two points in time: at retirement (the most common point of departure) and within the first 2 years. People leaving during the orientation period, years 1 and 2, did so typically because they did not fit the culture. Fitting in required emphasis on details, technical competence, and willingness to commit to Lakeside for the duration of their careers. This screening out of misfits by early attrition created a relatively homogeneous organization of loyal members (consistent with Schneider's, 1987, description of homogenizing forces in organizations). Barring egregious conduct (e.g., stealing), variance in performance was acceptable.

When asked about the contract they had with the company 5 years ago, Lakeside plant managers report:

"Career path."

"Paternalism."

"Opportunity to grow and succeed."

"Increased rewards not altogether linked to results" offered in exchange for "overtime and willingness to become a process technology expert."

Today that same contract continues for many with the addition of

"Continued employment, higher challenge, and uncertainty."
(and for some) "Limited opportunity, modest compensation, and uncertainty."

Thinking in terms of five years from now, members report a variety of different beliefs about their future relationship with Lakeside (possibly coinciding with signs of downsizing in older Lakeside facilities):

"Same contract as today with opportunity to grow and succeed, [more] challenge."
"Declining commitments: no overtime, no consideration of seniority. Challenge continues, [but with] limited opportunity."
"?????"

In the future, many Lakeside employees anticipate a continuation of the same set of responsibilities for their side of the contract including

"Work ethic, honesty, and dedication."
"Intelligent risk taking."
"Get[ting] the job done but with less commitment."

Key features of relational contracts are their emphasis on mutual commitment and continuity. Even though Lakeside may be in the initial phases of some strategic change due to the need to adopt technological innovations, its members see a mix of old commitments ("the same contract") as well as, in some cases, newer uncertainties ("limited opportunities," "less commitment"). Internal labor markets have been the major focus of their human resource strategy, providing predictable sources of employees and the ability to control their behavior. In return, organizations such as Lakeside have conveyed relational contracts in the form of extensive commitments to those employees. Change often feels threatening and restrictive to relational contract holders because of frequently diminished security and decline in rewards such as advancement. However, given the history of supportive work relations across levels, loyalty continues on both sides.

General Electric's Balanced Contract

Under the leadership of Jack Welch, General Electric spent a decade restructuring its business to compete globally, and has revamped itself into a highly customer responsive and internally team-oriented enterprise. Programs such as WorkOut foster continuous learning and innovation, along with skill building and mutual support.

In a 1992 statement to GE shareholders, Jack Welch conveyed four types of contract terms for GE managers/leaders, as described in Chapter 2.

1. Those who deliver on commitments and share GE values will go "onward and upward."
2. Those who do not meet commitments and do not share GE values are likely to leave.
3. Those who miss commitments but share the values usually get a second chance.
4. Those who deliver on commitments, make all the numbers, but don't share the values must change or "part company."

The contract terms described here include both relational features (shared values and commitments) as well as results (the need to attain specific business goals). This mix of shorter term transactional features with an emphasis on internalized values is the hybrid (relational and transactional) contract referred to here as a "balanced contract."

Such shareholder statements serve several purposes. They communicate what the organization promises to do in response to its managers' efforts and spell out what managers need to do to realize that promise. The text also expresses a number of related messages to both shareholders and employees: that culture change is a big part of GE's business strategy, that members will receive support in this change, that good faith efforts to change will be rewarded, and that if there are trade-offs between short-term performance and long-term development, they be will at the expense of the short term. This kind of statement both articulates a contract and signals developments in the organization's culture.

MAPPING CONTEMPORARY CONTRACTS TO PARTICULAR TYPES OF EMPLOYMENT RELATIONSHIPS

Contemporary contracts are tied to particular types of employment relationships. Commentators have proposed a variety of lexicons to describe new employment arrangements, from the shamrock organization (Handy, 1989) to the boundaryless career (Arthur, 1994). Terms like *core, contingent, peripheral, independent contractors,* and *networked employees* are widely used to identify different work arrangements. We propose a framework that integrates these commonly used terms in a fashion that helps us describe their implications for contracting.

Two basic dimensions of the worker-organization employment relationship are (a) the time frame of the relationship (short-term or long-term) and (b) the degree of internalization or externalization (embeddedness in the organization). With a long-term time frame, parties are more likely to rely on the relationship. Employees acquire skills and knowledge of limited use anywhere else (what Williamson, 1979, refers to as asset specificity) and the employer invests time and money in training that is lost if employees leave. Reliance makes exit costly. Internalization/externalization is the degree of embeddedness of the individual in the organization, through employment status, socialization, training, and development specific to the firm. In common terms, internalization creates insiders and externalization makes for outsiders. The depth of knowledge individuals acquire about both the organization and its technology and markets will be higher in insiders as will be the psychological attachment of people to the organization. Organizations internalize members when learning specific skills and behaviors offers a competitive advantage. They externalize when knowledge is widely available and of little competitive advantage (e.g., janitorial services) or too costly to learn or acquire (e.g., specialized technical skills). Based on the intersecting dimensions of relationship duration and internalization/externalization, a diverse array of employment relations can be mapped (Figure 4.3).

Traditional employees in internal labor markets were highly internalized and long term: Workers were embedded in the organization, working within its walls and its boundaries (legal and administrative), with both a history and a future of employment with that firm. Outsourcing work in contemporary organizations has created short-term arrangements with high externalization: The organization's work is performed not by its members but by those who work elsewhere often under someone else's guidance, with no history or future with that organization—a trend referred to as the hollowing of American industry (Bettis et al., 1992).

Historically, control was built into the employment relationship. Bureaucratic organizations excelled at management's technical and social control, both of which require employees to be insiders. Yet, despite our discussion of historic trends toward control through culture and long-term relationships, many short-duration, external relationships exist. Perhaps the best exemplars are the entertainment industry (e.g., music, television) and construction, where uncertainty in customer demands is dealt with by maintaining one's freedom to continually contract with others in a classic spot market type of fashion. Construction organizations, too, often can be truly hollow companies (Bettis et al., 1992) with virtually no full-time, long-term employees.[1]

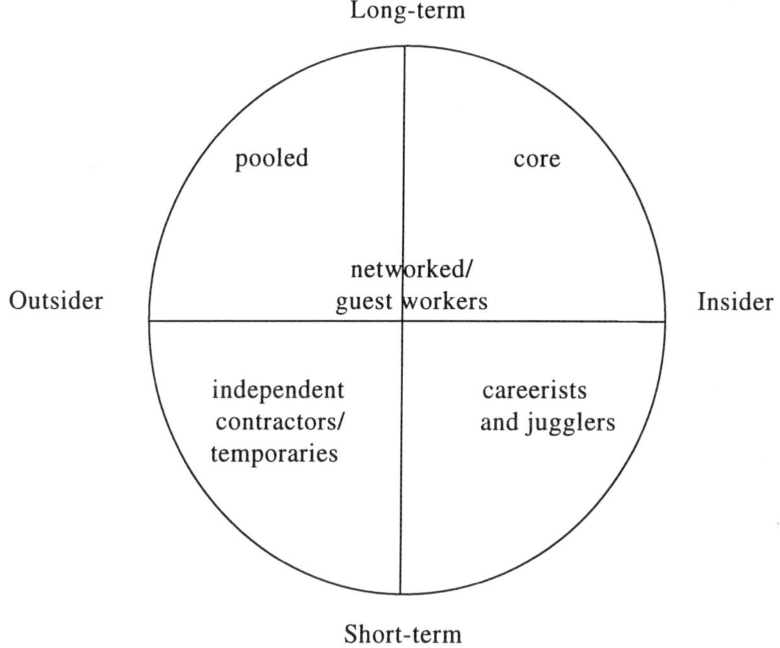

FIGURE 4.3. Attachment Map

Both long-term internalized (e.g., civil servants) and short-term externalized (e.g., migrant farmworkers) relationships have existed for centuries. Innovations in employment have occurred in the off-quadrant domains (see Figure 4.3) of short-term internalized and long-term externalized relationships. Such patterns are becoming increasingly complex as organizations seek simultaneously to adapt and change while meeting demands for consistency and quality (as in "well made," "supportively serviced," "reliable," and "environmentally sound").

Long-Term Insiders (Core Employees)

Core employees are those around whom organizations are built. They provide a focus for its activities, based on their critical skills and expertise, which constitutes a distinctive competitive advantage for the organization. Core employees and the ILMs that support them are characteristic of work high in technical complexity. Retention in the core promotes organizational stability as well as continuity and learning. This long-term relationship complements the development and assimilation of shared values and beliefs. Core employees participate in some form of ILM, not necessarily through hierarchical advancement but through deployment in a variety of roles over the course of a career with the organization. Core workers know the ropes, including the organization's priorities. They are rewarded both for *how* they work and for *what* they produce. Core workers typically can be used flexibly across jobs. As organizations come to compete more on technological innovation or service, core employment arrangements will grow to develop greater technical capabilities and organization-/customer-specific knowledge regarding service delivery. Core employees are expected to be highly relational and loyal, to be work-involved, and to hold work as a central life interest. It becomes clear from a consideration of core relationships that attachment can work two ways: Core employees are highly attached to the organization, and it is highly attached to them.

The mutual attachment of core employees and organization is consistent with research on commitment that demonstrates high affective commitment (emotional identification with the organization) by employees experiencing high degrees of organizational supportiveness (a form of organizational identification with the employee; Shore & Wayne, 1993). Core employees are likely to be party to contracts with many relational terms (i.e., relational or balanced).

Short-Term Insiders (Careerists)

Careerist workers are employees who expect to make their career in an industry, not with a specific firm. Demands for performance quality coupled with the need for flexibility have created new forms of internalization in which workers employed by the organization can be monitored on the results of both how they work and what they produce without assimilation into an organizational culture. Firms with careerists offer jobs that provide training as a stepping stone to jobs elsewhere and promote individual career growth without creating internal labor markets (e.g., consulting). Careerist roles are probably undergoing the greatest change as evaluations are made regarding the need for internal control (with the overhead burden this brings). Such arrangements cover types of work amenable to outsourcing. However, by permitting such work to be outsourced, organizations do not themselves solve their critical problems, thus forgoing opportunities down the road based on that learning (Bettis et al., 1992). If outsourcing is used as a general solution to organizational problems, in time the firm can become what Bettis refers to as a "hollow organization" with few distinctive strategic competencies.

However, in a chaotic and unpredictable marketplace, there may be only a few distinctive competencies an organization can muster. Here, careerist workers provide the necessary flexibility for organizational survival, consistent with the traditional freedom that transactional contracts offer the employer—to readily terminate one employee and seek out others when it is in their interest to do so. Hall (1993) argues that transactional-type roles serve several purposes for individual job holders too. They offer employment opportunities to people seeking low-involvement roles to help integrate work and family responsibilities. Also, transactional arrangements offer a host of career options for people highly involved in work who seek psychological success through achieving personal goals other than promotional success.

Long-Term Outsiders (Pooled Workers)

Call-ins, substitutes, and other periodic employees can work irregularly for an organization, though in many cases over some period of time. A form of temporary employee, many pooled workers are employees whose time commitments have changed due to such factors as educational opportunities or family demands. Hospitals coping with nursing shortages create pools of nurses who want reduced hours and flexibility. Schools employ substitute teachers to replace ill and absent ones. Many pooled workers actually are part-time employees with erratic schedules. Contract terms can be quite varied for pooled workers, depending on whom they believe their employer to be (e.g., an agency, the school district) or if they view themselves as freelancers. Generally speaking, the more externalized the role, the narrower and more specific the contract's performance terms. Thus pooled workers are likely to be party to transactional arrangements. But when they are intermittently employed in the same organization over a period of time, relational elements can drift into the contract.

Short-Term Outsiders (Temporaries and Independent Contractors)

Externalization is a human resource strategy to promote flexibility and lower costs. Many varieties of temporary or "peripheral" workers have developed to promote flexibility for organizations as well as lifestyle options for individuals. Temporary work is used to meet various needs (e.g., call-ins when regular employees are absent, and limited duration hires for seasonal work or special projects). Temporaries are hired and managed directly by the firm and thus are not totally externalized. There are two classes of temporary workers, those hired as individuals and those hired through agencies. Individual temporary workers tend to be younger or much older, low in experience, and often women (Davis-Blake & Uzzi, 1993). Jobs where temporaries are employed typically are lower on technical and information complexity. Agency-based temporary workers are typically used when union-management relations are poor (Uzzi, 1993) or when there is no union (as in the case of nurses).

Extensive reliance on temporaries has been identified as a potential problem both for organizations and for employees. From the employee perspective, extensive use of temporaries creates two classes of employees: secure workers with high-paying employment and temporaries with sporadic and low-paying jobs (though some temporaries such as agency nurses are paid more per hour than staff nurses). Bettis et al. (1992) raise this issue as a long-term threat to the well-being of the workforce economically as well as socially. Problems can emerge if temporaries are demographically different than core workers, especially regarding minority group and socioeconomic status. However, from the core employee perspective, hiring temporaries increases the core worker's mobility (with fewer people available to fill more responsible managerial and professional roles). Prolonged reward inequality can potentially lower the productivity and increase conflict within organizations (Cowherd & Levine, 1992).

An interesting challenge to the conventional wisdom on use of temporaries is found in research on employee benefits. Conventional wisdom argues that organizations use temporaries to avoid paying benefits (which can be upward of 25% of total labor costs). Little evidence exists regarding the tangible benefits to firms for offering fringe benefits. Davis-Blake and Uzzi (1993) report little concern over benefits in firms electing to use high rates of temporaries.

However, use of temporaries is positively related to unionization. Temporaries may thus be a way of gaining flexibility in allocation of labor rather than a benefits cost-reduction strategy per se. Firms with formal mechanisms for joint union-management problem solving are less inclined to employ temporaries. Use of outsiders may be sought where internal relationships are either troubled or constrained. Thus it is possible that problems in maintaining contracts with core employees promote expanded use of temporary workers.

Independent contractors are another form of short-term outsider. People providing paid services to an organization without employment status are independent contractors. In effect, they work for themselves. Typically, they have a career within a profession such as accounting or consulting. Use of contractors permits firms to offer a range of products without risking large fixed investment in labor. Firms do not exercise day-to-day control over independent contractors and thus may not use them for tasks critical to their core business. Bureaucratic firms, larger organizations, and those with multiple sites tend to use independent contractors. However, use of contractors in core activities can depend on whether contractors have experience with the firm, as is often the case with consulting arrangements that develop into long-term relationships.

Some Floating Employment Arrangements

Some employee relationships cut across categories. Although core workers by virtue of their key role are long-term insiders, other types of relationships such as networked and long distance can occur in virtually any quadrant. *Networked employees* is the term used by Miles and Snow (1986) to refer to individuals whose work is performed outside the boundaries of their home organization. Networked employees are typically a sort of "guest worker" whose organizational home is elsewhere. Engineers who work on assignment as part of a client team, end users who serve on their supplier's design team, and others participating in interorganizational strategic alliances all can be classified as networked. Whether this network is short or long term affects the development of new memberships, skills, and work norms. Networked employees who work in several organizations simultaneously will in fact need to be able to discriminate among various role relationships in identifying what behaviors are appropriate in a specific assignment.

Missing Workers Revisited: The Case of Part-Timers

It has been estimated that a quarter of the U.S. workforce is part time (Belous, 1989), making this one of the most common types of employment relationships. We have not mapped part-time workers in our relationship map. One of the few organizational treatments of part-time workers (Rotchford & Roberts, 1982) referred to part-time employees as "missing workers." But, of course, we are not overlooking them here. Rather, we argue that part-time workers actually represent many distinct employment relationships. The actual conditions of employment differ considerably among part-timers. Some part-timers are veteran employees scaling back their workday as they transition to retirement. Some are parents of young children reducing their hours temporarily. Other part-timers are short-term employees (such as teenagers who work the lunch counters of fast-food restaurants). People with limited time commitments to the organization can vary in terms of their degree of both internalization (some part-timers evolved from full-time status, changing due to lifestyle factors—children, health, aging—but others begin and remain only marginally integrated into the organization) and employment duration. Part-time instructors in universities can come to have "moral tenure" by virtue of their long-standing relationship, scheduled to teach the same classes year after year. Elsewhere, part-time status coincides with temporary employment that has limited involvement and virtually no training or orientation of employees. Our analysis suggests that to understand the work experiences of part-time employees we must play closer attention to the nature of their individual employment relationships. Part-timers can in fact be party to any of a number of contracts with their employer.

IMPLICATIONS

Contracts can be woven out of myriad terms. The "dead old psychological contract" is very likely the pure relational contract, in its many iterations, which has undergone expanded performance requirements, the erosion of internal labor markets (though not in all sectors of the economy), and the relaxing of organizational boundaries. Emergence of new contemporary contract forms has many implications for organizations:

- Any organization can potentially have many distinct contracts to create, manage, and maintain at the same time.
- Consistency across human and administrative contract makers is likely to become even more difficult to achieve than it was when organizations maintained only a few contracts with workers. This inconsistency should be particularly evident if current ways of making contracts (e.g., existing uses of performance appraisals) are not altered to suit new working conditions.
- Presence of widely dissimilar contracts can create perceptions of inequity and other by-products of social comparison, similar to the effects of great wage disparity between workers and executives.
- Protracted change can undermine the organization's ability to maintain efficient contracts with workers because predictability is a basic feature of contracts.

To understand what is happening to existing contracts, we need to consider the events leading up to the introduction of changes in the organization. How these changes are implemented can spell the difference between contract violation or renegotiation.

NOTE

1. Not all construction firms operate in this short-term transactional fashion—some have relations with employees that go back generations. However, unstable housing markets and other economic fluctuations are moving this industry toward a transactional approach.

Violating the Contract

> They promised me a job in marketing and here I am doing telephone sales.
>
> The company promised that no one would be fired out of the training program—that all of us were "safe" until placement. In return for this security, we accepted lower pay. The company subsequently fired four people from the training program.
>
> Original representations of the company's financial and market strength [were] clearly fraudulent.
>
> *Quotes from recently hired employees*

Contract violation can run the gamut from subtle misperceptions to stark breaches of good faith. In organizations, violated contracts are at the heart of many lawsuits brought by customers (Kaufmann & Stern, 1988) and employees (Bies & Tyler, 1993). Although potentially damaging to reputations, careers, and relationships, violations also appear to be both frequent and survivable.

The basic facts of contract violation, detailed in this chapter, are these:

- Contract violation is commonplace.
- Violated contracts lead to adverse reactions by the injured party.
- Failure to fulfill a contract need not be fatal to the relationship.

To explicate the hows and whys of contract violation, this chapter will define violation and describe the factors that lead victims to believe their contract has been breached. A model is presented detailing the role of relationship strength, monitoring, remedies, explanations, and procedural justice in the experience of contract violation. Because individual victims respond differently to violations (some end the relationship, others suffer in silence, and some renegotiate), alternative reactions to violations will be described along with ways in which violations can be remedied.

WHAT IS CONTRACT VIOLATION?

In the strictest sense, violation is a failure to comply with the terms of a contract. But, given the subjective nature of psychological contracts, how people interpret the circumstances of this failure determines whether they *experience* a violation. Violation takes three forms (Table 5.1). *Inadvertent* violation occurs when both parties are able and willing to keep their bargain, but divergent interpretations lead one party to act in a manner at odds with the understanding and interests of the other. Two people who misunderstand the time of a meeting will inadvertently fail to honor their mutual commitment to attend. *Disruption* to the contract occurs when circumstances make it impossible for one or both parties to fulfill their end of the contract, despite the fact that they are willing to do so. A plant closing forced by a hurricane can prevent an employer from providing work. Similarly, a car accident can keep an employee from showing up to work on time. *Reneging* or *breach of contract* occurs when one side, otherwise capable of performing the contract, refuses to do so. A sales representative who agrees to stay on the job for three years when hired may quit after 6 months. Whether the victim understands the source of violation to be unwillingness or inability to comply has a tremendous impact on how violation is experienced and what victims do in response (Bies & Moag, 1986).

Given the subjectivity of contract terms, a contract could hardly exist without some inadvertent violation. Because contracts are continually being created and sustained, we can assume that organizations, members, suppliers, and customers make accommodations for many inadvertent violations. Misunderstandings may be ignored, some remedied by rationalization. A person who has been passed over for a promised promotion may decide that next time it will be her turn. Victims do not interpret all instances of noncompliance as violation; thus we cannot understand violation simply as noncompliance. If contract terms are in the eye of the beholder, then violation will be as well. Subjectivity might make it easier to *feel* that violation has occurred but harder to *know* if it has. Some contract failures result not from an actual break but from a failure to communicate.

It is our thesis that experienced violation occurs when failure to keep a commitment *injures* or causes damages that the contract was designed to

TABLE 5.1 Sources of Experienced Violation

Inadvertent	Able and willing (divergent interpretations made in good faith)
Disruption	Willing but unable (inability to fulfill contract)
Breach of contract	Able but unwilling (reneging)

avoid. Failure to keep commitments can be based on opportunism, negligence, or failure to cooperate. *Opportunism* is active, self-serving behavior by one party at the expense of another (e.g., quitting an employer with whom there was an agreement to stay). *Negligence* is more passive than opportunism, involving failure to perform specified responsibilities (e.g., mentors who do not follow through on promised support for those they counsel). In situations where the long-term nature of the relationship between the parties makes exit costly, violations arise not just because of specific terms but from breaches of good faith that jeopardize the relationship itself. Such breaches of good faith are a *failure to cooperate.* Based on norms regarding good faith and fair dealing, failure to cooperate involves behavior that undermines the ability of the parties to maintain their relationship (e.g., refusing to participate in attempts to resolve disputes and misunderstandings). In personal relations, for example, when a spouse in a troubled marriage refuses to talk or seek counseling, such a failure to act in support of the relationship is a failure to cooperate. Opportunism, negligence, and failure to cooperate are the bases of contract violation.

A bank manager who wants to spend more time with his family leaves a high-demand/high-pay job with one bank for another with a smaller financial institution. The major attraction of the new bank for the manager is its low-pressure environment, which is played up by the officers who recruit him. Within two weeks of taking the job, the manager learns that the smaller firm is starting an aggressive marketing campaign he is expected to head, which will keep him away from his family for even longer hours than before. Damages include increased stress and family conflict along with loss of reputation if he tries to change jobs again soon. The sense of betrayal and entrapment this manager feels exacerbates his personal costs from the organization's actions. If the bank manager were deliberately misled, the violation is based on opportunism. If critical information was denied him because recruiters were ill-informed themselves, this is an example of negligence. And if a new strategic plan was made without his input, this constitutes a failure to cooperate. In any case, the circumstances can feel like betrayal.

TABLE 5.2 Sources of Violation by Contract Makers and Systems

Sources	*Violations*
Contract makers:	
recruiters	■ unfamiliar with actual job ■ overpromise
managers	■ say one thing, do another
coworkers	■ failure to provide support
mentors	■ little follow-through ■ few interactions
top management	■ mixed messages
Systems:	
compensation	■ changing criteria ■ reward seniority, low job security
benefits	■ changing coverage
career paths	■ dependent on one's manager ■ inconsistent application
performance review	■ not done on time ■ little feedback
training	■ skills learned not tied to job
documentation	■ stated procedures at odds with actual practice

Although contracts can be violated in innumerable ways, there are a number of common forms (Table 5.2). Recruiters may overpromise a job's opportunity for challenge, growth, or development, but at the same time eager job seekers may read into a promise what they want to hear. Managers, coworkers, or executives who say one thing and do another all can engender violation. A common cause of violation for many employees involves a change in superiors. When one's boss or mentor is promoted, terminated, or retired, old deals may be abrogated. Similarly, changes in human resource practices, even with constructive intent (e.g., to align with a new business strategy), can appear to break old commitments (e.g., introducing new results-based performance criteria among veteran employees used to a seniority system). Then there is the phenomenon of mixed messages, where different contract makers express divergent intentions. A mission statement can convey that the organization rewards employees based on merit ("commitment to excellence") while the compensation system is based on seniority. Different contract sources may each convey mutually exclusive promises.

The *experience* of violation appears to be quite common. A longitudinal study of M.B.A. alumni reported that over half experienced a violation of a preemployment commitment within the first two years on the job (Robinson & Rousseau, 1994). The types of violations reported ran the gamut of employment conditions, from pay and promotion opportunities to the nature of the work and the quality and character of coworkers and the organization itself (Table 5.3). Changes in personnel (new managers or top executives) were frequently at the root of these other changes. However, despite the high rate of reported violation, M.B.A.s reported that some of these violations were repaired by actions they and their employer have taken. Others reported that even though they disputed what had happened between them and their employer, their contract was still basically fulfilled. The differences between violation and contract fulfillment can be analyzed by examining the dynamics of contract violation.

HOW CONTRACT VIOLATION OCCURS: A MODEL

To understand the dynamics of contract violation, we need a model to explain instances such as these:

- A sales representative whose lucrative accounts are reassigned reacts angrily. Meanwhile, another sales rep readily accepts the same change.
- One customer receives a replacement for a damaged shipment and is pleased with the service while another remains outraged at the supplier's unreliability.
- One plant's closing leads to angry protests in the city in which it is located, but another's leads the local newspapers to praise the company.

A major "problem" in contract violation is understanding why some events, seemingly at odds with a contract, do not provoke adverse reactions, but other events that appear innocuous engender outrage and anger. Based on research on relationships (Clark & Reis, 1988), social cognition (Fiske & Taylor, 1984), justice (e.g., Bies & Moag, 1987; Lind & Tyler, 1988), and remediation (e.g., Rousseau & McLean Parks, 1993; Rousseau, Robinson, & Kraatz, 1992), a model is proposed (Figure 5.1) to account for the dynamics of contract violation.

TABLE 5.3 Types of Violations

Violation Type	*Definition*	*Frequency*	*Examples*
Training/ Development	Absence of training, or training not as promised	65	"Sales training was promised as an integral part of marketing training. It never materialized."
Compensation	Discrepancies between promised and realized pay, benefits, bonuses	61	"Specific compensation benefits were promised and either were not given to me, or I had to fight for them."
Promotion	Promotion or advancement schedule not as promised	59	"I perceived a promise that I had a good chance of promotion to manager in 1 year. Although I received excellent performance ratings, I was not promoted in my first year."
Nature of Job	Employer perceived as having misrepresented the nature of the department or the job	40	"[My] employer promised I would be working on venture capital projects. I was mainly writing speeches for the CEO."
Job Security	Promises regarding degree of job security one could expect were not met	37	"The company promised that no one would be fired out of the training program—that all of us were 'safe' until placement (in return for this security we accepted lower pay). The company subsequently fired four people from the training program."
Feedback	Feedback and reviews inadequate compared to what was promised	35	"[I did] not receive performance reviews as promised."
Management of Change	Employees not asked for input or given notice of changes as they were promised	29	"I was promised more knowledge and control over my future."
Responsibility	Employees given less responsibility and/or challenge than promised	27	"[I was] promised greater responsibility. More strategic thinking/decision making."

People	Employer perceived as having misrepresented the type of people at the firm, in terms of things such as their expertise, work style, or reputation	25	"I was promised a dynamic and challenging environment . . . rubbing elbows with some of the brightest people in the business . . . a big lie. The true picture started to come out . . . after the initial hype . . . of working at one of the best 100 companies in the U.S. had worn off."
Other	Unfulfilled promises that do not fit into above categories	26	"It became clear that original representations of the company's financial and market strength were fraudulent."

SOURCE: Robinson and Rousseau (1994). Violating the psychological contract: Not the exception but the norm. *Journal of Organizational Behavior 15*, 256. Reprinted with permission.

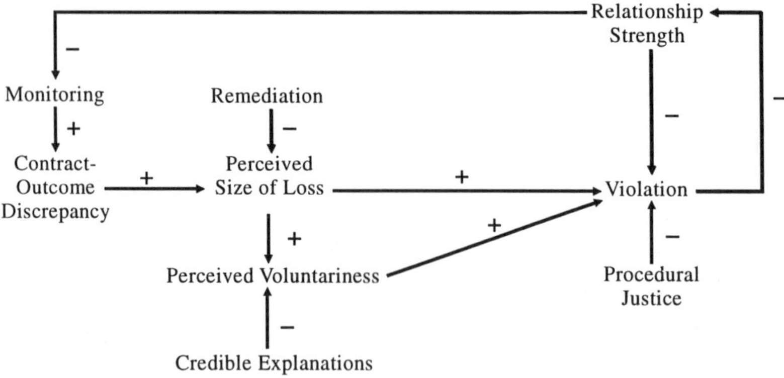

FIGURE 5.1. A Model of Contract Violation

Contract-Outcome Discrepancy

Contract violation begins with the perception of a discrepancy between a relied-upon outcome (e.g., a choice assignment, extra support) and the actual outcome that occurs. But not all discrepancies are noticed and not all that are noticed are perceived as violations. What turns contract-outcome discrepancy into a violation? Three basic factors increase the likelihood that a discrepancy will be interpreted as a violation: monitoring, size of loss, and relationship strength.

Monitoring. Monitoring is the indirect seeking of information by scrutinizing the behavior of others (Clark & Reis, 1988). Monitoring is not constant in all situations. Some discrepancies are more likely than others to be noticed. People pay particular attention to the behavior of others when they feel a special need for information. Unless someone is watching the clock, a coworker's arrival five minutes late can go unnoticed. But if that coworker's lateness is chronic and a source of frustration to others, people are more likely to note when the tardy individual arrives.

Unless a person is actively comparing outcomes with his or her understanding of the contract, many discrepancies may go unrecognized. If no one checks an employee's work to see if it is up to standard, the employee may come to believe that the quality he or she has been giving is good enough. Unless we have reason to check the employee's work, we may not do so, and thus discrepancies pass by unnoticed—and continue. The extent to which people monitor the behaviors of others affects the *experience* of violation. Monitoring in the form of quality control may not occur until a particularly poor performance occurs. Other things being equal, larger discrepancies are more likely to be noticed than smaller ones.

Perceived Size of Loss. The perceived size of the loss is an important factor in determining whether the victim perceives a contract-outcome discrepancy as a contract violation. Not only are large discrepancies more salient, but we interpret them differently than small ones. In making judgments regarding the amount of harm done, people tend to attribute more responsibility for events such as accidents that produce severe rather than mild consequences. Calling these "defensive attributions," Fiske and Taylor (1984, p. 81) offer the example of a clumsy friend, Debra, who bumps into a table, knocking its contents everywhere. As she didn't mean to do it, we don't blame her too much for any damage done. But if our priceless Ming vase was on the table and is now in a hundred pieces, our attributions are likely to change. She is no longer just clumsy but also careless and inconsiderate. Fiske and Taylor argue that this intensified blame when losses are great helps us avoid feelings of personal responsibility. Similarly, perception of contract violation is likely to be greater when one party's actions engender considerable harm to another party. Failure to deliver a promised promotion may not be seen as violating a contract if other benefits accrue to the promisee or if a sense of good faith is maintained before the delayed promotion is obtained. However, when there has been a history of trouble in the relationship (e.g., between employee and organization, work group and team leader, or customer and supplier), monitoring is more likely to occur. Once trust has eroded, minute discrepancies can take on a special, aversive significance.

Relationship Strength: The Context of Violation. When a contract is violated, the relationship on which it rests can ultimately be damaged too. If a person robs a bank and is caught, giving the money back is not typically treated as sufficient compensation to restore the robber to society's good graces; the damage constitutes more than just the money taken. Violation is a trauma for a relationship and undermines good faith. But the relationship's strength and especially its history influence the experience of violation. If there is a history of adversarial behavior, grievances, or other symptoms of mistrust, victims are more likely to perceive any adverse event as intentional. Repeat offenders are treated more harshly by the criminal justice system than first-timers. First-timers might blame their circumstances and be believed. But, for repeat offenders, attributions tend to focus on the person rather than on his or her situation. Once the person is implicated as the cause of discrepant outcomes (e.g., poor performance, failure to provide promised rewards), trust has eroded. The person, not the situation, is seen as responsible for any wrongdoing. Trust once lost is not easily restored. Good relationships tend to manifest high tolerance of the behaviors of others, even when they result in discrepant outcomes. However, troubled relationships often go from bad to worse.

Organizations and individuals may both go through cycles of escalating violation, because each may be inclined to perceive adverse events as part of a larger pattern of untrustworthy conduct. The escalation cycle is brought about because people who perceive their relationships as troubled react differently to adverse events than those in more stable relationships. Healthy relations relax monitoring, but troubled relationships fuel it (Clark & Reis, 1988). In romantic relationships, partners who feel insecure may monitor their significant other to find out if he or she still loves them. Casual statements and ordinary actions are analyzed for the motives they reveal. The use of monitoring to gauge the status of a relationship has been labeled "secret testing" (Baxter & Wilmot, 1984). A classic example of a secret test goes something like this: "If you love me you'll do what I want you to do (e.g., take out the garbage, bring me flowers, praise my work) *without me having to tell you.*" Not surprising, because troubled relations lead to monitoring, monitoring tends to identify many more *negative* judgments than positive ones. It is difficult to pass a test when one is unaware of being tested; thus many secret tests are failed by the testee. Marriage counselors report that counseled couples are more likely to end up divorcing when one or the other party believes that the other should be able to "read their mind," know what is expected of them without being told.

In sum, several factors operate on the experience of a discrepancy between contract terms and actual outcomes:

- Monitoring increases the number of observed discrepancies in contract performance.
- Larger contract-outcome discrepancies are more likely to be seen as violations than smaller ones.
- In troubled relationships, small discrepancies associated with contract outcomes are more likely to be seen as violations than they are in healthy relationships.

CHANGING THE MEANING OF A LOSS: THE FUNCTION OF REMEDIATION AND CREDIBLE EXPLANATION

Because violations are injurious and often willful, strategies for reducing the experience of violation target both the actual losses incurred as well as the perception of these losses. The following example illustrates such a strategy. In England, the palace announced that Queen Elizabeth II was no longer permitting her staff the perks they had historically enjoyed. As part of a plan "to rationalize and streamline" palace pay and administrative costs, the 350 staff members no longer would be allowed to take home, for their own consumption, miniature bottles of alcohol drawn from the royal bar stocks. Instead of the spirits, staff were given an extra $45 in their pay packet. Servants once given free bars of bath soap received an annual stipend instead. Senior courtiers lost the privilege of buying a new suit on the queen's account for every other trip they made with her. According to the *New York Times* ("In Her Majesty's Service," 1993): "The palace insisted that none of its workers would be worse off as a result of the changes, even though the new cash allotments would be taxable" (p. 6).[1]

Other statements by the palace reminded staffers that one perk would still be provided—their annual Christmas pudding from the queen. The palace example illustrates several strategies for managing the size of reliance losses incurred by the contract violation: (a) reducing actual losses by substitution (e.g., money in exchange for gifts), (b) reducing perceived losses (e.g., downplaying the tax liability), (c) recognizing the symbolic features of the contract (e.g., continuing to offer the Christmas pudding), and (d) offering a credible explanation or justification for the actions taken (e.g., streamlining the household and cutting costs).

Remediation. Remedies substitute one outcome for another and thus can be thought of as forms of "buyout." In some fashion, remedies are a way of honoring the spirit if not the letter of a contract. Reliance losses often will not result in termination of the contract if remediation of comparable value is offered. Because contracts are designed to reduce the reliance losses parties incur, living up to the contract may not necessarily always involve delivering its specific terms. A sales trainee offered one territory at hire may believe her deal is being kept when, due to a market decline, she is given another equally attractive territory. The issue here is comparable value between what is promised and what is delivered.

Substitution is actually a common form of contract keeping. Early retirements often occur along with beefed-up benefits packages for veteran employees. Workers with obsolete skills are retrained. A vendor loans a customer a personal computer while the one he purchased is being repaired. All these substitutions can be seen as cushioning reliance losses. The closer the cushion comes to the perceived value of the original contract term, the better the deal is honored. Thus a psychological contract of long-term employment with an employer can be honored during a period of downsizing if efforts are taken to ensure the worker's long-term employability somewhere else.

Nevertheless, substitution strategies for reducing losses (e.g., money for the queen's soap) can change the *meaning* or nature of the relationship. The symbolic value of being able to take home some of the queen's special household items conveys a sense of closeness to the royal family, but additional cash puts the household staff on more formal footing. Efforts made to manage actual and perceived losses can be thought of as *remedies* for reliance losses. Increasing a servant's pay can serve to reduce the resources (household goods) lost by the change. Keeping the traditional Christmas pudding might mitigate the status losses that monetary buyouts can create in relational contracts. When substitutions are used as remedies, the troublesome issue of comparable value arises. Can we reduce the value of a bar of soap to "mere" money? Obviously, the answer is "yes" in most cases. But doesn't it matter that the soap belongs to the Queen of England, or that employees have become accustomed to a position of special trust and privilege? Symbolic value makes the equation of one resource with another problematic.

Another illustration of the importance of symbolic value in substitutions comes from the experiences following the breakup of the Bell system in the 1980s. For generations of people employed by AT&T, working for the "phone company" had a meaning of its own: a secure, responsible, good job. Employees joked about having "bell-shaped heads." Following divestiture, the individual operating companies with interests beyond telephone service (e.g., information systems support and technological development, as in the case of Ameritech) now were differentiated from the local telephone companies providing phone service to customers. Some former Bell employees were transferred into Ameritech, a newly created organization, where they spent the rest of their careers. But upon retirement, many former phone company employees requested to be transferred *for their last day of work* to Illinois Bell, the local phone company. Fulfillment of this request allowed people who had once begun their careers with the phone company to be retired from it as well. Symbolic value in substitutions may be as critical as the monetary value of any other arrangements made in contracting.

Severance pay and advance notice are frequent substitutes for employment. These remedies have been found to reduce perceptions of the employers' obligation to retain terminated employees (Rousseau & Aquino, 1993). Other efforts to promote a just or fair way of allocating adverse outcomes (e.g., job loss or benefit take-aways), through employee participation and offering legitimate reasons (poor performance, economic necessity), may enhance fairness but not necessarily reduce obligations (Rousseau & Aquino, 1993). Efforts to assuage negative reactions to changes involving take-aways and losses may make the perpetrator appear more fair without reducing its obligations to keep commitments. Unless remedies actually substitute for some loss, they may do little to help fulfill the obligations between the parties.

The difference between remedies honoring the spirit of a contract and remedial efforts that fail is evident in the way in which remedies have been applied in plant closings. Based on their study of plant closings in the automobile industry, Yoder and Staudohar (1985) argue:

> The impact on workers of plant closings is fourfold: (1) their jobs are lost; (2) the old job experiences are not readily transferable to new jobs in growing industries; (3) their new jobs typically provide pay and benefits that are significantly reduced from previous levels; and (4) they and their families experience high levels of anxiety and stress. During the period of transition to new jobs, displaced workers usually need help in such areas as retraining, counseling, job search, and income maintenance. Thus, management and public policies are judged by their effectiveness in cushioning adversity. (pp. 45-46)

Yoder and Staudohar contrast shutdowns at GM and Ford. In the 1980s, assembling cars and trucks in California was no longer economically feasible in light of the diminished market and long distances involved in shipping parts. Faced with the same market pressures, GM and Ford conducted plant closings in distinct ways that yielded different outcomes (Table 5.4).

The GM Fremont plant was closed indefinitely in 1982. Employees were given 3 weeks' notice. With a history of labor-management dispute since the plant's opening, neither the union nor individual nonmanagerial employees were involved in the planned shutdown. At the time of closing, with no plans for retraining or other postshutdown support, employees believed that the closing was temporary. Employees who did not know their job loss was permanent waited for GM to reopen. Only a few sought retraining. Postemployment programs, largely offered by state and federal agencies, were not well coordinated. Little retraining occurred, and existing programs emphasized finding jobs without offering retraining. Local television and newspapers accused GM of abandoning its workers. Two years later, less than half of GM's former employees had found jobs. Dysfunctional behavior was also evident in the aftermath of the plant closing. Community records indicate that eight employees committed suicide following the plant closing. There was a 240% increase in reported child abuse in the community at large.

In contrast, the Milpitas plant of the Ford Motor Company, with a history of cooperative union-management relations, announced its closing 6 months in advance. Employees were told that the closing was permanent and a joint union-management planning process was begun. Planning entailed development of skill testing and job placement programs within the plant along with stress counseling. The program emphasized retraining and developed employability plans for individual workers. Production continued to the last day at a relatively high rate. The final car off the assembly line was donated by Ford to the city of Milpitas in recognition of its support. A little over a year later, 63% of employees had found new jobs.

TABLE 5.4 Contrasting Management of Plant Closings

	GM	*Ford*
Plant	Assembly Plant, Fremont, (approx. 6,000 employees)	Assembly Plant, Milpitas, (approx. 2,500 employees)
Climate	Adversarial, conflicted union/management relations, high substance abuse	Cooperative, participative, high productivity, positive union/management relations
Date	March 1982—closed indefinitely April 1983—closed permanently (Thirteen months delay in final decision)	May 1983—closed permanently (No delay in decision)
Notice	Three weeks' notice before 3/82 shutdown; workers did not believe closing was permanent	Six months' advance notice; workers believed closing was permanent
Shutdown process	Management controlled	Joint union-management planning of shutdown process
Assistance prior to shutdown	None	Employee testing, stress counseling, job placement, and other programs provided at plant
Post-closing assistance	Income security—state unemployment insurance combined with UAW supplement benefits—95% base pay for hourly. Some relocation to other plants (670). Some state-company-federal retraining efforts after shutdown, not well-coordinated. Program stressed direct placement.	Program emphasized retraining and employability plan for individuals
Community	Company chastised by print and broadcast media for abandoning workers	
Outcomes	— 46% employed over 2 years later — Eight suicides following shutdown — 240% increase in incidence of child abuse 4 months after closing	— 63% employed 14 months later — No suicides following shutdown — N/A

SOURCE: Yoder and Staudohar (1985). Management and public policy in plant closure. *Sloan Management Review, 26*(4), 45-58. Reprinted with permission.

How GM and Ford handled these closings was strikingly different:

1. Ford's notice 6 months in advance created opportunity for employees to adjust to the idea of job loss, to plan how the shutdown would occur, and to provide members with support through the change. At GM, employees were still reeling from the announcement when the plant shut down. A sense of disbelief was pervasive.
2. Worker-management cooperation in Ford's shutdown planning gave people a voice in creating programs to meet their needs. Employees had no voice in GM's abrupt shutdown.
3. Ford's closing was announced as definite and permanent, creating a shared sense of the need to plan and respond to the change. GM's closing was initially "indefinite," fostering denial and failure to confront the job loss.
4. Ford offered preclosing support for employees. GM offered little, if any.
5. Ford's postclosing assistance programs focused on long-term employability. GM's focused on providing temporary salary and benefits.

The history of long-term employment in both of these organizations makes it likely that employees would believe in a relational contract. Ford offered employees the opportunity of employability elsewhere along with a variety of efforts designed to reverse the adversities of job loss. By cushioning employees from present stresses and future losses, the organization in effect can honor the spirit if not the letter of its contract with employees.

The more suddenly an adverse outcome occurs, the more negative the likely reaction will be. Advance notice gives people time to understand the inevitability of some losses, and it also provides potential victims a time frame, or window, in which to plan ways of reducing these losses. A Kraft cheese manufacturing plant in the Midwest participated in a team-building program for several years before it was announced that the plant would be sold. Although a profitable operation, its product did not fit into the larger corporation's strategic plan. As part of the team-building effort, there had been widespread discussion of the strategic plan at the plant for several years. By the time the plan to sell the facility was announced, the plant's production staff and management understood both the corporation's perspective as well as the critical features required to operate the plant effectively. The plant found a buyer within two weeks—the plant's employees.

Organizations are often reluctant to give employees time to adjust to upcoming job loss out of fears of sabotage and lowered productivity. However, where cooperative employment relations exist, such dysfunctional actions need not occur. Advance notice does not lower productivity or commitment in companies where supportive relations exist and where employers are seen as behaving in good faith (Weber & Taylor, 1963; Yoder &

Staudohar, 1985). At Ford's Milpitas plant, absenteeism dropped following announcement of the closing. Similarly, after the state of Maine introduced its advance notice law, unemployment rates were substantially lowered, probably because employees were able to look for and find other jobs (Folbre, Leighton, & Roderick, 1984). Risk of turnover and decreased performance can also be reduced by offering a bonus for remaining with the organization until closing occurs and by providing incentives for sustained high performance. Such incentives may help mitigate unintended consequences of closings where employee commitment has been low and where employment has largely been transactional. In the instance of small firms, employers may fear giving advance notice because premature loss of *any* employee is costly. Incentives for staying (e.g., bonuses) are particularly important in such cases.

Voluntariness. Any event at odds with the perceiver's understanding of a contract can be interpreted as a violation. A breach of contract occurs when one party reneges on the agreement despite their ability to fulfill it. From the perspective of the victim, there may be a fine line between ability and inability to fulfill the contract. How the perpetrator acts cues the potential victim as to whether to interpret a given behavior as a violation. Behavior, both before and after the violation, matters in the interpretation of an event as contract breaking.

If the circumstances inhibiting contract completion are perceived to be under the control of the perpetrator, victims are more likely to experience a breach of contract. Economic downturns may cause wages to flatten, but victims may still blame poor management practices and strategic planning for a business's problems. A steelworker at an aging facility that makes railroad wheels complained that the company had not invested in new technology or market analyses in the past 20 years: "With three changes of owners, what profits this plant made were never put back into it to help it catch up with changing times." If the company's owners are seen as having acted in bad faith, the steelworker and his peers may believe that their contract has been broken. Similarly, escalating workloads may cause an employee to unwillingly miss deadlines or turn in poor quality work. However, if that person missed opportunities to plan or to organize better, disappointed colleagues may still blame the poor performer. "You knew we might get last minute requests," they might ask, "so why did you wait until today to start the work I gave you last week?" It is a truism that we judge others by their behavior and ourselves by our intentions. However, attributions regarding the intentions of others are fundamental to the experience of violation.

Credible Explanations. Whether the potential contract violator is perceived as responsible for the occurrence of an adverse outcome is a function of the information available to victims. Perceived voluntariness is based on the attribution of intent. What would-be violators convey to victims can shape their understanding of motives and circumstances. Although natural disasters and other "acts of God" are usually obvious, the reasons underlying most other losses are not. Events whose causes are unambiguously interpreted as beyond control will not violate contracts. However, when ambiguity exists regarding how controllable or anticipatable the situation really was, as in the case of economic downturns, causal attributions can be shaped by information offered before, during, and after the experience of a contract discrepancy. People who don't receive the expected raise, special assignment, or other opportunity look for explanations to help them understand and adjust to their losses. Much of how people make sense of losses stems from what perpetrators communicate to victims. A corporation that gives an account of its actions can reduce its culpability by

Communicating positive intentions
Providing information on constraints (economic, external competition, and so on) or other extenuating circumstances that limit available courses of action.

Causal accounts claiming mitigating circumstances create a perception of fairness because they attempt to eliminate "worst case scenario" interpretations of a decision maker's intentions (Schlenker, 1980). Bies and Shapiro (1993) use the example of a journal editor who remains silent as to why there has been a delay in the manuscript review process. If that editor continues to offer authors no explanation, they may expect the worst, that is, that he is unfair and even prejudiced against them. But if an account is offered explaining that the delay was due to a vacation or misaddressed letters, feelings of unfairness are reduced, and the behavior appears more inadvertent than deliberate. Credible accounts that claim mitigating circumstances reduce perceptions of unfairness and volition.

In sum, managing outcomes and their meaning are two major ways of reducing the size of the reliance losses that contract parties experience. Outcomes and meanings are influenced by a variety of interventions that reduce the experience of violation:

- Reducing the actual size of the loss
- Reducing the perceived loss
- Explaining the loss in such a way that violators seem less responsible

PROCEDURAL JUSTICE

People make distinctions between outcomes that favor their own self-interest and outcomes that are fair (Lind & Tyler, 1988). Although contract discrepancies work against the self-interest of the victim, people do react more favorably when the decision-making process behind the discrepancies is perceived as fair. If an employee notices a discrepancy or loses a dispute that leads to a negative outcome, the decision will be perceived as more legitimate and understandable when the process used was believed to be fair.

Procedural justice refers to the fairness of the decision-making processes underlying the allocation of outcomes or the resolution of disputes. Although *distributive justice* refers to the fairness of the outcomes, and contract violations are, by definition, unfair in distributive terms, procedural justice affects the magnitude of violation. Fairness in processes has been characterized by six procedural rules (Bies & Moag, 1987; Levinthal, 1988):

- *Consistency:* Allocative procedures should be consistent across people and over time.
- *Bias suppression:* Personal self-interest and blind allegiance to narrow preconceptions should be prevented.
- *Accuracy:* Decisions must be based on good information and informed opinion.
- *Correctability:* Opportunities must exist to modify or reverse decisions based on inaccurate information.
- *Representativeness:* Allocation process must represent the concerns of all important subgroups and individuals.
- *Ethicality:* Allocation process must be compatible with prevailing moral and ethical standards.

Losses experienced by individuals will seem more serious and generate more adverse reactions when others have been or are treated differently. If an organization that gave notice before previous layoffs does not for a subsequent layoff, the experienced violation will deepen. On the other hand, careful attention to due process, especially those specified in personnel manuals and handbooks, is essential to creating a sense of consistency.

Bias is manifested in losses that seem to unduly benefit particular individuals or where forms of prejudice are evident. Family businesses that give preferential treatment to a low-performing family member over a nonfamily employee who contributes highly breach the bias suppression rule.

When employees are to be terminated for cause or punished for substandard contributions, the quality of the performance data on which such a decision is made influences the accuracy associated with the decision. Performance-based decisions such as merit pay or terminations-for-cause necessitate high-quality performance appraisals (e.g., well-informed raters, including bosses and peers, who employ the measures consistently).

Correctability implies that if the decision is based on false, inaccurate, or limited information, it can be reversed or altered. Decisions to terminate many employees for business-necessity reasons do not usually offer the option of correctability, because job loss occurred regardless of performance. However, when there is a merit basis for the decision, fair procedures permit people to voice their objections, argue their case, and exercise the opportunity to reverse unfair decisions.

Representativeness is a special concern when losses are borne unequally across organizational subgroups. The outcry over executive-level pay raises at General Motors in the face of flat wages for union workers is a potential violation of the representativeness rule. To avoid such inequality, and the resulting perception of violation, companies might use across-the-board cuts in pay for all employees, including management, when economic difficulties precipitate such cuts. An example is Hewlett Packard, which cut payroll costs through use of the 4-day workweek across the board, from senior management to production workers.

The ethicality rule is a sort of "mother of all rules." The way in which decisions are made must be consistent with ethical standards, which change over time and with the prevalence of contract violations in the larger society. Business practices tend to develop into trends. In the 1980s, the rate of corporate takeovers was initially low, because the strategy was used by only a few firms positioned to benefit from related acquisitions (buying businesses related to their core business). But by the end of the 1980s, an explosion of mergers and acquisitions occurred, in part due to the imitative behavior of business executives who served on boards with other executives who had themselves already participated in an acquisition (Haunschild, 1993). Haunschild notes that these later imitators tended to make decisions for non-business-related reasons and therefore experienced more losses due to their acquisitions than did the early-adopter leaders. If executives copy the behaviors of others in determining appropriate courses of action for their firms, it is highly likely that the prevalence of downsizing and widespread employee terminations makes it easier for other firms witnessing these behaviors to consider cutting their own staffs and terminating employees. Similarly, employees who have friends who quit without notice or who read such headlines and titles as "Promises Don't Pay Off" (1993) and *Pack Your Own Parachute* (Hirsch, 1987) might believe that acting similarly is appropriate. The prevalence of contract breakdowns can provide available justification for subsequent violations. Contract violation may lower the subsequent standards to which people hold themselves accountable both within an existing relationship as well as in a larger society where such actions become commonplace. In effect, behaviors involved in honoring or breaching a contract may themselves shape the moral context of subsequent decisions.

Adherence to procedures affects the quality of treatment victims and witnesses perceive. The quality of treatment a person receives in the context of a violation can reflect on one's social standing: in the organization, among peers, and in the individual's broader personal life (Wade-Benzoni, 1993). Information about one's standing in a group is often communicated by the quality of the treatment received, especially from those in authority (Tyler & Lind, 1992). When one is treated with dignity and shown respect (e.g., through soliciting opinions, creating an opportunity for correctability or recourse), social standing is enhanced (Bies & Moag, 1986). Disrespectful treatment, especially by a boss, carries the implication that the person is not a full member of the group. These effects are enhanced when losses are made public, for example, when family and coworkers become aware of them (Wade-Benzoni, 1993). Public losses make incidents harder to dismiss or forget, especially when isolated individuals are affected, as in the case of the firing of an individual as contrasted with a large-scale termination. Violations can humiliate victims when they involve public losses, public attributions of personal wrongdoing or negligence, and disrespectful treatment (e.g., denial of a promised promotion without possibility of corrective action or voice).

Creating Just Procedures. Procedural justice involves a number of practices. First and foremost, procedures must exist for promoting consistency, accuracy, and correctability. Compliance with prespecified routines, such as procedures specified in employee handbooks governing terminations-for-cause, enhances the sense of fairness, particularly among witnesses but also for those directly involved in the process. Moreover, procedures may be more apt to be updated as circumstances change than are more subjective contract features. Typical procedures promoting consistency, accuracy, and correctability include the following:

- Warnings, such as an announcement of intended termination
- Documentation of the reasons behind adverse outcomes, such as evidence of substandard performance
- Remedial actions—if termination-for-cause is considered, the organization may offer to provide an employee with the support necessary to improve performance

Established procedures are especially important when substandard performance by one contract party is the basis for termination of the contract. When subjectivity exists in contract terms (occurring more often in relational agreements than in transactional ones), understanding performance standards and one's own level of compliance is critical to a felt fair process. Many organizations have what is in effect a "justice cycle," a set of procedures to follow in cases of terminations-for-cause. A frequent motivation for such processes is the desire to avoid legal action for wrongful termination (Bradshaw & Deacon, 1985). Justice cycles might entail gathering evidence of substandard performance (valid performance appraisal measures, attendance records, customer complaints, and so on), an oral warning with an offer of assistance (e.g., training), a written warning if the substandard performance continues, followed by leave without pay. If such efforts to signal the importance of performance to continued employment fail, dismissal results.

Disciplinary measures with less severe consequences than dismissal also need to involve procedural justice features to be perceived as fair. The "hot stove rule" exemplifies attention to procedural justice in disciplining employees. The principle behind this rule is that discipline should be similar to our reaction upon touching a hot stove: immediate (we know instantly to get our hand off the stove), consistent (every time we touch the hot stove we feel the consequences), and unbiased (anybody touching the stove risks getting burned).

Procedural justice mechanisms have both positive and negative aspects. On the upside, use of procedures is critical to protecting people from inadvertent contract breach (e.g., due to misunderstandings of performance terms). Procedures can establish more dignified treatment of people who are disciplined by allowing them recourse, voice, and the opportunity to change. But their downside is the escalation of both expectations and bureaucratization. Growth of formalized procedures (e.g., grievance mechanisms) has the effect of creating higher aspirations and expectations for the employer among employees (Selznick, 1969). Employees perceive managers to have obligations to act ethically (Folger & Bies, 1989) and, as a consequence of rising expectations, managers have to meet higher standards of fairness, thus increasing the potential for even greater perceived unfairness (Folger, 1977). This search for justice has been termed "the quest for law" by Selznick (1969), as it generates new aspirations and increasingly more comprehensive goals. The pursuit of fair mechanisms for making unfavorable decisions can at once enhance procedural fairness while undermining both the employer's and the employee's sense of social justice. Highly restrictive labor agreements often have the effect of lowering productivity, which frustrates both management, which seeks change, and labor, which seeks economic stability. Each is likely to blame the other for the consequences of the rules to which they have bound themselves (Kochan, Katz, & McKersie, 1986). Grievances and litigation can distance parties from each other while amplifying existing differences and disputes.

Folger and Bies (1989) argue that the dilemmas associated with escalation of expectations and procedural justice mechanisms may best be "solved" by the interpersonal and moral conduct of managers who enact the policies and procedures. This code of behavior involves careful consideration of the implied and psychological nature of various commitments. For example, a firm manufacturing gaskets may hire many of its employees from a select number of families to promote loyalty. The plant manager may be able to deal with a tardy employee by first having one of the employee's relatives talk to him. A strategy that won't work everywhere has the effect here of keeping performance standards high and reducing the use of bureaucratic means of enforcing contract terms. The procedures serve as backup when an interpersonal approach fails.

Procedural justice mechanisms protect the interests of contract parties by providing a means for enforcing sanctions (e.g., against poor-performing employees, who themselves are in effect contract violators) in a way that seems fair to both victims and witnesses. It would be difficult to create contracts if there were no way to enforce them. But fair enforcement is necessary if the organization wishes to save a relationship with a particular employee as well as to protect its reputation from the perspective of other employees. Promoting procedural justice means

Establishing procedures for allocating discipline and sanctions before they are needed,

Adhering to procedures consistently,

Basing decisions on accurate information and permitting the other party to provide input,

Using both interpersonal relations and due process procedures when enforcing the contract (e.g., disciplinary action) as well as when acting at odds with the contract (e.g., changing its terms).

When is a discrepancy a violation? The three instances this chapter opened with involved contract discrepancies with very different outcomes:

- A sales representative whose lucrative accounts are reassigned reacts angrily but another rep readily accepts the same change. Both reassignments occurred in metropolitan Chicago due to an organizational restructuring aimed at creating sales areas based on customer needs rather than geography. The second sales rep had been participating in ongoing training in support of a new strategy that could potentially position him to advance within the company. The first rep had no such preparation.
- One customer receives a replacement for a damaged shipment and is pleased with the service but another remains outraged at the supplier's unreli-

ability. Not surprising, service recovery works well for the first customer, who has a long history of quality service from this vendor, but fails with the second, who recently has put up with a series of shipping problems due to the vendor's ongoing poor interdepartmental coordination.

- One plant's closing leads to angry protests in the city in which it is located, but another's leads the local newspapers to praise the company. As in the case of Yoder and Staudohar's (1985) discussion of Ford's and GM's different plant closing strategies, an abrupt, indefinite closing generates much greater loss for employees than a closing that is announced well in advance and supported by programs that assist employees in coping with the change.

These instances demonstrate how events before, during, and after the appearance of contract discrepancies shape whether they eventually turn into violations.

WHEN IS VIOLATION MOST LIKELY?

Based on the above discussion of contract dynamics, we can conclude that violation is most likely when the following occur:

- There is a history of conflict and low trust in the relationship.
- Social distance exists between the parties such that one does not understand the perspective of the other.
- An external pattern of violations exists (e.g., an era of business retrenchment).
- Incentives to breach contracts are very high or perpetrators perceive themselves to have no alternatives (e.g., organizational crises).
- One party places little value in the relationship (e.g., alternative parties are relatively available and there are few sunk costs).

WHAT FEATURES CREATE RESISTANCE TO VIOLATION?

The factors that reduce experienced violation include the following:

- Strong relationships
- Frequent interactions
- Sacrifice and other previous investments that serve to bind parties to each other

WHEN A CONTRACT IS VIOLATED

Responses to violation take many forms. Violated contracts promote mistrust, anger, and attrition (Robinson & Rousseau, 1994) and change the way people behave in subsequent interactions (Rousseau et al., 1992). The aftermath of contract violation can be seen in declining corporate loyalty (Hirsch, 1987) and increased litigation (Bies & Tyler, 1993). Managers decry the decline of employee loyalty, but at the same time the workforce has been counseled to eschew reliance on job security and employer commitments, and to "pack its own" parachute instead (Hirsch, 1987). In both instances, there is the suggestion of contract violation and the implication that at least one party has failed to keep its side of the bargain.

Types of Responses

Whether organizations and individuals choose to end their relationship, resolve their dispute, sue, or suffer in silence is a function of both situational factors and the predispositions of the parties. Previous research on responses to the more general phenomenon of dissatisfaction has largely focused on four courses of action: exit, voice, loyalty, and destruction. Although studied in various combinations (e.g., Hirschman's, 1970, *Exit, Voice, and Loyalty*) and labels (e.g., Farrell's, 1983, exit, voice, loyalty, and neglect), these courses of action reflect two essential dimensions (Farrell, 1983; Robinson, 1992): active-passive and constructive-destructive (Figure 5.2).

These responses to violation can be induced by both personal predispositions and situational factors. Personal characteristics predisposing the victim to believe that the relationship is valuable or can be saved should promote relationship-building behaviors of either voice or loyalty. Without this belief, behaviors that undermine the relationship—exit or destruction—are more likely. Research on individual reactions to inequitable situations suggests that people differ in terms of their willingness to tolerate unfair or inequitable exchanges (Huseman, Hatfield, & Miles, 1987). "Equity-sensitives" are people who tend to monitor their exchanges with others very carefully. "Beneficient" individuals are those who tend to be other oriented, or comfortable when exchanges benefit others more than themselves. There is some evidence that men are more likely to be equity-sensitive and women more beneficient, although personality and other factors also enter in. Situational factors promoting certain behaviors and inhibiting others also affect responses to violation. Social learning and the presence of behavioral models tend to induce certain types of behaviors. Thus employees in organizations where other victims have left might be inclined to leave themselves. Simi-

	Constructive	Destructive
Active	Voice	Neglect/Destruction
Passive	Loyalty/Silence	Exit

FIGURE 5.2. Responses to Violation

larly, individuals who have observed others successfully complain about their treatment might themselves be inclined to complain (Robinson, 1992). It is likely that the culture of the organization shapes the type of violation responses people make. A very bureaucratic organization that stifles communication and deviant behavior probably engenders little voice and more neglect and disloyalty. An open, communal organization might foster more overt complaints as well as attempts to repair the contract by communicating with superiors.

Exit is voluntary termination of the relationship. Employers can terminate workers whose performance does not meet standards (e.g., too frequently tardy, absent, or careless), and workers can quit an untrustworthy or unreliable employer (e.g., one that fails to deliver promised training or promotions). Exit is most likely in employment with transactional terms, where its costs are relatively low. Failure of either to honor commitments is typically unambiguous, because terms are discrete, objective, and frequently measured. Transactional arrangements are self-regulating, in that parties to such arrangements can more readily exit unsatisfactory contracts and find new, more appropriate partners. Both active and destructive, exit terminates the relationship. The vast majority of people quitting jobs within the first two years of employment report that their employer had violated commitments it had made (Robinson & Rousseau, 1994).

Exit is most likely following violation when

1. The contract is transactional
2. Many other potential jobs or potential employees are available
3. The relationship is relatively brief
4. Other people are also exiting
5. Attempts to remedy a violated contract have failed

However, it should be pointed out that violations don't always lead to exit. Robinson and Rousseau (1994) found that although 79% of leavers reported violated contracts, so too did 52% of stayers. While enduring violation, stayers can manifest three forms of response: voice, loyalty/silence, or neglect/destruction.

Voice refers to the actions victims take to remedy the violation. Any attempt to change the objectionable features in the situation, such as complaints to one's boss or to human resources, or the filing of a grievance, are efforts made to remedy or compensate for the violation while remaining in the relationship. As a means of expressing general dissatisfaction, voice has received wide study in terms of grievance filing (Allen & Keaveny, 1981), willingness to vote for unions (e.g., Getman, Goldberg, & Herman, 1976), and whistle-blowing (Near & Miceli, 1986). However, as a means of remediating a contract violation, voice has features distinct from reparations for dissatisfaction. Voice in contract violation focuses on (a) reducing losses and (b) restoring trust.

As a response to dissatisfaction, voice often has been associated with relationship-threatening alternatives, where members in effect burn their bridges (e.g., whistle-blowing). Voice in response to contract violation is an active, constructive effort and is manifested in a number of ways. In a study of M.B.A. alumni, there were three major types of employee voice behaviors: talking with superiors, threats, and changes in behavior (Rousseau et al., 1992).

Talking with superiors was the most frequent type of voice:[2]

> I discussed my disappointment with my boss and also with my mentor. I was assured that, although I did not receive a bonus, my performance was above average. I was promoted and received a salary increase 6 months later.
>
> They moved me to a more challenging job . . . after I asked them to do so. This required two formal requests for a transfer.
>
> [My boss and I] had a heated discussion face to face. He took notes on what I felt I needed to have in order to complete the transition. He carried through 110%.
>
> I am in the process of negotiating with higher management. . . . I do have places to go with my concerns and have never felt the need to remain silent.

Some complaints obtain some sort of substitution:

> They said the situation was out of their hands and gave me a substantial salary increase.
>
> Management attempted to rationalize the decision to explain it was a capricious process and then gave me a larger bonus to assuage my discontent.
>
> Their system of training has come around a little . . . but they do not place as high a priority on training as they first sold me.

Some complaints elicit no response:

My boss paid lip service to making changes, but nothing actually occurred.

Senior management listens to me very well and then does nothing.

I went through all the necessary channels and have met with no success.

They just said no.

Voice can take the form of a threat in a smaller number of cases:

I threatened to leave based on my work assignment, training, and development opportunities. I was given new assignments, more training, and was allowed to stretch for development . . . however, I believe that happened primarily because of my director; another director probably would have let me leave.

I had to appeal my case and threaten legal action to get my record changed to a layoff from firing and also to get a settlement.

In a few instances, a change in the victim's behavior generates a response:

I was unhappy with the situation and my performance reflected it. The decision was made by [my] managers to reverse the situation. I now report to the marketing manager with a dotted line reporting relationship with the financial manager [a reversal of the previous situation].

Exit was the final resort for some:

First there was a confrontation on my part to bring the problem forth, then following further unkept promises, I left the company [giving over a month's notice].

When turnover is already high in the firm, exit may follow soon after a voice channel failure:

Many colleagues left the organization, including myself, eventually. Several colleagues prepared a memo protesting the repeal of a promised salary increase. [Management's response was a memo] simply stating "salary matters are dealt with on an individual basis."

I made clear my observations as to the discrepancy between their public assertions and the apparent reality. . . . Because I already was involved with many of their major dealings . . . they could not easily just fire me. The result was their effort to smooth over any ripples I'd created and impose conditions upon which I'd choose to leave so that they would not actually have to fire me. As I write this I am a witness for several of their creditors'/investor groups' lawsuits.

Voice is most likely when

1. A positive relationship and trust exist
2. Voice channels exist
3. Other people are using voice
4. People believe that they can influence the other contract party

Silence is a form of nonresponse. Manifested as loyalty or as avoidance, silence reflects a willingness to endure or accept unfavorable circumstances. Silence can imply pessimism, in terms of believing that one has no available alternatives. Or silence can reflect loyalty—optimistically waiting for conditions to improve (Rusbult, Farrell, Rogers, & Mainous, 1988). As a passive, constructive response, silence serves to perpetuate the existing relationship.

> I started spending more time with my family and worrying less about what was happening at work.
>
> The last few years have really changed things with new owners and little investment back into the business. Where else could I go?

Silence is likely when

1. There are no voice channels or established ways of complaining or communicating violations
2. No available alternative opportunities exist elsewhere

Neglect, which entails passive negligence or active destruction, is a complex form of response. It can involve neglect of one's duties to the detriment of the interests of the other party. Passive-aggressive employee behavior, as in work slowdowns or providing customers with poor service, is a form of neglect, as is an organization's failure to invest in certain employees while developing others. Even when passive, neglect reflects erosion of the relationship between the parties. *Destruction* involves more active examples of counterproductive behaviors, including vandalism, theft, and interpersonal aggression (e.g., violence at work).

Neglect/destruction is most likely when

1. There is a history of conflict, mistrust, and violation
2. No voice channels exist
3. Other people demonstrate neglect or destruction

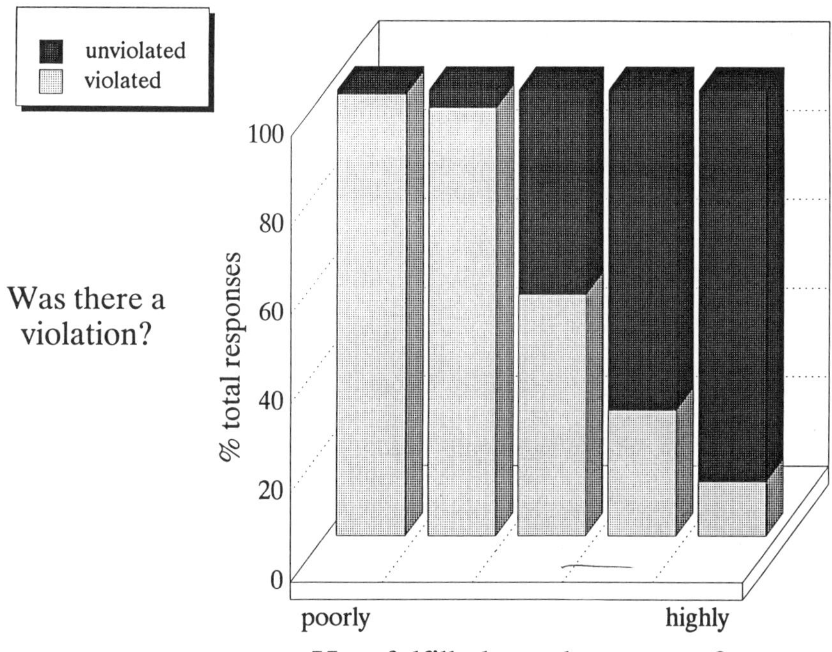

FIGURE 5.3. Worker Contracts

VIOLATION ISN'T THE END OF THE CONTRACT

Exit is only one of many results of contract violation. The fact that so many people with violated contracts remain with their employer suggests that although violation may be based on a discrete event (e.g., a willful breach of contract terms), a contract's fulfillment is more a matter of degree. When Robinson and Rousseau (1994) asked employees to indicate *whether* their contract had been violated, using a yes/no format, a total of 55% indicated "yes." However, when respondents were asked if their contract had ultimately been fulfilled by their employer, a large proportion (73%) indicated that their employer had honored its commitments at least moderately well. Among those employees reporting a violation at some point in the first two years of employment, 48% indicated that their contract had been honored at least somewhat by their employer. (The major difference was that for victims of violation, the modal rating of fulfillment was 3 on a 5-point scale—mean = 2.65—but for nonvictims it was 4—mean = 3.93) (Figure 5.3). Extent of contract keeping was affected by what benefits the employee received (e.g., if not the promotion as scheduled, then one later) as well as whether the violation was an isolated incident or part of a larger pattern. These findings suggest that although violation is a discrete event, contract fulfillment is not. Rather, fulfillment is a continuum shaped by both the quality of the relationship and the postviolation behavior of both victim and perpetrator.

SUMMARY

Contract violation erodes trust. It undermines the employment relationship, yielding both lower employee contributions (e.g., performance and attendance) and lower employer investments (e.g., retention and promotion). How people respond to violation is largely a function of attributions made regarding the violators's motives, the behavior of the violator, and the scope of losses incurred. To understand how events are experienced as violations, it is necessary to take into account the perspective of the victim and the behavior of the perpetrator. For the prospective victim, the experience of violation is heightened when

- Losses seem greater (experienced violation is a matter of degree rather than a discrete event)
- The event occurs in a context where it poses a threat to the relationship between the parties (e.g., a history of previous breach or conflict)
- The violation event appears to be voluntary, as opposed to inadvertent, accidental, or due to forces beyond the violator's control
- No evidence of good faith efforts to avoid violation (the appearance of irresponsibility or neglect) is perceived by the victim

The strength and quality of the relationship not only affects the extent to which violation is tolerated or leads to dissolution of the contract but also affects the ability of the parties to repair the relationship. How people are treated following violation can repair the relationship or exacerbate its problems.

NOTE

1. Schmidt, 1993, p. 6. Copyright © 1993 by *The New York Times*. Reprinted with permission.

2. The following quotations were obtained from the M.B.A. alumni constituting the sample also used in Rousseau et al. (1992), Robinson, Kraatz, and Rousseau (1994), and Robinson and Rousseau (1994). The quotes appear here for the first time.

6 Changing the Contract

It isn't the changes that do you in, it's the transitions.

—*William Bridges (1991, p. 3)*

It used to be that working for the company meant being part of a family. Now they say we're supposed to be a team. There's a difference. You can't fire one of the family but you can in a team.

—*Employee, telephone operating company*

In a sense, contracts are designed to accomplish two often impossible tasks: predicting the future and forestalling change. Employers want to know in advance the kind of effort they will get from workers. Employees try to anticipate how their employer will treat them before taking out a mortgage for an expensive house or going to night school to advance their career. Predictability is a major motivation in contract making. We know a contract has been kept when neither party is surprised by the behavior of the other. Making and obtaining future commitments is a way to "lock in" the future, creating an image of tomorrow that can be relied on today. A contract makes predictability easier. The irony is that contracts sometimes need to change so as to be kept.

Contract change ranges from subtle, imperceptible shifts in understanding to traumatic upheavals, and affects both the work experience of individuals and the dynamics of work groups. Emerging contract forms have introduced new standards for gauging business practices while altering how the public thinks about careers (upward mobility versus the boundaryless career), job security (golden handcuffs versus golden handshakes), and loyalty (dead and gone versus alive and well).

Contracts are a model of the future based on past experience. Many forms of contract making are rooted in an earlier era when people and organizations operated in more stable environments. Predictability was easier then. Now it's becoming tougher to achieve, but perhaps even more valuable. Radical change in the nature of work, as described in Chapter 4, calls into question the meaning and nature of employment contracts in environments that can be both dynamic and unpredictable. Increasing instability and unpredictability certainly affect a contract's terms and may also affect the strategies needed to manage change.

This chapter describes the major forms that contract change takes. It addresses how internal and external factors alter contract terms and their performance. It also details how change can be managed to meet organizational and personal needs for predictability and flexibility.

FORMS OF CONTRACT CHANGE

Contract change occurs in several ways (Table 6.1). Changes that develop in the contract parties themselves modify their understanding of the contract, a process referred to here as "contract drift." External developments affecting the work people do, the setting in which they work, or the larger environment can also intervene in the contract, leading to changes ranging from minor additions, modifications, and adjustments in contract terms or to radical reformulation of the entire contract. These external changes take two forms: evolutionary accommodation or revolutionary transformation. With the possible exception of one-shot transactions, all contracts are subject to change.

INTERNAL CHANGE: DRIFT

Psychological contracts can change without any formal effort to alter their terms. This contract drift can be evident when

long-tenured employees do different kinds of work than their more junior counterparts with the same job title,

organizations permit greater flexibility in hours and work practices for veterans or top performers than they do for other workers,

performance requirements expand gradually over several years—and workers don't complain.

Time is the single most important cause of contract change, but not simply because the outside world might be changing. Rather, contract parties them-

TABLE 6.1 Three Kinds of Contract Change

Location	*Dynamics*	*Examples*
Internal:		
contract drift	■ internally induced ■ self-focused ■ maturation	■ evaluating self as fulfilling contract more than others ■ acquiring more relational terms over time ■ adjusting interpretation to suit changing personal needs
External:		
accommodation	■ consistency ■ equilibrium	■ introduce additional related performance requirements ■ take away bonuses while continuing regular salary
transformation	■ disruption ■ irreversibility	■ redefine relationship, that is, a team, not a family ■ terminate one contract, initiate another

selves change in ways that influence their understanding of the contract's terms and the terms' meaning or fulfillment. Terms such as *satisfactory performance* or *growth potential* only have meaning compared with some standard, and that metric of comparison varies according to the experiences of each party. Personal development, maturation, aging, and the contract's duration can alter a psychological contract. A company priding itself on its employee benefits package can find that the mix of health care and retirement benefits that satisfied employees when most were young and single may be woefully inadequate once many of them have married and started families. Junior-level employees in a consulting firm who have sacrificed their personal lives to travel and work long hours can, over time, come to believe this exchange is unfair or inequitable. Older manufacturing workers find themselves doing less physically demanding jobs than they once did, putting aside

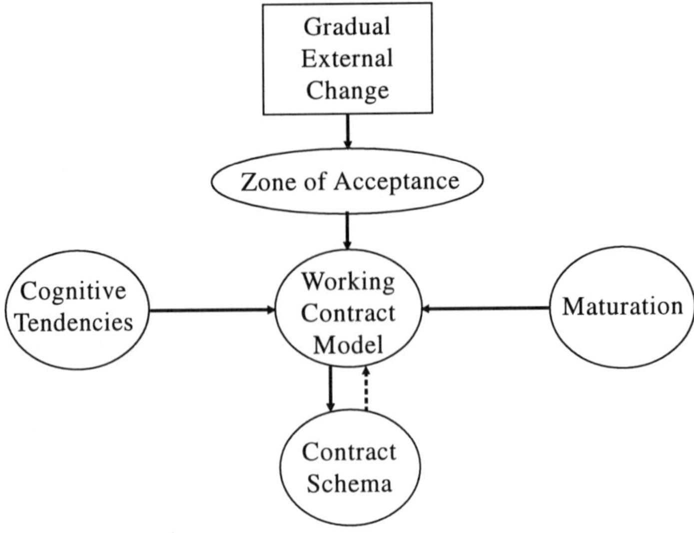

FIGURE 6.1. Contract Drift

their tools and picking up a clipboard. This "contract drift," or change lacking an external cause, is one reason that mutuality between contract parties can be difficult to sustain.

Drift refers to internally induced shifts in how the contract is understood (Figure 6.1). It occurs when beliefs gradually diverge regarding whether terms are performed, when terms come to mean something different than they did initially, or when the contract acquires new terms without one party becoming aware of the addition. The major forces behind contract drift are general cognitive tendencies and the maturational effects characterizing the life cycle.

Cognitive Tendencies. In general, people gather information in selective ways. Most information processing is full of incomplete data gathering, errors, and shortcuts (Fiske & Taylor, 1984). In particular, self-focused interpretations and prior expectations weigh heavily on judgment. In contracts, how people gauge their own and their partners' contributions shapes their subsequent interpretations of that contract's terms (Robinson et al., 1994). Some of the more common cognitive tendencies, described below, include availability, judgments of intentionality, and unrealistic optimism.

The Bias of Availability. Readily available information is most likely to be self-relevant, focusing on our own accomplishments, experience, or needs (Fiske & Taylor, 1984). Contract fulfillment is often interpreted in terms of what the individual has contributed while downplaying what the other party has given. Easily available information also tends to include salient and well-publicized actions to the neglect of less visible efforts. Thus people in one firm might think that their employer provides them with terrific benefits while employees in another firm are dissatisfied—despite the fact that both employers offer comparable benefits. The difference can be explained by the fact that the first organization has distributed information to each employee on the dollars spent annually on their individual benefits (health care, disability insurance, pension, and so on), but the second organization never provided individuals with these details. Contributions that people do not see may not be credited. In sum, perceptions of how well parties fulfill the contract over time are affected by the availability of information regarding each party's contributions.

Judgments of Intentionality. We tend to judge ourselves by our intentions and others by their behavior (based on the most easily available information). When making judgments, we tend to credit ourselves with good intentions. However, because other people's intentions are not readily known to us, we typically judge them by their behavior, and tend to judge it less positively than our own. As described in our discussion of violation, if this behavior produces adverse consequences for us, we are more likely to see it as intentionally harmful. Thus individuals are likely to weigh their own and others' contributions to contract performance differently. Individual contract holders tend to credit themselves with fulfilling their end of the contract to a greater extent than their counterparts do.

Unrealistic Optimism or Self-Confidence. Unrealistically positive views of our own ability and performance apply to both past recollections and future expectations. Most people remember their successes better than their failures and remember positive information about themselves better than negative information (e.g., Greenwald, 1980). Rosy past memories lead both managers and workers to overestimate their past contributions to the firm and to each other. Having less recall of our failures than our successes, it becomes easy to be optimistic about the future, including our ability to continue to meet commitments we make to others.

Future optimism is also caused by an exaggerated belief in personal control. People typically attribute their successes to personal factors (e.g., effort or ability) and the successes of others to luck or easy circumstances.

(The pattern reverses for failure: Individuals typically attribute their failed efforts to job difficulty or to unlucky circumstances.) Moreover, most people believe they will be less likely than others to encounter problems or impediments in their own performance.[1] When asked to predict their chances of experiencing accidents (Robertson, 1977), unemployment (Weinstein, 1980), or illness (Perloff & Fetzer, 1986), people typically report that they are less likely than their peers to experience such negative events. Taylor and Brown (1988) illustrate this belief with the proclamation: " 'The future will be great, especially for me' " (p. 197). The result of this optimistic view of one's future is the tendency to overpromise, ignoring the likely constraints on one's ability to fulfill commitments. This optimism can create unrealistic expectations of the other party and unrealistic beliefs about one's own contributions.[2]

Implications of These Cognitive Tendencies. These pervasive tendencies to view the self positively, and especially as better than others, have tremendous implications for contractual thinking. Generally speaking, people are more likely to believe they themselves have fulfilled their side of the bargain and less likely to think the other party has. Ross and Sicoly (1979) asked married couples to indicate which spouse had responsibility for each of 20 household chores. Responsibility scores for each member of the couples totaled over 100% in most cases—typically husbands rated themselves as having more responsibility for household chores than their wives believed the husband had, and vice versa. Further, each provided more examples of his or her own contributions than those of the spouse (Ross & Sicoly, 1979). Having more information about our contributions than our partner's and remembering it better are primary factors in a self-centered bias. What's more, knowing how well intentioned we were in entering a voluntary agreement with another makes it likely that we will believe we have held up our end of the deal. These biases apply to all contract parties, including workers, managers, stockholders, and customers.

Recently graduated M.B.A.s describe performance of the contract in ways consistent with self-focused cognitive tendencies (Robinson et al., 1994; Figure 6.2). When they were hired, M.B.A.s indicated what they owed to their employer and what their employer owed them. Employer obligations included providing rapid advancement, high pay, training, and job security. M.B.A. obligations included working overtime, loyalty to their employer, willingness to accept transfers, staying a minimum length of time, and respecting their employers' proprietary rights (to knowledge and customers). Two years after taking their first job, alumni were again asked to indicate what they and their employer owed each other. Strikingly, out of eight employee obligations, five declined over time (none increased significantly), whereas, out of seven employer obligations, three increased significantly

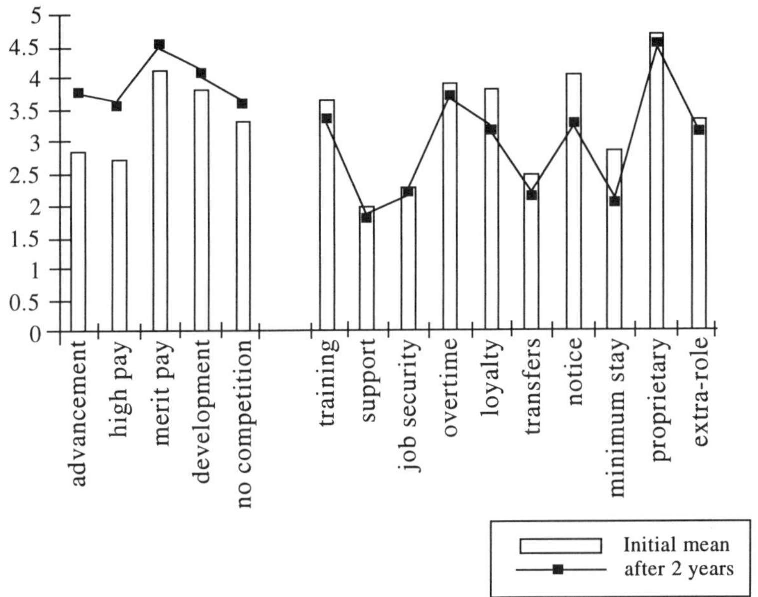

FIGURE 6.2. Perceived Obligations
NOTE: Data from Robinson, Kraatz, and Rousseau (1994).

(advancement, high pay, and merit-based pay) and only one significantly declined (training). The increase in employer obligations can be interpreted as the "payback" organizations owe employees who have fulfilled their end of the deal. Consistent with this explanation, an organization would no longer owe training (the one significantly declining employer obligation) if its employee had successful completed the work required. On the other hand, employees who focus on their own contributions to their organization can be expected to believe their own obligations have been fulfilled.[3]

Maturation. The passage of time brings substantial physical and social changes. The needs of workers and organizations can change with age and new adult roles and responsibilities. Time can make what was once a normal work activity almost impossible to fulfill. "Thirty-something" workers with family responsibilities, dual career demands, and ensuing time crises can find that expectations they might have welcomed in their twenties (e.g., travel or entertaining clients) have become difficult to comply with. A person who sees herself as a well-motivated, dedicated employee might accommodate her definition of the job to changing family demands. Such shifts may happen more easily when people are part of a work cohort who share the same experiences. A medical director in an intensive care unit complained of the changing culture in his unit brought on by the aging of its staff:

> It used to be like a MASH unit around here. Back when most of us were in our twenties and thirties, the camaraderie was tremendous. Nurses and doctors would go out drinking together after hours. Now everybody is married and has kids. They finish their shift and rush home to their family.

Personal growth and development can also alter the way individuals enact their employment contract:

> The closer I get to retirement, the more I think about this company as my legacy.
>
> —*Owner of small manufacturing firm*

> What it means to be successful to me is different today than when I started here—I want to enjoy what I do at work.
>
> —*Investment banker*

For many people, changes in their personal lives modify the way they view their work role. These changes can be subtle shifts in time allocations or more major adjustments in activities. Nonetheless, the changes can create a new taken-for-granted definition of one's responsibilities at work. Maturation and personal development lead to changes in the interpretation and value of contract terms such as employer-provided benefits. For example, the promise of "great career flexibility" and a "supportive environment" is more important to the parent of young children than to a preretiree. The life cycle can change the meaning of contract terms. Drift occurs when terms undergo unannounced shifts in importance to suit an employees' emerging needs.

Both employees and employers can modify their expectations without the other party experiencing a change in the deal. Herbert Simon (1958/1976) describes the "zone of acceptance" (adapted from Chester Barnard's notion of a "zone of indifference") wherein organizations can ask new things of employees without people noticing. Whether secretaries place a letter in the mail or fax, it is probably a matter of indifference to them; these tasks fit into the larger performance term of *processing correspondence.* Some changes can occur so gradually that they create drift in the zone of acceptance, for example, gradually increasing the educational demands required for promotion or workers performing more job tasks at home as family demands increase. In time, new standards may be created against which contract performance is gauged. In all these instances, employee or employer creates drift, or unannounced shifts in interpretation of the contract. Contracts drift most readily when internal changes can be fitted into an old schema. We already know that people typically prefer to maintain a schema. In a peculiar way, drift makes an old schema easier to keep.

The zone of acceptance is more readily altered for either employee or employer (or any other contract parties) when there is a strong positive relationship between the parties. This positive relationship is often the case in long-standing employment relations. An older employee with a bad back may not have to do the heavy lifting that young workers do. Members of a family business may be quite comfortable helping each other with assigned tasks. Simon (1958/1976) originally characterized the zone of acceptance as the area "within which the employee will accept the authority of the organization" (p. 116). Certainly, legitimacy of authority is important to accepting change without perceiving it as a break with preexisting commitments. Yet employers also may accept certain demands from highly valued employees without renegotiating the contract. The value people place on the relationship, including incentives offered and losses risked if the relationship flounders, can promote an essentially unconscious change in the zone of acceptance. Changes in the zone of acceptance are essentially changes in the contract.[4]

Contract Duration: Escalation of Commitment to the Relationship. Both employer and employee are affected by the duration of their relationship. The longer a relationship exists with repeated cycles of inducements and contributions, the greater the investment each has in the other, and the more difficult and costly it can be to break, both economically (investments in organization-specific learning and training) and emotionally (due to attachments based on familiarity, shared beliefs, and identification). Over time, boundaries blur as employees fail to differentiate between themselves and the place they work, and as the organization becomes what its employees have made it. Time expands a contract's relational terms. Think of the stories of Bell system employees with "bell-shaped heads," "blue-blooded" Federal Express employees (to match their uniform), only to be rivaled by the "brown blood" (that uniform again) of United Parcel Service employees. Time escalates commitment to relationships and can mean that what began as limited transactions can become highly valued, trusted relations between person and organization. Such escalating, relational contract terms are most likely in organizations that have provided support to employees in terms of help both in doing their jobs (e.g., training and guidance) and in their personal lives (e.g., flexible hours; Barksdale & Shore, 1993). Customers can also become more relational toward the organization based on accustomed contact with certain sales staff or support people representing the firm (Seabright, Levinthal, & Fichman, 1992). In some instances, customers develop a loyalty to those people that can transcend loyalty to the organization itself. As the duration of any contract increases, expanded entitlements and investments occur that lead to relational contracts with an array of socioemotional terms (e.g., support, concern for personal welfare, loyalty).

Older workers who have spent years in the same firm exemplify drift in contracts. Job analyses reveal that the longer someone does a particular job, the more idiosyncratic are the tasks performed and skills demonstrated (e.g., Miner, 1987). In organizations where experience is valuable, this drift can reflect an exchange: the opportunity to do the job the way the worker prefers in exchange for making tacit knowledge and unique experience available to the organization. This expanded contract differs from the initial contract; nonetheless, it is experienced more as continuity than change.

An Illustration of Contract Drift. Drift can create a series of interim interpretations or working models of the contract (Figure 6.3). Michelle Roberts, a market researcher who was hired some years ago at the age of 25, operated with a contract schema that committed her to loyalty, best efforts, and dependable work in exchange for the opportunity to work for a supportive employer. Her working model of this schema at age 25 held that she should work an 8-hour day at the office, 5 days a week. Gradually, competitive pressures on the company made it difficult for it to hire new people as demand increased. An escalating workload over a period of 3 years caused Michelle then to work between 50 and 60 hours a week, though much of it through telecommuting. Ten years after hire, 35-year-old Michelle added an elderly parent to her household. Expecting support from her typically flexible employer, Michelle makes her "best effort" by working a 40-hour week over a 7-day period, spending some of that normal work time at home to provide care for her parent. Her employer has been experimenting with a variety of family leave arrangements and other benefits for workers caring for children or elderly relatives, and is supportive and accepting of her adjusted work patterns. After 13 years with the same firm, this market researcher, when asked, says, "I have basically the same employment arrangement with this company that I had when I started." The robustness of the contract over time is probably due to the fact that the employer was accepting of Michelle's shift to telecommuting, and she in turn had no strong objection to expanding the workweek if the employer had a good reason to increase the load. Both Michelle and her employer have a zone of acceptance that is large and expandable. If, however, down the road, Michelle's employer becomes increasingly demanding, or Michelle's lifestyle becomes more

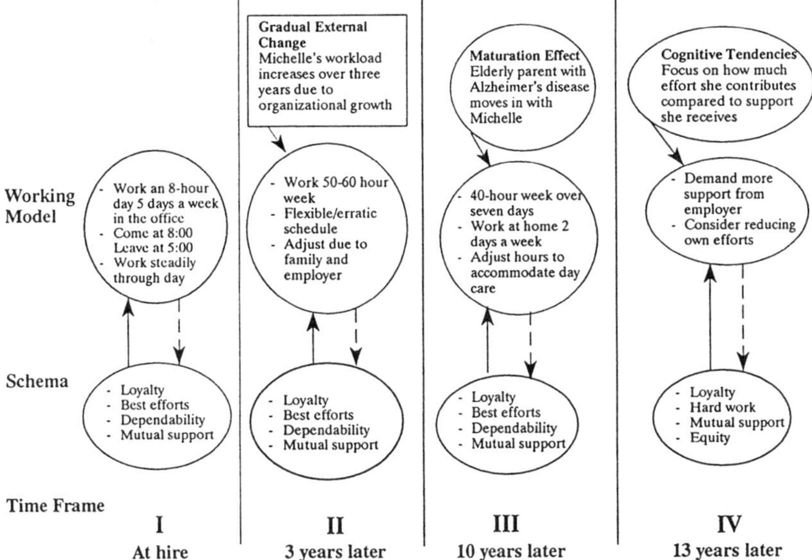

FIGURE 6.3. A Drift Time Line: The Case of Michelle Roberts

more removed from work, she or her employer may begin to believe the contract is being breached.

Practical Implications of Drift

Drift clearly has its good and bad points. It creates flexibility in response to life cycle developments and gradual organizational changes. On the other hand, drift can inadvertently create violation when one party's psychological contract drifts beyond the other's zone of acceptance. It is in the interest of all parties to work to achieve continuity and mutuality in contract terms.

The following describes how can drift be managed effectively:

1. *Periodic conferences,* that is, discussions and reminders of contract terms (e.g., performance requirements and benefits), can prevent erosion or expansion of contract terms due to drift. Perhaps one of the most useful applications of the performance appraisal interview is the maintenance of the psychological contract. A two-way conversation regarding performance criteria, incentives, and support to be anticipated from achieving the criteria are key aspects of contracting.

2. *Training and development* exercises in which managers and subordinates each list their joint expectations and then share and compare the two lists can promote mutual recognition of shifting needs and priorities.
3. *Updates* are another antidrift tactic. In the case of marriages with prenuptial agreements, a cynical tactic is to have a spouse sign such a contract again and again to prevent expanded entitlements over the life of the marriage. Similarly, organizations seeking to establish and maintain at-will employment policies may communicate through personnel manuals or memos this at-will status to prevent employment that is transactional from becoming a relationship. In this manner, drift is managed by keeping entitlements from expanding and understandings from eroding.

Arresting or even reversing the process of contract drift is advantageous for prolonging predictable, stable employment relations. But the flip side is that some drift is quite adaptive. People and organizations do change and develop different needs over time. If every change that surfaced were viewed as a threat to the relationship, there would be many more perceived violations and far fewer viable contracts. Adjustments to the psychological contract caused by drift often serve to keep people in stable relationships while permitting personal growth and development and organizational flexibility.

EXTERNAL CHANGE

The contract changes people notice are more than likely brought on by external factors. Such undeniable changes in existing contracts include the following:

- Shifts in job duties from individual efforts to teamwork, and from short-term financial results to customer satisfaction (Handy, 1989)
- Reduction in adversarial union relations in favor of increasing labor-management cooperation (Kelly & Harrison, 1992)
- Moving from offering "a job for life" to stressing "employability" (Snow, Miles, & Coleman, 1992)
- Different contracts for newcomers than veterans, such as the two-tiered wage systems used in the airline industry (Capelli & Scherer, 1990)
- Increasing variety in types of employment contracts within the same organization, as seen in the recent headline declaring that designers are to be hired on a contractual basis by a Japanese carmaker ("Toyota to Hire," 1994, p. A39; see Handy, 1989)
- Outsourcing all functions except those deemed to be core or critical (Bettis et al., 1992; Handy, 1989)

A global economy, growing competitiveness, escalating rates of technological innovation, shorter product life cycles, and fluctuating economic growth have created new demands for organizations and the people who work in them. Innovations in products or services can alter the work people do, and thus affect their contracts' performance conditions. Rapid and unpredictable change makes longer term commitments difficult to make and keep in some industries.

There are two distinct kinds of externally induced change processes. *Accommodation* makes adjustments within the framework of the existing contract. *Transformation* marks a fundamental shift in the nature of the relationship between the parties, redefining it and the contract on which it is based. Accommodations modify, clarify, substitute, or expand terms within the context of the existing contract. Isolated changes in performance criteria, benefit packages, or work hours are likely examples of accommodation. This contract change is comparable to the single-loop learning that Argyris and Schön (1978) describe and the first-order changes detailed by Bartunek and Moch (1987). Transformations, in contrast, create a shift in meaning and interpretation comparable to double-loop learning and second-order organizational change (Figure 6.4). Systemic changes that alter the scope and nature of the exchange, such as a switch from a "family business" to a "team," are an example of transformation.

ACCOMMODATION: ADJUSTMENTS WITHIN THE EXISTING CONTRACT

When contract changes can be successfully subsumed under the existing contract, accommodation occurs. The underlying philosophy of accommodation strategies can be thought of in terms of a statement President Jimmy Carter made in his inaugural address, in which he quoted his former schoolteacher, Julia Coleman: "We must adjust to changing times and still hold to unchanging principles" (January 20, 1977).

Because of the continuity it offers, accommodation is often the contract change strategy of choice. The following are just a few examples:

> Our customer representatives have always had job security and reasonably high pay compared to the market. Now they get that from helping grow the company. We've uncapped the incentive system and moved from paying for number of shipped units to gross margin profit.
>
> —*General manager, industrial marketing firm*

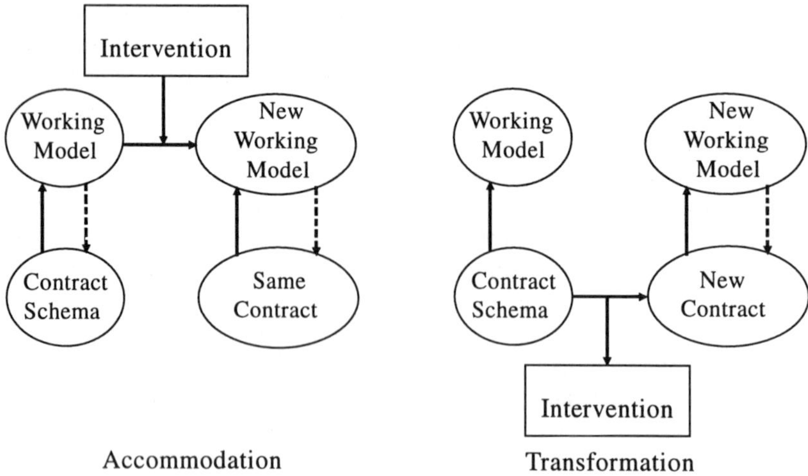

FIGURE 6.4. External Change in the Psychological Contract

> We've always paid based on performance. It used to be the individual contributor loyal to his or her personal dollars was the best paid. Now it's more the team player who helps bring the division average up who makes the most.
>
> —*Pharmaceutical firm executive*

> [There has] never been a layoff in the company's history. A few years ago when the market was down, everybody—managers, operations people, everyone—shifted to a 4-day work week. People really hung in there.
>
> —*High-technology firm spokesperson*

Accommodation can mean honoring the spirit if not the letter of an existing agreement when adjustments become necessary. A consultant unable to deliver a scheduled report on time because of a sick child might negotiate an extension of the deadline. Technological changes may necessitate fewer operators on a production line, so surplus operators receive training to perform new tasks. Accommodation occurs when the same schemas remain despite acknowledged changes in working conditions.

When there is a good faith relationship between contract parties, changes are more likely to be interpreted as existing within the framework of the existing contract. Good faith relationships lead to accommodation because (a) parties are not actively looking for contract violations and (b) good faith relationships include some relational contract terms that increase the zone of acceptance. Relationships with a positive history manifest a willingness to be flexible, which makes it easier for both parties to ask for changes. In the words of a veteran manager in a family-owned manufacturing firm: "When we hit tough times, old Mr. ______ [the owner] calls a 'family meeting' of all employees, whether they're from the family or not, and tells us we need to tighten our belts or work harder. You do what needs to be done." Contrast that description of accommodation with the statement of the founder of Shea and Gould, a New York-based law firm that voted to disband after several years of financial trouble, reported infighting and difficulties in managing the transition once the founders had retired:

> I was reared in the tradition where a law firm was a family—we supported each other from a motive of general benefit. . . . But I have suffered a betrayal by people who owed a lot to me: they didn't discuss it with me, and they used bad judgement to further objectives that were selfish and unjust. ("An End," 1994, p. A1)[5]

Maintaining the Status Quo. A cardinal rule in fairness is that one party should not benefit by simply imposing an equivalent loss on another. Thus a firm that cuts wages to put more money in the owner's pocket is very likely to be viewed as exploitative and opportunistic. On the other hand, cutting wages or the workweek at the risk of otherwise going out of business is likely to be seen as more fair, perpetuating the basic contract requirement of acting in good faith. Actions are deemed more unfair if they achieve a gain for one party at the expense of the other than if they avoid a loss.

How changes compare with the status quo affects whether accommodation occurs. There tends to be a strong preference toward maintaining the status quo (Kahneman & Tversky, 1979). Preference for maintaining the status quo yields considerable fairness efforts focusing on reducing losses. For example, organizations frequently tolerate people using up their sick time even when they are not ill if that sick time will be lost if not taken. One-sided gains are also acceptable if they come at no cost. Although taking reams of office paper to use on one's home computer can be seen as stealing, office secretaries might stay after work to use the office word processor for personal correspondence without any outcry because the organization's losses are minimal. One-sided losses are also more acceptable if they yield no positive gain (merely keeping up the status quo), for example, when bonuses are withheld during an economic downturn. They are also more likely to be acceptable when the reasons offered are interpreted as legitimate. These reasons tend to be external and beyond the control of contract parties, such as depressed conditions in the marketplace.

Core Versus Ancillary Contract Terms. Changes in established practices are more readily accommodated when adjustments are made in the "extra" or ancillary terms of the contract while core terms continue to be kept. Contract terms are interpreted as core when they are a well-established part of the status quo. When an organization has a long, successful history of paying a profit-sharing bonus, employees often react negatively when the bonus is cut due to declining profits. Bonuses regularly added to a weekly paycheck become the status quo—taken for granted when given, and resented when taken away. On the other hand, separating paycheck from bonus check can signal the conditional nature of the latter. Labeling a benefit as "special" makes its fluctuation or loss easier to bear. For the same reason, we may tell our children that a meal at a fancy restaurant is "special" to keep them from expecting it every time we eat out. When benefits are bundled, people have difficulty seeing their components as separate. Disaggregating the individual parts can maintain the flexibility to change their distribution. Other things being equal, contract change is easier to accommodate when it is the extras that are affected.

Participation and Voluntary Acceptance. Because the essence of contracting is voluntary acceptance, participation in the change process can promote accommodation, especially when it includes active information gathering and planning. Sending employees to visit customers who otherwise have little contact with them can create a felt need for change or service improvement. Organizationwide education on the need for change is another form of involvement. In the words of one CEO:

> We held a meeting for all the salaried people. . . . We gave them an overview of the . . . plan . . . then different staff heads talked about their strategy and where they're headed. . . . We do that on a quarterly basis now. Once you start doing that you can drive the plan down into the organization. People understand it, they embrace it. (Cameron, Freeman, & Mishra, 1991, p. 60)

Involvement in the planning process, as seen in the closing of Ford's Milpitas plant (Chapter 5), fosters a greater sense of control, provides more information to and from those affected by change, and leads to active use of that information through planning efforts. Active participation promotes contract change by permitting contract parties to exercise their understanding of the change in terms of their existing contract.

Limited Scope of Change. Staying within the framework of an existing contract is usually easier when only a few changes are made to it. Most forms of accommodation involve refinements and variations on preexisting contract elements. Just as one can repair a ship afloat by replacing one of its timbers while leaving the others in place, isolated changes (clarifying performance requirements, raising the standards for promotion) are more easily accommodated than multiple interventions. Focused change has the advantage of permitting simultaneous adjustments in several administrative contract makers (from performance review to selection processes) with attention to a specific contract term (e.g., promoting sales growth, improved innovation rates).

Punctuation: When Does Change End? Punctuation is important to both contract change and maintenance, as it signals when a change begins and ends. For a contract to function fully, people need to be able to rely on their understanding of its terms. If change goes on for prolonged periods of time, that predictability may be lost. An advantage of accommodation strategies and focused change efforts is that it often becomes possible to tell people when the change is over. Throwing a party to celebrate adoption of a new system helps mark the end of uncertainty, just as forestalling other major changes aids in the creation of a new equilibrium.

It is not uncommon for organizations to forget to tell people that a change has been completed. Sometimes this is because there is too much uncertainty to predict whether current changes are sufficient (in which case we are really dealing more with transformation—see below—than with accommodation). Often, however, change agents take it for granted that people are aware and understand the implementation plan, including when the change is complete and what is supposed to happen next. By eliminating the need for contract parties to read each other's minds, punctuating the end of change can help maintain and support the contract. Failure to do so generates prolonged anxiety and uncertainty, one reason many organizations experience high voluntary turnover when enduring protracted change over a period of years.

When Is Accommodation Possible? Appropriate use of accommodation is predicated on how well the existing contract fits the new circumstances. A request for more effort in the same established performance areas (e.g., sales, service) may be better accommodated than new and distinct performance demands that signal a change in the nature of work.

Accommodation is the strategy employed by Sheet Metal Company described in Chapter 2. Calling it a "renegotiation of our contract," top management responded to pressure from owners for increasing profitability. First, a corporatewide goal of "market dominance in 3 years" was communicated to all employees. Next, several steps were taken to legitimate this goal and help employees understand it. Sales representatives were first given training focusing on industry changes and new marketplace strategies. They were then asked to conduct a survey of present and potential customers, including their perception of SMC and its competitors. Sales representatives now had more information about how customers made their purchasing decisions, including their views regarding service reliability. An SMC tradition was to promise the customer the earliest delivery date regardless of customer need; because of this, missed delivery dates were common. Improved information links created more realistic delivery dates and also made it possible for the operations department to focus on improving its own scheduling. The incentive structure was also altered following the customer survey, from an activity-based system (with bonuses for numbers of units shipped) to one that rewarded individuals for gross margin profit. Thus setting customer-negotiated delivery dates resulted in more reasonable targets and also provided the organization with information on how to improve its internal coordination.

When the company decided to expand to two more plants, the sales force faced pressure to grow with the business's increased capacity. Incentives were further changed to permit greater earnings for high achievers. A long history of secure jobs with a well-understood compensation system had created beliefs about the company that were largely positive, and these beliefs continued throughout the change.

In the context of accommodation, changes to SMC's core contract features were largely accepted based on long-standing reliance and modifications of comparable value. Income potential for sales representatives increased due to both new incentives and improved information systems. Use of substitutions of comparable value was discussed in Chapter 5 as a means of reducing the experience of contract violation due to change. At Sheet Metal Company, the change strategy substituted a new reward system that sustained or increased compensation while protecting the vast majority of employees from losses due to lack of ability through training and support. Expressing changes in terms of an established cultural value or organizational belief can make it easier to substitute new terms for earlier ones. At SMC, core values were sustained throughout the change: Employee job security and income potential were protected, and the historically congenial relationship with customers was actually improved. A rapidly implemented change program is made easier when the changes are few and well focused. Changes at Sheet Metal Company took place within a 12-month period; intentions were announced up front and were consistently followed through on. Initiation of changes was focused and timely, creating few disruptions for employees. In terms of the contract forms we have described previously, Sheet Metal Company in many respects stayed within its existing framework, sharpening certain performance terms, removing barriers to existing performance demands, and adding incentives. Losses were offset by training, employee involvement, and incentive programs.

Continental White Cap (Harvard Business School, 1990) is another classic case of accommodation. In 1984, this firm was the market leader in the production and distribution of metal closures for glass jars. Peter Browning, its vice president and operating officer, was charged with revitalizing this division of the Continental Group in the face of a threatened change in the market: the introduction of plastic packaging. Competitors were now likely to cut prices and build market share. So despite the fact that sales were stable, Browning felt the need to create a more efficient and flexible operation that could cut costs by expanding into plastics:

> From the very start, Browning recognized two major obstacles. . . . Few managers or employees at White Cap acknowledged the need for change. Business results for more than 50 years had been quite impressive and when dips were experienced, they were perceived as cyclical and transient. Second, White Cap had a family-style culture characterized by long-term loyalty from its employees, long-standing traditions of job security, liberal benefits, and paternalistic management. Attempts to alter these traditions would not be welcome. (Harvard Business School, 1990, p. 2)

Browning's challenge was to convince employees of the need for change at White Cap. He recognized that because employees viewed the White family as patrons and parental figures (Mrs. White used to cook a free lunch every day for White Cap workers), any change introduced with the imprimatur of the White family would have legitimacy. Thus Mr. White attended a "family meeting" with Browning and White Cap employees to talk about the need for technological innovation in the shift to plastic packaging. Browning then sent White employees on plant tours and to the grocery store to see what consumers already knew: everything from catsup to peanut butter was being packed in plastic containers. Convinced by what they saw, hardworking White Cappers began working on the introduction of plastic packaging (and ultimately a new plastic packaging plant was built). Market share increased, costs declined, and White Cap achieved its goals thanks to such accommodation strategies as contract continuity, employee involvement, and the use of existing cultural symbols in framing changes.

Failed Accommodations. Attempts at accommodation can fail because of lack of continuity. When IBM acquired the Rolm corporation in the mid-1980s, performance demands for Rolm's sales force shifted from selling hardware to creating a relationship with the customer. As one ex-Rolm, now IBM, employee put it, "In the old days we used to drop the hardware and run. Now it is like we get into a marriage with the customer." The new service emphasis was not easily accommodated by the old short-term, sales-focused contract. The fact that the former Rolm employees had not voluntarily joined IBM made them resistant to adjusting contract terms. In the words of one former Rolm employee, "The cowboys got acquired by the sheep ranchers."

Accommodation assumes that changes can fit into the framework of the existing contract. When contract modification is undertaken, parties can be surprised that what seems to them to be a minor modification in the existing situation produces an "overreaction." Both contract parties and change agents tend to believe that contracts, like other schemas, are more similar than they really are (Bartunek, 1988). In an attempt to respond to student demands for more "challenging" courses, one university required faculty to grade more stringently, restricting the proportion of "A" grades. Student outrage over the resulting tougher grading caused a retraction of the policy within a matter of weeks. As one incoming student indicated, "I came here because there was supposed to be little competition in the classes"; to the students, "challenging work" apparently meant something different than tougher grades. Before modifying the contract again, administrators might consider exploring the meaning of "challenging work" from the students' perspective.

Conclusion

Successful contract change through accommodation has several basic features:

1. Expressing change in the context of an existing contract
2. Positive relationship between the parties
3. Few losses or use of loss-reducing strategies
4. Changes affecting ancillary contract terms ("the extras"), leaving the core terms relatively unaffected
5. Active participation in change by both parties
6. Relatively few changes made
7. Sending signals that the change process is ending and a new equilibrium is being created

TRANSFORMATION

From William Whyte's *The organization man* [*sic*] (1956) through Rosabeth Kanter's *Men and women of the corporation* (1977), the portrayal of the large successful American corporation, in social science and the business

> press . . . assumes long-term reciprocal commitments, careers within companies, attractive wages, and job security . . . this idealized recipe for success has come under vociferous attack. (Hirsch, 1994, p. 135)

> In the U.S. over the past hundred years . . . a common evolutionary dynamic is apparent—dramatic environmental change is accompanied by the appearance of a new market strategy, a new organizational form, and a new managerial ideology. (Miles & Creed, in press)

> Life is not a static thing. The only people who do not change their minds are incompetents in asylums, who can't, and those in cemeteries. (Everett Dirksen, quoted by MacNeil, 1970, in Carruth & Ehrlich, 1988, p. 122)

Transformations are radical forms of change. In contemporary organizations, there is little consensus about the nature of change, but there is agreement that organizations are changing at unprecedented rates. The change contemporary commentators note is a radical transformation in the psychological contract between employee and employer. In transformation, an existing contract ends, sometimes through breach, other times by completion, and a new contract is created. Losses are real and costs are high, but the gains may be too. Violation by definition is a willful breach of contract that costs the person violated. There is often a fine line between violation and transformation. Some argue that there is no difference between them; there is no real line at all. James March (1971) argues that change can be intrepreted as hypocrisy. Changes make liars of people who built the organization around one set of assumptions, only to later take it apart for reassembly around a different set.

The purpose of contract transformation is the creation of a new contract in place of an existing one, where the new contract engenders commitment and efficacy for all concerned. The process of transformation determines whether change degenerates into violation or transforms the basis of the relationship. In the last 100 years, organizations have undergone radical changes and in consequence employment contracts have changed too. As work shifted from an agency model, where workers contracted directly with owners, to the hierarchies and divisions of the internal labor markets, new organization forms have changed contract terms. Emergence of modern organizations has shifted contract terms to include more emphasis on behavior and culture and on membership (identification and relationships) and enhanced the degree to which managers have demonstrated trust of workers (broader job descriptions, flatter hierarchies). Miles and Creed (1995) observe that the meaning of trust in organizations has been evolving over the course of the century. In the more traditional functional organization, "trust" meant that subordinates were expected to be competent and willing to meet schedules and stay within budgets. In the newer, networked firms, managers must learn to trust upstream partners to deliver quality parts on time and downstream ones to assure customer satisfaction.

Another particularly telling illustration of contract change has been the successive redistribution of risk between employer and employee. One hundred years ago, employers put their money at risk when choosing a business strategy, and workers' wages remained fixed. However, workers bore almost exclusively the health risks of the pre-OSHA era. For much of the twentieth century, employers (and government) have taken on a greater share of the risks due to occupational injury. Risks are also being redistributed in the form of pay-for-performance compensation systems, contingent fees, and profit sharing, all of which link worker compensation to organizational success. Changes in trust, performance requirements, and risk distribution transform not just the discrete terms but the essence of the psychological contract.

Transformation and Schema Change. Transformation means that new schemas replace old ones, and virtually any contract is subject to transformation. Schemas offer many benefits—mutual understanding, order and predictability, cues to help people interpret ambiguous situations, speedy information processing and problem solving, and the supply of missing information with default options (Gioia, 1986, p. 346). But because schemas are a reflection of the past, they come at a cost. New information is transformed when it is fitted into an existing schema. Contracts, as schemas, transform information whenever new changes are viewed through the lens of an old contract. People fill in gaps with typical or previously useful information—not necessarily with accurate data. Discrepancies can be ignored, and the loss of important information can result. Existing contracts are seldom tested by the bearer once established. In effect, contracts resist revision. Transformation goes against the grain.

To understand how contract transformation occurs, we draw on insights from research on schema change (Sims & Gioia, 1986), organizational transformation (Bartunek, 1988), and learning (Argyris & Schön, 1978). As shown in Table 6.2, Bartunek (1988) describes a four-stage process that can be used for transforming contracts. The basic phases are as follows:

- *Challenging the contract:* The reasons for change must be perceived, understood, and interpreted as legitimate.
- *Preparing to reframe:* The old contract is unfrozen and efforts are taken to reduce or offset losses.
- *New contract generation:* A new contract is created to supplant the old.
- *New contract testing and reliance:* Acceptance of the new contract must occur so as to complete the process of transformation.

TABLE 6.2 Transformation

Stage	*Dynamics*	*Intervention*
Challenging the contract	—stress —turbulence —disruption	■ Provide new discrepant information
Preparing to reframe	—ending old contract —loss reduction —bridging	■ Participation in information gathering ■ Interpretation of new information ■ Creation of a felt need for change ■ Acknowledgment of the end of old contracts ■ Creation of transition structures
Contract generating	—sense making	■ Evoke "new contract" schema ■ Manage meaning ■ Make contract makers readily available ■ Involve affected people in transition ■ Active participation in new contract creation
Contract testing and reliance	—reality checking	■ Consistency in word and action ■ Follow-through

CHALLENGING THE CONTRACT: CREATING LEGITIMACY AND FELT NEED FOR CHANGE

Consider the following scenarios:

A photocopying shop has one employee who has worked in the shop for 6 months and earns $9 per hour. Business continues to be satisfactory, but a factory in the area has closed and unemployment has increased. Other small firms have now hired reliable workers working at $7 an hour to perform jobs similar to those done by the photocopy shop employee. The owner of the photocopying shop reduces the employee's wage to $7.

Is it fair for the employer to cut the employee's wage from $9 to $7 an hour?

Now consider this scenario:

> A house painter employs two assistants and pays them $9 per hour. The painter decides to change his business and go into lawn mowing, where the going wage is lower. He tells the current workers that he will keep them on if they want to work, but will only pay them $7 per hour.

Is it fair for this employer to cut the employee's wage from $9 to $7 an hour?

These two scenarios have been widely applied in laboratory studies of students and classroom discussions with executives, and have consistently yielded opposite answers to each in the vast majority of cases. When first employed by Kahneman, Knetch, and Thaler (1986), the photocopy scenario led approximately 85% of respondents to say it was "unfair." The reverse happened in the lawn mowing situation: A comparable percentage of respondents indicated that cutting the wage was "fair." The major difference between the two scenarios is that in the second one, the $2 loss is framed in terms of an external change (i.e., the nature of the business).

These scenarios highlight some of the major issues surrounding changing contracts:

- The tendency toward conservatism and contract maintenance
- The prevalence of beliefs regarding appropriate and inappropriate behavior when contracts exist
- The need for externally validated reasons for change

In investigating the history of organizational development and change, it is important to ask how the change process was legitimated and whether externally anchored reasons were offered. The slow adoption and in many cases frustrating failures of the Quality of Work Life movement in the United States can be attributed to a lack of any widely understood legitimate reasons for contract change. Quality of Work Life programs (e.g., in the Rushton coal mine; Goodman, 1979) were introduced in the Nixon years to address declining productivity. However, there is ample evidence that the threat of foreign competition, particularly from Japan, was not perceived by many managers and employees in large companies such as General Motors and IBM. QWL efforts were frequently disbanded because this external motivation for change went undetected. A similar set of difficulties arose in the 1970s with the introduction of the matrix organization (Davis & Lawrence, 1977). Most of the reasons cited for shifting to a matrix form were internal, such as the need for managerial efficiency. The failure of organizations to adopt the theoretically more efficient matrix form may partly be due to the absence of externally validated reasons for contract change. A turning point in organizational change efforts came with the Total Quality Movement of the 1980s. The widespread use of benchmarking made it more likely that organization members would look at the competition for knowledge about their organization's relative health and look to firms in unrelated industries for information on best practices and innovations.

Externally validated reasons for contract change range from imminent crisis conditions, such as a major decline in market share, to a felt need for preemptive strikes against anticipated changes in the marketplace. When employees are poorly prepared to receive a new message, change is often resented and ultimately fails. This can also occur because the reasons offered are not perceived as relevant. One extreme example is the defense contractor that downsized 10% of its workforce under the banner of "improved shareholder value." With great fanfare, it gave each of its (over 100) top managers in the firm a share of company stock—encased in a handsome frame suitable for hanging on the walls of the executive suite. The companywide response was one of resentment, surreptitious conversations behind closed doors, and mistrust of hierarchical superiors. The message sent touted shareholder interests, not the corporation's interests generally or the organization members' particularly. Unless one is a stockholder, such a message doesn't generate a lot of motivation to change.

A more effective message is that offered by Xerox in the early 1980s following its major loss of market share (to Japanese competitors). The CEO, David Kearns, saw a need to foster greater employee involvement and customer responsiveness to improve corporate competitiveness:

> Part of the problem was this was not a high-priority item at the time with top management. We were fixated on costs and the Japanese. Although I wasn't opposed to employee involvement, I clearly didn't see it as a vehicle to turn around the business. To me, it was something on the level of a suggestion program. It was nice to have, but it wasn't going to solve the company's central ills.
>
> And by this time things had already started to cascade down on us like Niagara Falls. . . . It was obvious to me that we had service problems and had never addressed them . . . we dispatched a team of people to Japan. It included plant managers, financial analysts, engineers, and manufacturing specialists. . . . Our team went over everything in a thorough manner. It examined all the ingredients of cost: turnover, design time, engineering changes, manufacturing defects, overhead ratios, inventory, how many people worked for a foreman, and so forth. When it was done with its calibration, we were in for quite a shock. [One manager] remembers the results as being "absolutely nauseating. It wasn't a case of being out in left field. We weren't even playing the same game." (Kearns & Nadler, 1992, pp. 120-121)[6]

Results of these analyses revealed that the Japanese carried six to eight times less inventory, had half the overhead, and a near 99.5 quality rate on incoming parts compared with Xerox's 95%. Unit manufacturing cost was two thirds that of the American firm.

> This was no gap. That was a chasm. . . . For a long time, we had been getting engineering reports on the Japanese cost structure and now we realized that they had been hopelessly wrong. . . . Was it bad analysis? I doubt that it was a case of the information not being available. I think it was purely denial. (p. 122)

The product of these insights was a strategy designed to improve business effectiveness at Xerox through two underpinning concepts: employee involvement and benchmarking. Commitment to Excellence and Team Xerox were the titles given to these strategic change efforts. Benchmarking is the active monitoring of other organizations for the purpose of establishing performance standards, best practices, and unfreezing what people believe is possible in their own organization. Although benchmarking helps identify new schemas, involvement serves to promote schema refinement and active use.

A legitimate message regarding the need for fundamental transformation in the contract would focus on either protection against losses from the status quo (e.g., the need to respond to declining market share) or the acquisition of unilateral gains caused by implementing the change (e.g., maintaining employee job security and improved working conditions through continued organizational growth). The message must be expressed in terms understood by its intended audience, which often means that affected individuals and groups need to participate in the gathering of data such as customer surveys to determine the need for change.[7]

Transformation is often accompanied by a prevailing sense of "change it or lose it." Perception of threat, however, is not enough for contract reframing to occur. Contracts are less likely to be constructively challenged if the reasons for their change are business difficulties that are understood to be top management's failure to exercise their fiduciary responsibilities in the past. Lack of innovation and ongoing investment by the major steel corporations in the United States over a period of years made it unlikely that the steelworkers or their unions would perceive a legitimate need for change when the corporations at last recognized their declining market positions: "One of the problems in the mills is that no union man would trust any of the companies. To the average union man, they're always crying wolf" (Joseph Odorcich, Vice President, United Steelworkers of America, quoted in Hoerr, 1988). New leaders might be necessary to effectively challenge and renegotiate such a contract rather than those perceived to be responsible for the business failure.

History is another important factor in how people react to contract challenge. If there is a history of mistrust, challenges can appear to be less legitimate. Organizations with a history of attempted and failed changes engender little faith among employees that real change can occur. Two kinds of organizations have special problems at this phase. Among those that have never changed, such as Defender firms, those that stay in the same niche for generations, the belief that change is possible is virtually nonexistent. The other type of highly change-resistant organizations are those with a history of attempted, announced, and short-lived change efforts. A firm that operates on a "Plan of the Year" approach (usually accompanied by frequent replacements of the CEO and top management team) trying out Management by Objectives in the early 1980s, Quality Circles in 1985, Self-Managing Teams in 1987, Total Quality Management in 1988, and Rolfing the top management team in 1989 probably creates another layer of employee disbelief with every change announcement. Firms that change constantly never really change substantively, because employee reactions are of the "this too shall pass" variety. "Plan of the Year" and Defender firms need to use different tactics to convey the message that "this time we really mean to change." "Plan of the Year" firms need to keep the CEO and top management team in place and see a change through to completion. The never-changing Defender firm, however, often needs new management, particularly from outside the firm, to initiate innovation and signal the firm's commitment to change.

Challenging the contract requires creating a *deep*—vivid, actively obtained, and legitimate—understanding of the reasons change is necessary. Sending production workers to scout the competition's product can send a powerful message regarding the need to change production processes and alter the nature of the business. Successful challenge to an old contract involves understanding the importance of the change in the affected individuals' own terms.

PREPARATION FOR REFRAMING: LOSS REDUCTION STRATEGIES

> Intractable problems are usually not intractable because there are no solutions, but because there are no solutions without severe side effects. . . . It is only when we demand a solution with no costs that there are no solutions.
>
> —*Lester C. Thurow (1980, as quoted in Carruth & Ehrlich, 1988, p. 204)*

The goal of reframing is to unfreeze or take apart the old contract while readying the parties for the next phase, creating the new contract. There is a three-pronged approach to effectively managing reframing: creating credible signs of change, reducing losses, and implementing transition structures to bridge the new contract. Credible signs of change demonstrate a commitment to follow through on the challenge conveyed in phase one and creating an appropriate ending for the earlier contract. Reliance losses people incur begin to surface with loss of tangibles such as job security and intangibles such as certainty and predictability. The loss reduction initiated here serves to create a relationship on which a new contract would be based. Transformation is seldom an all-at-once phenomenon. Too many complex things must change, and the nature of the new contract is often not fully known to the executives or change agents who initiate the transformation. For these reasons, transition structures are created. Transition structures, or temporary arrangements designed to reduce losses, gather further information on implications of change, strengthen commitment to the change, and serve as bridges from one contract to another.

Credible Signs of Change. In the early stages of contract transformation, some mourning for the old relationship is likely. Glorifying the past, as in the case of ex-Rolm employees' old "cowboy days," can make it difficult for a new arrangement to appear as desirable as the one recalled. Nonetheless, respecting the past is part of respecting the people who believed in the old contract. William Bridges (1991), author of *Managing Transitions,* uses the example of the Almaden winery's sale of its beautiful garden to which employees were greatly attached. When business reasons necessitated sale of this property, employees began surreptitiously taking clippings from rose bushes as mementoes. Managers discovered this and began passing out rose clippings to help all employees share in the transition and to acknowledge widely shared sentiments. Similarly, a party held to celebrate old successes before closing a contract could be another form of punctuation. A defense contractor might celebrate the success of its efforts during the cold war and declare victory before going on to reorient its business to new markets. By whatever means, before initiating a new contract, the old one needs to be completed.

Loss Reduction. Most changes involve "take-aways"—in the form of lost pay, greater uncertainty, or rising fears regarding personal capacities to deal with the change. Take-aways are losses, and an effective change strategy seeks to reduce losses. Loss reduction efforts must begin early in the transformation process, because escalations similar to the violation cycle are likely if losses are not addressed quickly. Major forms of loss include departures from the status quo (e.g., security, status), emotional distress due to change, and greater uncertainty.

A classic issue in change resistance is the loss of status, role, and responsibilities experienced by managers:

> One of the greatest surprises when an organization grows into a matrix comes in regard to the changing role of the functional managers. In functional organization, managers have authority over the objectives of their functions, the selection of individuals, the priorities assigned to different tasks . . . in a matrix organization none of these responsibilities remains solely the purview of the functional manager. He or she must share many of the decisions with program or business managers. . . . Thus, for functional managers a matrix organization is often experienced as a loss in status, authority, and control. It is a step down. (Davis & Lawrence, 1977, pp. 84-85)

Offsetting such losses involves both substitutions in the form of trades and remedies (Chapter 5) and the use of procedures that create greater information and control in the hands of the people affected by the change. Loss of control and certainty typically accompanies changes but can be offset by involving individuals in planning the changes that will affect them. For example, when downsizing through early retirement is part of the change process, making it possible for affected people to choose their date of retirement can maintain their sense of personal control. Changes in the nature of work effectively deskill the people who worked in the old system. Introduction of job-specific training as well as process skill development (e.g., teamwork, customer relations) can offset the loss of former skills. Changes in status may be addressed by making senior employees responsible for supporting and implementing changes with special recognition (feedback, titles, support).

Downsizing is a common tactic used in transformation. What was once done only in a crisis is now a part of long-term strategic planning in many firms. This means that what constitutes a "legitimate" reason to terminate employees in 1960 was gauged by a different standard than might apply today. Kozlowski, Chao, Smith, and Hedlund (1993) identified a hierarchy of downsizing strategies commonly used today: natural attrition, induced redeployment (incentives to transfer, quit, or take early retirement), and involuntary terminations. Alternatives to downsizing include job reengineering, in which workers propose how to make their job a value-adding one. Poor planning reduces motivational qualities in survivor jobs (e.g., high workloads, disruption in social support). Potentially, downsizing can promote job enrichment because usually it occurs with delayering. But there is a major difference between reactive (crisis-oriented) downsizing and proactive planning, as lead time makes transition management possible.

Transition management during downsizing has been described as having a two-pronged approach (Kozlowski et al., p. 37): support for victims (information, financial incentives, and more direct interventions such as therapy to aid coping) and concern for survivors (regaining trust, confidence, and commitment, and rebuilding a positive image). The managerial/practice literature on downsizing is very rational—focusing largely on information needs. The emotion and trauma involved receive less attention and even less is given to creating meaning during these experiences. Nonetheless, image and reputation losses for firms are considerable (Sutton, Eisenhardt, & Sucker, 1985). Loss reduction strategies must address not only economic loss but also emotional losses associated with eroded security, predictability, and comprehension of events.

Transition Structures. Few transformations occur all at once. Their scope and complexity take time to fully implement. The fact that transformations often occur during major external upheavals (political or economic) means that the full scope of the change cannot be known at the beginning and therefore could not be implemented all at once even if one intended to. Everyone involved is searching and sense-making, from top management to veteran employee to newcomer. Transitions are usually iterative processes involving a series of new programs, adjustments, activities, learning, and course corrections. For contracts to change successfully, transition structures should be used to promote the effort.

Gradual change strategies reduce losses by phasing in new practices for incoming members while continuing the contracts of veterans (i.e., "grandfathering"). Organizations that create new contracts among new hires while honoring existing ones with veterans seek to transform contracts gradually. Often, a two-tiered wage system is used to distinguish veterans from newcomers. The downside of such a gradual transition strategy is that veterans can feel insecure about their continued benefits, and newcomers experience relative deprivation, receiving less than veterans for the same work or effort. Not uncommonly, however, newcomers brought in following realistic recruiting are themselves better suited to the transition than veterans. Low-wage workers in an airline with a two-tiered wage plan reported feeling significantly more satisfied with pay, work, and supervision and more optimistic about future pay and job security than did higher paid veterans (Capelli & Scherer, 1990).

Departing from its practice of lifetime employment, the Toyota Motor Corporation hired automobile designers under 1-year contracts:

> The mentality on the part of young people in Japan is changing . . . an increasingly number of young people want to come and go from a company. . . . Toyota said the program would be restricted at first to only a handful of designers, but that it would consider broadening the program to other types of work. ("Toyota to Hire," 1994, p. A39)[8]

Little research exists on the impact of having multiple contract forms within the same firm over a long period of time. Although such arrangements are becoming more commonplace, the "shamrock organization" Charles Handy describes, in which some workers are core, others are short term, and still others are peripheral outsiders, is relatively recent. We do know that wide differences exist in compensation and benefits and that this perceived inequity can result in dissatisfaction and lower performance (Cowherd & Levine, 1992), particularly when the differences are between senior executives and lower level workers. It may be that phased-in change using two-tiered wage systems also requires some form of phase-out strategy to help veterans adhere to new performance criteria.

Other transition structures can take on the form of task forces that enable people to look into ways of effectively introducing or managing change. This was the case of the employee groups that assisted in the planning of the Ford plant closing in Milpitas (Chapter 5). Such structures are often critical in transformations to new contracts, because conventional communication channels have become insufficient to convey information to affected individuals whose anxiety levels and information needs have skyrocketed. To maintain trust, it is important to have rich information channels, which convey both bad news and any other relevant information in a timely way. Having task forces that cut across several functions, areas, and levels can aid transformation planning both by the information they gather and by what they share.

A lack of transition structures that respond to escalating information needs is a common cause of transformation failure. When information flow dries up, affected individuals are left with little alternative but "mind reading." Absence of information leads to sense-making (monitoring, informal questioning, and reliance on otherwise poor quality information), which in turn creates untested and often harmful assumptions. Ideally, transition structures such as task forces should be created at the same time that transformations are initiated.

A third transition structure is actually a form of contract in itself. Change breeds transitional behaviors. Reactions to uncertainty vary from overt displays of emotion and frustration, to purposive information gathering, to passive withdrawal. Downsizings in particular create tremendous tension and excessive vigilance such that survivors might actually get little work done, preferring the following strategy: "Keep your head down and you might not get shot." When old certainties go and nothing (yet) takes their place, the transitional, or "no guarantees," contract (see Chapter 4) results. A likely transition from this state is the creation of temporary transactional contracts. When specific commitments cannot yet be made, it is useful to specify short-term objectives (e.g., project orientation) that give people clear tasks, provide support to make those tasks a success, and encourage them to ask questions. Creating an interim, transactionlike contract can provide a bridge to a more comprehensive contract later on.

CONTRACT GENERATION: CREATING A NEW SCHEMA

In the process of formulating a new and different commitment, contract generation is the most creative stage. This transition period, which has also been labeled "thaw" or the "neutral zone" (Bridges, 1991), can be painful but also pathbreaking. New commitments are needed that shift attention from the past to the future. At this juncture, contract generation creates images of the future and renders them current and relevant.

The formation of a new schema requires the identification of contract terms that both parties view as mutually beneficial. Organizations that enter this phase without a willingness to create new commitments are likely to continue in a protracted transition without ever putting a more efficient contract into place. This absence of employer commitment undercuts the contractual nature of the new arrangement, generating employee compliance until a better opportunity comes along at a different company.

When contract makers offer an understandable statement of new terms and solicit commitment to them, the supplanting of one contract by another can occur. The terms Jack Welch used to represent his 1992 model of an effective member of GE—"one who produces the results and has the values" (Chapter 4)—are the perfect example of a contract-making statement (see Welch & Hood, 1992). In most cases, however, contract generation is a process rather than a single event. New contracts, just like the ones they replace, tend to be created by interaction and sense-making. Because even strong statements by top managers can be incomplete reflections of a new deal, employees must still inquire, observe, and monitor to understand the scope of the new contract.

New terms of agreement must be identified, conveyed, and interpreted during contract generation. During transformation, many former contract makers continue to convey old contract terms to employees. Although change agents work at aligning the various contract makers, their conflicting messages have to be sorted out by employees. For example, in the wave of professional firm mergers in the 1980s, two of the former Big Eight accounting firms merged. Despite the two distinct cultures and geographic differences, the new firm continued on for a few years in accommodation mode while gradual integration of practices occurred. Several years into the change,

TABLE 6.3 Examples of Contract Change in an Accounting Firm

Partner Obligations	*Past*	*Now*	*Future*
1. Anna	Loyalty	Hard work	To try
Firm	A career	A job	Uncertainty
2. Bill	Take business seriously Work hard	Work hard Do more	Ability to grow self and client services Develop staff
Firm	Financial reward in secure environment Long-term future together	Performance-based compensation Tenure remeasured annually	Opportunity to increase profit Become leader of local firm
3. Chris	Loyalty Develop skills	Conflicting messages	Grow people Grow self
Firm	Support growing compensation	Risk taking feared by top management yet rewarded if goals are attained and no mistakes are made	Clearly identified strategy Clear culture

NOTE: All three partners survived the postmerger downsizing. They provided both their own perspective and their perception of the postmerger firm's perspective of the contract's terms.

poor customer economic conditions and increasing competitive pressures led to substantial downsizing. In a move virtually unheard of before the merger, hundreds of partners were terminated, with the stated intent of reorienting practices around specific industries to provide more integrated client services. But with no clear industry models regarding the meaning of this reorientation for surviving partners, several years after the change, widely divergent interpretations emerged about what the new partner contract meant (Table 6.3). Three partners whose contracts are shown here are typical of the divergent points of view partners hold regarding their contract. Most would agree on what the old contract had been: loyalty, hard work, and a long-term future. The new contract was, however, less certain. Hard work was a continuing message, but what was promised in return was less commonly understood. And the future had several different meanings, depending on what the partner had heard regarding an identifiable strategy for the future and on what he understood his new role to be in dealing with clients and services. How long it takes to align contract makers to communicate consistent contract terms is a major factor in determining the duration of transformation.

Transforming a contract can require what Weick has called a "complicated understanding." Change agents need to be able to interpret organizational and environmental events from several perspectives (e.g., veterans and newcomers, higher and lower level members), going beyond their individual narrow frames of reference. It is probably abundantly clear by now that contracts are beliefs in mutuality rather than the actual fact of mutuality. Weick's (1979) advice to managers, "Complicate yourself!" (p. 261), can lead to complementary ways of understanding change—from the viewpoint of its multiple constituents and the many contract makers shaping understandings of the deal. How do people operating out of one perspective get into the mind of someone else? Bartunek, Gordon, and Weathersby (1983) argue that people have to be willing to discuss "messy" issues, which encompass not only more than one point of view but more than one reality. Focus groups and other qualitative surveys have been successfully used to tap diverse contract perspectives (Guzzo & Noonan, 1994).

Transitions and the Newcomer. During contract generation, we expect that individuals and work groups will reflect varying degrees and phases of transition. Some may still be wrestling with the ending of the old contract, feeling a sense of loss and separateness from events around them. Others may already feel committed, seeing themselves as a part of the whole organization. In the process of new contract generation, one truly precious resource is the newcomer.

Newcomers can promote transition in a number of ways. Recruiting practices can change and communicate a message to newcomers distinct from that conveyed to veterans when they were hired. Thus organizations seeking to be a team rather than a family may find this goal easier to achieve in an era of rapid growth when many people are hired. In fact, it may be much more difficult to transform an organization's contract with employees without some new hires. Socialization efforts involve different activities than normal day-to-day events. Recruiting a different kind of newcomer can alter the culture and the associated contract:

> A newcomer who is strongly committed to a work group will try to acquire whatever information he or she needs to help the group achieve its goals and to gain acceptance from other members. In contrast, a newcomer whose commitment to a work group is weak will be less motivated and may even actively avoid new information if it conflicts with his or her prior beliefs. (Resnick, 1991, p. 267)

Newcomers explicitly recruited to be part of a change effort, turnaround, or transformation are likely to have a different contract than their senior colleagues. The presence of newcomers can alter the behavior of veterans in several ways. For example, a critical mass of newcomers can create a new reality by exposing veterans to an entirely new model. According to Levine and Moreland (1987):

> The simple act of explaining group culture can cause old-timers to think more deeply about their beliefs and alter some of them (e.g., new faculty). And newcomers often ask disturbing questions or make unsettling references to other groups that can raise further doubts in the minds of old-timers. Newcomers may also try to produce change, especially if they are dissatisfied with the group. Newcomers are more likely to produce cultural change when they elicit more commitment from old-timers than they feel toward them. (p. 273)

Employee Involvement and Active Information Search. New contract terms are understood when organization members begin to act again like newcomers actively seeking new information. Holding focus groups to share employee perceptions and creating task forces to flesh out new performance terms simulates the information gathering individuals engaged in during recruitment. Survey results fed back to organization members also create a social process for generating and making sense of the data (Nadler, 1977).

Reinventing the contract is aided by employee involvement. Ameritech, which has been involved in a culture and contract change for a decade, has a contract written by senior managers that has been the topic of discussion at many training sessions, focus groups, and organizational gatherings. The document, shown to but not copied for people outside the organization, stresses the importance of innovation and growth and the continuing invention of the organization. Ongoing discussion of the meaning of its terms gives the document wide application in how people think about their roles, a group's task, and the organization's strategy.

CONTRACT TESTING AND RELIANCE: PROMOTING NEW CONTRACT ACCEPTANCE

Once new contract terms are identified, communicated, and understood, the critical concern becomes their acceptance and implementation. Voluntary entry into a new contractual arrangement means that people have a sense of choice and personal commitment. Creating new contract acceptance is helped along by evoking a "new contract script." Acting in ways associated with commitment making—public statements, new titles, joining up, or signing on the dotted line—signal acceptance. Goal setting research finds that the presence of goals is not enough to motivate; however, once goals are accepted, they become highly motivating to the people who commit to them. Acceptance is symbolized by such activities as signing the new contract, recruiting for a new job within one's current company, or actively participating in a "new employee" orientation. A printing firm in the midst of a major culture shift transferred many people from its core business to its high-tech information services division but required them to be treated like new employees in the process. The transferred employees submitted résumés, interviewed, took tests, participated in new employee orientation, and signed an employment contract stressing the importance of innovation and customer service. McLean Parks and Schmedemann (1994) describe the signing of a new employee handbook as a behavioral event signifying the reader's assent to the deal, especially if the signature follows a statement that the employee has read and understands the handbook provisions. Such behavioral events may signal the beginning of a new contract and create a sense of active acceptance.

In sum, acceptance of new contract terms is enhanced by the following:

- *Adopting a new frame of reference:* transferring to a new job or new organization within the same parent company
- *Actively expressing a choice:* bidding for a new job, filling out an application, and participating in other recruitment-related activities
- *Conveying commitment vividly and publicly:* signing a written agreement, completing a new employee orientation
- *Publicly demonstrating acceptance:* participating in planning the changes
- *Developing a critical mass of people with the same contract:* creating a normative contract widely shared and understood by members

Once the new contract has been accepted, it is up to the parties to implement it. Key employee concerns include whether people know specific behaviors are required of them and whether they believe they are able to perform them. Setting and supporting realizable short-term goals (e.g., cross-training for team members) can build momentum for individuals and groups to follow through. From the employer's perspective, consistency in word and deed is a major issue at this juncture. Some reality-testing is part of the implementation process; because terms are inherently incomplete, people may wonder what will happen if someone breaks the contract by reverting to old ways of doing things.

Reality-testing is evident in the U.S. Navy's attempt to integrate its combat units. The aftermath of the Tailhook scandal led to a public commitment on the part of the Navy to improve the environment for its female members.

Allowing Navy women to become combat pilots and aircraft carrier personnel is one sign of change, as these roles were previously forbidden by both custom and an act of Congress. When a 31-year-old female pilot and lieutenant telephoned a repair office on the carrier the USS *Eisenhower,* a male sailor answered and called to his boss, "Hey, there is a lieutenant chick on the phone for you." Minutes later, the sailor's angry supervisor hauled the young man before the lieutenant to formally apologize ("Navy Women," 1994, p. A1). Such events are part of the reality check that should occur when work roles, norms, and contract terms change. Reality-testing yields a more consistent result when efforts have been made to garner support for the change, align contract makers, and train members in new behaviors.

SUCCESSFUL TRANSFORMATION

In sum, the elements of successful contract transformation include

1. well-articulated externally validated reasons for the change;
2. member involvement in gathering information on environmental factors contributing to the change;
3. acknowledgment and even celebration of the old contract;
4. scrupulous efforts to assess and then offset the losses involved in the change;
5. building strong communication links up and down during transition to a new contract by using planning tasks forces and frequent cross-level meetings;
6. responding to the need for more information and structure during uncertain times by creating interim transition arrangements emphasizing short-term projects and activities that benefit the long-term change effort (e.g., training, task forces);
7. managing the meaning of change by expressing current efforts in terms of long-term objectives;
8. aligning the many contract makers (people and structures) by integrating the change efforts into training and human resource (HR) activities;
9. promoting acceptance by evoking new contract-making events such as orientations, internal recruiting, and participation in planning;
10. soliciting input on how thoroughly the new contract is implemented, and taking corrective action quickly when reality tests fail.

CONCLUSION

The issue is not whether change will occur—there is no doubt that it will—but whether it maintains, enhances, or disrupts the existing contract.

There are several kinds of contract change, ranging from natural drift to evolutionary accommodation to revolutionary transformation. Individual contracts drift and evolve, accruing baggage with the passage of time. Certain contemporary HR practices serve to promote mutuality and limit undesirable drift, including two-way feedback in performance appraisals, survey feedback, and focus groups.

Global competitiveness has pressured many organizations into actively modifying their employment relations. Changing the contract by accommodation strategies leads to the fashioning of new terms onto existing frameworks, promoting the adaptability of the contract. Accommodations gain strength from continuity, but transformation strategies are built on new frameworks. Their shared advantage lies in a readiness to create a new relationship based on an articulated model of the future.

NOTES

1. Of interest, the belief in personal control extends to games of chance. People tend to believe that they have greater control when they throw the dice than if someone else does it for them (Fleming & Darley, 1986, cited in Taylor & Brown, 1988).

2. A punch line, of sorts, to this litany of cognitive tendencies is that these "biases" are not just normal—they are healthy. Taylor and Brown (1988) persuasively argue that people who hold these "positive illusions" are happier, more successful at work and in life in general, and demonstrate better mental functioning than their more realistic counterparts. In fact, those people who are realistic in their assessment of themselves and others are more likely to be labeled as clinically depressed.

3. Another potential source of drift lies in the thinking styles of individuals, that is, their *stable individual traits*. Contract parties can have very different accounting rules by which they gauge what is fair. How they weigh their efforts in comparison with someone else's, what they count as their contributions, and what they recognize they have received in return vary among individuals.

Several personality styles are postulated to explain the kinds of accounting rules people use (Huseman et al., 1987). "Equity-sensitives" use strict accounting rules in trying to maintain a quid pro quo. They are likely to look to specific features in exchanges to obtain reassurance of the fairness of their deal to both parties. Given their focus on both sides of the exchange, we might expect that equity-sensitives demonstrate less drift and more stability in their interpretation of the contract and its fulfillment.

"Beneficients" are those who prefer to give more than they get, often due to heightened sensitivity to the fairness perceptions of the other. An other-orientation and desire to maintain relations makes beneficients construct more elaborate and extensive contracts than their counterparts. Beneficients are inclined to think in relational terms with an emphasis on relationship-maintaining conditions (loyalty and support). Recruits interpreting their contract in relational terms desire to stay with the organization longer than those with transactional contracts and thus adopt a longer term view of contract fulfillment.

In contrast, "exploiters" take more than they give, and feel most comfortable in circumstances where they are assured that no one takes advantage of them (Huseman et al., 1987). Exploiters are more inclined to seek immediate adjustments whenever they feel they "overpay." This short-term view is evident among newly graduated M.B.A.s who seek a first job as stepping stone to some better opportunity later. Robinson et al. (1994) observed that these "careerists" tend to be party to transactional contract agreements. The time frames people use to compute equity and contract fulfillment may be a major individual difference in contractual thinking. Some individuals can see equity as a goal to work toward over time (Birnbaum, 1983; Mellers, 1982) while others operate on a more "pay-as-you-go" model. Contract drift can occur when these dispositions color how exchanges are interpreted and how and when contributions are counted.

4. Simon (1976/1958) placed the zone of acceptance squarely in the hierarchical organization, where a subordinate's zone of acceptance defined how much influence the superior had over that person. But in contemporary contracting, the zone of acceptance has much broader implications for the relationships between contract parties, from subordinates, to team members, to suppliers, and customers. It raises the issue of how much the contract's performance terms can be changed without parties recognizing a difference.

5. Hoffman, 1994, p. A1. Copyright 1994 © by *The New York Times.* Reprinted with permission.

6. Selected excerpts from *Prophets in the Dark* by David T. Kearns and David A. Nadler. Copyright © 1992 David T. Kearns and David A. Nadler. Reprinted by permission of HarperCollins Publishers.

7. One argument for advance notice in plant closings is to give unions the opportunity to renegotiate a new contract that conceivably could change the economic reasons for the closure (Harrison, 1984). Some advance warning in preparation for transformation may be critical to generating, sending, receiving, and interpreting the message that change is essential and legitimate.

8. Pollack, 1994, p. A39. Copyright 1994 © by *The New York Times.* Reprinted by permission.

7 Business Strategy and Contracts

Words are nothing but words; power lies in deeds.

—Mali griot Mamadou Kouyate
(from Sundiata: An Epic of Old Mali,
1217-1237 A.D., quoted in Riley, 1993, p. 3)

This chapter describes how contracts in contemporary American organizations are linked to business and human resource (HR) strategies. Several writers have linked human resource practices to specific business strategies that they help implement (Jackson, Schuler, & Rivero, 1989; Miles & Snow, 1984). In executing business strategies, certain HR practices tend to be used together. For instance, firms competing through distinctive forms of customer service tend to train employees extensively and attempt to foster a service-oriented culture. These practices encourage employees to develop organization-specific skills, share cultural norms supporting good customer relations, and remain with the organization. We can describe such firms as "making" their workers. Firms competing by retaining flexibility in the markets they serve and customers they seek tend to use such HR practices as short-term performance criteria and minimal training. These firms experience rapid employee turnover. We can describe such firms as "buying" workers. These clusters of practices for making or buying appropriately skilled workers form what Miles and Snow (1984) refer to as human resource strategies. This chapter develops the linkage between business and HR strategies, expanding the Miles and Snow framework to include the employee psychological contracts that emerge from these strategies. The link between strategy and contracts will also be expanded to include the impact of HR practices on relations with customers.

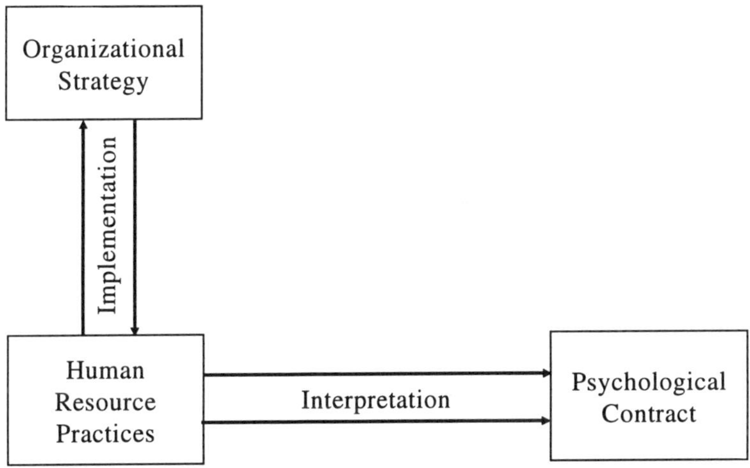

FIGURE 7.1. Framework

CONCEPTUAL FRAMEWORK

Our framework (Figure 7.1) rests on the link between organizational/business strategy (the position the organization seeks in its market or environment), its human resource practices (workforce resources available for implementing business strategy), and the psychological contracts that arise from these practices (employee beliefs regarding the terms of their employment). Whether an organization makes or buys its talent results in the kind of customer relationships it achieves.

Business Strategy and Human Resource Practices. Choosing which HR practices to use is itself a strategic decision. Human resource practices are a primary mechanism for implementing business strategy. Moreover, human resource practices and the capabilities they make available are critical determinants of the organization's human capital. The knowledge, skills, abilities, and motivations of its workforce constrain or amplify an organization's choice of strategies. Investments in employee skill development affect both product cost and product quality. If training costs lead to higher product costs in a market where the product is just another commodity, those training costs will reduce the organization's competitiveness. On the other hand, investments in training targeted to improve customer relations can enhance competitiveness in a business competing on service quality. Business strategy shapes the criteria used to assess employee performance. For instance, different relations with customers arise from performance appraisals focusing on customer satisfaction than from appraisals emphasizing sales (Jackson et al., 1989). As organizations shift toward more intensive relations with customers, as described by Davidow and Malone's *Virtual Corporation,* we expect significant alterations in incentives, performance reviews, and employee selection criteria to implement such a change. In effect, human resource practices are a major way in which organizations *implement and support* their business strategy. Firms that focus on interpersonal skills in hiring employees or on customer relations in monitoring performance are in effect deploying their resources in ways that can have a significant impact on product or service quality and cost as well as on responsiveness to customers. HR practices thus can provide many resources critical to successful adoption of a business strategy.

To implement is to translate strategic plans into organizational actions. In the case of HR practices, this means that knowledge of market demands (e.g., service standardization in tax accounting, or customization in management consulting) and their performance requirements (e.g., innovation, speed of response) translate into how employee performance is measured, the way members are trained, and whether they work cooperatively or independently. Consistent with Miles and Snow's (1984) position, we argue that certain HR practices are more appropriate in implementing some business strategies than others. Alignment of business and HR strategies is a key issue in implementing strategy. Yet misalignment is common. In many organizations, the strategy that top management claims it has is at odds with the actual strategy its HR practices support—an instance of the widespread phenomenon Steven Kerr (1975) has labeled "the folly of rewarding A while hoping for B."

Consider this example. Partners in a major accounting firm claimed its strategy was to be a full service management consulting firm. Brochures, presentations to staff, and discussions with customers played upon this full service capability. Yet its performance review and promotion processes rewarded only development of very narrow functional skills. Instead of being a full service consulting firm, this firm became known in the industry as "the auditor's auditor"—the epitome of deep but narrow specialization. The strategy the firm claimed to have and what it practiced every day were quite different. The HR practices of the organization often convey a more accurate picture of its *real* strategy than any claims top management might make.

Human Resource Practices and Psychological Contracts. HR practices shape the day-to-day behaviors of members. As we have seen in Chapter 3, these practices are also the major means through which workers and the organization contract with each other. HR practices send strong messages to individuals regarding what the organization expects of them and what they can expect in return:

how jobs are advertised ("great advancement potential," "opportunity for salary growth"),
the way the organization is portrayed by recruiters ("lots of training," "we expect you to hit the ground running"),
performance appraisal feedback ("keep up the good work and we'll move you up"),
compensation systems (e.g., whether wages are based on rank or time on the job).

In effect, HR practices tell us what strategy is currently implemented and how contracts are being created to support that strategy.

TYPES OF ORGANIZATIONAL AND HUMAN RESOURCE STRATEGIES

Four contemporary business strategies make specific demands on HR systems in their implementation. In doing so, they have a profound impact on the contracts that define their employment relations. Miles and Snow (1984), in their seminal paper on human resource management as a strategic activity, proposed a model linking business strategy and HR practices consistent with business practices prior to the 1980s. They proposed a typology to cover the broad array of business types. Based on the idea that there are two kinds of environments (stable and unstable ones), their framework contrasted Defenders in historically stable settings (e.g., the pre-1980 automobile industry) with Prospectors (e.g., investment banking and high-technology firms) whose markets were subject to radical and unpredictable changes from year to year. Analyzers, firms that were large enough to operate in diversified markets (e.g., Xerox), have some divisions in stable markets and others in more unpredictable ones.

The 1990s brought the emergence of a fourth strategy—the Responsive organization. Responsive firms have environments that are changing but where scarce resources (e.g., qualified people) and high interdependence require coordination of efforts to respond to the market changes and opportunities. Competitive industries in which service and innovation are valued often are populated by Responsive firms (e.g., Rubbermaid, General Electric). As this developing organizational form will suggest, it is likely that any organizational strategy framework we propose will be modified with time as unforeseen environmental changes and new organizational forms occur (Table 7.1).

TABLE 7.1 Linking Strategy, Human Resource Practices, and Contracts

Strategy	*Defenders*	*Prospectors*	*Analyzers*	*Responsive*
Goals	Retain market share and position	Adapt to environmental changes Innovation/early entry into market	Adapt to different market segments	Focused business strategy Innovation/first to market Develop relationship with market members
Assumptions	Stable environment Organization's culture is competitive advantage Organization-specific experience is valid and valuable Deep, functional expertise required to be competitive People not substitutable	Dynamic and unpredictable environment Organization-specific skills are not valuable/state-of-art skills are valuable Rapid response to change is competitive advantage Abundant labor Low interdependence between employees People are substitutable	Businesses are segmentable Market is diversified Little advantage to coordination across divisions	Dynamic environment Resources are scarce High interdependence between employees Experience and state-of-art skills are both valued
Human Resource Practices	*Make*	*Buy*	*Make and Buy*	*Make With Buy*
Recruiting	Almost exclusive recruitment at entry	Recruitment at all levels	Mixed recruitment depending on division	Considerable entry-level recruitment Can recruit at all levels

Training	Extensively Long time in job Career development within firm	Little training on the job Career development within industry	Mixed training depending on division	Extensive training in organization-specific skills Orientation even for senior hires Continuous development Career progression
Placement	Functionally focused CEO/top managers promoted from within	Limited advancement within firm Pass-through system	HRIS identifies staffing needs Some lateral and inter-divisional transfers Tends to fill positions from within	Cross-functional/ SBU rotation
Performance review	Reward desired behaviors Focus on minimum levels/ error avoidance	Reward for results Short-term/easily measured criteria	Management by objectives (corporate strategy cascades down to local goals)	Trusted, valid performance appraisal Training in appraisals Peer, customer, self, and team leader reviews Performance criteria both objective and subjective
Retention/ turnover	Select *out* early in career/ eliminate cultural misfits Retain Turnover often <5%	High turnover (>25%)	Varies by division	10%-15% turnover Retain those with good performance and values
Learning	Strong tacit knowledge Functional expertise	Externalized	Strong local knowledge Difficulty transferring across divisions	Emphasis on continuous learning

(continued)

TABLE 7.1. *continued*

Human Resource Practices	*Make*	*Buy*	*Make and Buy*	*Make With Buy*
Culture	Dominant/widely held	Weak culture, especially for norms involving relations with others/task norms stronger, competitive, and short term	Dominant/corporate culture with divisional subcultures	Strong dominant culture (both task and relationship norms)
Employment contract	Relational	Transactional	Diverse	Core: balanced Peripheral: transactional
Internal customer	Diverse	None	Diverse	Relational
External customer	Diverse	Transactional	Diverse	Relational

Defender firms pursue a strategy of maintaining market share and furthering an already established position. They do so by continuing existing initiatives (traditional products and services) with incremental developments. Like Lakeside Company described in Chapter 4, the top management of Defenders essentially interprets the environment as stable, with continuing trends in customer demand and technological capabilities observed in the past. Environmental stability makes it possible for the Defender to accumulate in-depth knowledge regarding customer preferences, technological know-how, and efficient ways of organizing to maintain its strategy. Defenders can be characterized as "strong culture" organizations where members have been socialized in well-established norms (e.g., how to relate to each other and to customers). Firms such as General Dynamics, with an established track record of producing submarines, tanks, and weapons systems largely for the U.S. government, have well-established ways of relating to their customers ("give them more than they ask for") as well as to each other (through channels and in writing to conform to government requirements and work standards). Customer requirements (often highly institutionalized as in the case of government contracting) make it difficult for new members to know how to relate to their clients without extensive training and time on the job, necessitating training in organization-specific skills.

Human resource practices in Defender organizations are essentially "make" oriented:

1. Most people hired are recruited at entry.
2. Promotion practices create internal labor markets and long-term careers with the firm.
3. Extensive socialization to a distinctive organizational culture exists where lack of cultural fit is a major reason for (early) termination.
4. Turnover tends to be low as the organization reaps the benefit of extensive training over time and the employee pursues a relatively predictable career path.
5. Top managers work their way up from the lower levels of the organization.
6. Performance appraisal processes are often behavioral with subjective ratings of such items as "dependability," "teamwork," "communicates effectively," and "develops subordinates." This behavioral focus fosters further adaptation of the individual to the organization's culture.

Given the strong emphasis on employee retention and lower emphasis on results, the employment contracts in Defender firms are typically relational (Table 7.2). Members manifest loyalty and commitment to the organization's values and a tendency to stay with the firm during lean times, which is partially due to their development of very organization-specific skills not

TABLE 7.2 Types of Contracts by Strategy

Strategy	*Employee Contract*
Prospector	Transactional
Defender	Relational
Analyzer	Transactional, relational, or a mix
Responsive	Core: balanced Peripheral: transactional
Uncertain	No guarantees

easily transferred elsewhere. Personnel stability in Defenders permits stable customer relations and reinforces strong cultural norms within the firm. Organizational learning is often deep and tacit with strong institutional memory, but insularity and limited environmental scanning make it difficult to respond to new demands for learning.

Prospector firms operate in environments seen as dynamic and unpredictable by their top management. Sports and entertainment are classic examples of industries where Prospector organizations dominate. From year to year, the types of talents and capacities needed by the Prospector organization are difficult to anticipate. Prospectors compete by continually adapting to environmental changes and scanning the environment for opportunities to be "early to market"—essentially a strategy for continual innovation in new products and services (and, in sports and entertainment, new talent). This emphasis on early adoption of innovations occurs in conjunction with a view of labor as abundant at the right price. Given the need for flexibility, prospectors tend to scan the potential workforce for strong individual contributors who can hit the ground running when hired. Low interdependence between subunits and among employees is a basic assumption of Prospectors that makes people more replaceable.

The HR activities of Prospectors tend to focus on recruitment; they may be constantly "on the market" pursuing a strategy of "buying" new talent:

1. New hires are brought in at all organizational levels (no internal career path).
2. Training is minimal with emphasis on present performance, not future potential.
3. Performance reviews emphasize current results.

New hires in Prospectors typically view the organization as a stepping stone to opportunities elsewhere, as in the case of public accounting's recruitment of newly minted undergraduates who want experience, their C.P.A.s, and their eventual outplacement. Given the flexible focus of prospectors, HR is often very lean in such organizations where standard practices (i.e., bureaucratic procedures) are minimal. There may or may not be a formalized performance appraisal, given that great emphasis is placed on easily measured production results (e.g., audience ratings, billable hours, sales quotas). In essence, the reward system focuses on short-term, tangible outcomes. Organizational learning is actually minimal in Prospectors—especially because memory is a key feature of learning. Lack of personnel continuity and few systems (e.g., handbooks or other documents) means that learning is essentially externalized (people bring it with them and take it when they leave).

Contractually, Prospector firms tend to create transactional agreements in which both parties are given easy opportunities to enter as well as exit the relationship. To the employee, transactional employment offers work experience useful elsewhere (e.g., a "ticket punch" as in public accounting or for lawyers working for the Internal Revenue Service before starting their own tax practice), high pay for high performance (e.g., investment banking), or easy access jobs for people with marginal skills (e.g., crew members working the lunch counter at McDonald's). Turnover rates are highest in Prospectors, by design, from 25% a year in some public accounting positions to over 400% for McDonald's crew members. (In fact, McDonald's has boasted that eventually 50% of the U.S. workforce will have worked for them at one time or another—from high school students to retirees.)

Analyzers diversify and evolve. This strategy is a hybrid, where certain subunits pursue a Defender strategy while others pursue a Prospector strategy. Firms don't start out as Analyzers. Analyzers typically developed from Defenders that decided to become more adaptive (e.g., Lakeside in its move to expand from the print/graphics business to information systems). Or they were once Prospectors using one successful area as a "cash cow" to promote more innovative product lines, as in the case of pharmaceutical companies such as Searle, where holding a trademark on aspartame (Nutrasweet) permitted it to use profits from that division to support innovation elsewhere.

Positioned to respond to several different market segments concurrently, Analyzer firms mix their "make and buy" HR strategies:

1. Mixed recruitment and training strategies depend on the specific needs of their divisions.
2. Decentralized HR strategy is employed at the division level.
3. Corporate human resource personnel employ HR information systems to identify staffing needs. When new positions open up in Analyzers, the tendency is to fill from within, using existing talent and creating career opportunities consistent with the internal labor markets of Defender firms. The advantage of internal placements is exposure of Analyzer employees to

diverse aspects of the business, creating cross-divisional knowledge and careers.

4. Barriers to interdivision mobility can exist because compensation systems differ between internal labor market-oriented Defender subunits and the externally oriented Prospector one.
5. Results-oriented, Management by Objectives (MBO) types of performance review exist in most Analyzer organizations. As a formal process for linking unit and individual performance to the larger organization's strategic objectives, MBO-type systems involve a cascading down of goals, timetables, and plans that yield distinct types of targets for specific divisions and management levels.
6. Turnover is expected to vary across divisions, with Defender divisions having less and Prospector divisions more. However, some turnover will actually be cross-division movement and a source of flexibility and internal career as well as organizational development.

Lakeside is an example of an Analyzer, moving from Defender to Analyzer in the late 1980s. It has continued to develop its professional/technical people to produce managers to fill the hierarchy in the graphics side of the business, which has been its historical foundation, while bringing professionals in marketing or sales into its more dynamic information services businesses.

Several conflicts or tensions exist in Analyzers. One tension involves integrating the divisions to promote better coordination as opposed to continuing to permit divisions to develop distinctive competencies and mechanisms for dealing with their diverse market segments. The decision regarding whether to promote distinctive competencies or integration affects the performance of individual divisions as well as the organization as a whole. The performance review system is directly affected by this decision. In Analyzers, divisions, subunits, and individuals are held accountable for "bottom-line" results; however, the nature and types of goals may differ widely among them. It is not uncommon in Analyzers for one division to be held accountable for the rate of new product innovation (e.g., 33% sales from new products every year) but another division in the same firm is accountable for profitability or sales volume. Such differences in performance objectives can make between-division cooperation difficult, because they don't share the same goals, values, or incentive structures. Divergent goals across divisions have a significant impact on Analyzer performance when competitive pressures and scarce resources escalate problems of managing interdependence.

This interdependence creates *internal customer* relations among Analyzer units (e.g., corporate to the divisions, one division's staff to those of another). Interunit cooperation is a chronic difficulty for many Analyzers due to divergent goals and incentives across divisions. Rewards for interdivisional innovations and other cooperative ventures can create a greater *lateral* relationship between Analyzer subunits while creating for the firm some of the advantages characterizing Responsive firms (see below). In effect, such benefits stem from a relational contract with internal customers when Analyzer employees identify with the firm as a whole.

Employment contracts in Analyzers are of necessity diverse, depending on divisional strategies and the degree of emphasis the Analyzer gives to developing its internal labor market. Varied contracts in Analyzers can send mixed messages to employees, some of whom may have been hired under very different deals from other employees. Auditors hired in the Defender division of a public accounting firm are likely to have career paths and incentive systems very different than MIS consultants hired by a more Prospector-oriented division of the same firm. Analyzers tend to use different performance criteria across divisions and levels in the company, introducing distinct performance conditions to employees' performance contracts.

Responsive firms operate in environments seen by their management as changing and where resources (especially suitably skilled people) are seen as scarce. Such firms seek to leverage their ability to compete in a changing environment by creating and managing interdependencies between employees and business units. Characteristic of these organizations are increasingly shorter product life cycles, which require the involvement of designers, operators, marketing, and sales as well as customers in product design and production (i.e., concurrent engineering; Davidow & Malone, 1992).

This business strategy targets particular niches on which the firm focuses, often with an emphasis on a close customer relationship. General Electric developed a team-building, continuous improvement system called WorkOut to move its somewhat centralized functionally structured divisions into internal teams. From 1987 to the present, the Medical Systems Division of GE (manufacturing magnetic resonance imagers, or MRIs) has applied problem-solving and quality improvement processes to create and manage interdependencies across functional groups. GE Medical Systems has employed its WorkOut program as a means of creating a stronger relationship with its primary customers (hospitals and health maintenance organizations). By training the customer itself to use WorkOut, a new dimension is added to GE's customer relationship: Customers trained in WorkOut may be better able to use GE equipment. One health maintenance organization was able to increase the number of patients undergoing MRI procedures because use of WorkOut helped it coordinate better with hospital floors, enabling nurses to send patients to MRI appointments without interfering with ongoing activities such as meals and therapy. Such customer relationships create a barrier to entry because few GE competitors offer this form of gratuitous consulting.

The team development HR strategy of Responsive firms reflects their more boundaryless character. (Indeed, though employees in Defender organizations and in some Analyzer divisions may coordinate *within their subunits* in a teamlike fashion, it is more likely that Responsive firms will employ teamwork both *within and between* units; Ancona & Caldwell, 1992; Rousseau, 1993.)

In Responsive firms:

1. Retention of skilled people is emphasized; however, turnover does occur due to environmental pressures on business and employee marketability.
2. Rotation across jobs and divisions is made possible both by comparable compensation systems across units (e.g., broadbanding) as well as broader member identification with the firm as a whole (rather than the local division).
3. Both objective (short-term results) and subjective (staff development and adherence to values) performance criteria are used.

Teams tend to train people (managers as well as peers) in the proper use of performance appraisal forms and in how to give feedback. Peer appraisal is common in team-oriented organizations such as AT&T Credit, a New Jersey-based organization that handles financing arrangements for corporate phone systems. Peers know more about individual contributions than the team leader can (who may head a group of up to 20 people). Moreover, being rated by one's team signals the importance of working with that team.

Contracts in team-oriented organizations tend to be of the balanced variety, with an emphasis on both short-term results and long-term contributions to the development of the team and the business. Learning is a distinctive competitive advantage requiring openness to inputs from others in the organization and from the market. Retention of a critical core of people provides stable relations both to customers and to organizational memory. Team-oriented organizations tend to have core employees with balanced contracts and access to a more peripheral workforce that provides flexibility as new product or service demand increases. (Peripherals have transactional contracts permitting termination when demand declines.) Hewlett-Packard has traditionally had a two-tiered contract: core team members and, in its production facilities, a pool of "permanent temporaries" who are regularly brought in when demand is high and terminated when it declines. At HP, peripherals can remain in the pool, being "on call" as needed. Such people may work weekend shifts or other nontraditional hours well suited to college students and parents of small children. Two-tiered systems allow organizations in cyclical businesses to make commitments they can keep.

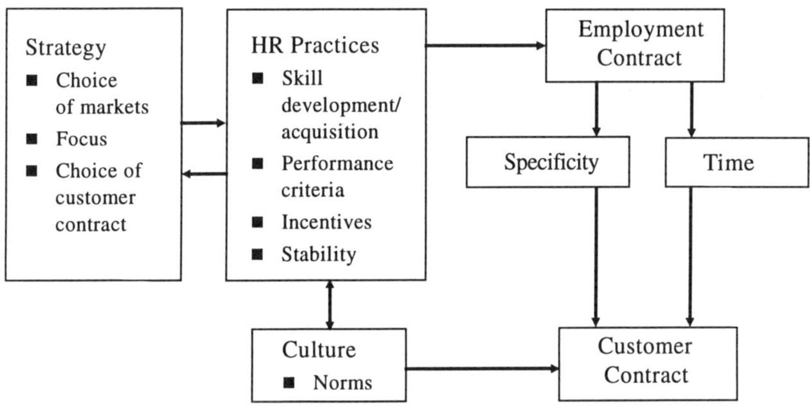

FIGURE 7.2. Strategy, HR, Employment Contracts, and the Customer

EMPLOYMENT CONTRACTS AND CUSTOMER RELATIONSHIPS: CONTRACTS IN PARALLEL?

Organizational strategy affects the employment contract through the HR practices that implement that strategy. Strategy dictates the choice of customers, their range and variety, and the array of products and services offered. But it is through the linkage of business strategy to HR practices that customer service and support are affected (Figure 7.2). Contract dynamics characterize both consumer marketing and industrial marketing channels.

Consumer Marketing. Employment contracts affect the depth of service and quality of after-market support. Lands' End, the successful mail order house, advertises: "We accept any return, for any reason, at any time . . . GUARANTEED. PERIOD" (Heskett, Sasser, & Hart, 1990), which is a pretty good statement of a relational contract—needs based with no performance terms on the part of the customer. Responsive organizations and other firms seeking long-term stable relations with customers may pursue essentially a Relational contract with those customers. However, those firms seeking to actively involve customers in their own service (e.g., concurrent engineering efforts in which customers help plan new product development) are fostering a balanced contract that includes performance terms for customers. The fundamental question here is: Is a particular *employment* contract required to maintain a particular type of *customer* contract?

Conventional wisdom holds that treating employees like customers creates more motivated employees more willing to satisfy customers. Of course, there are many ways to treat a customer depending on customer expectations. Mail order computer companies such as Gateway offer minimal postsale involvement with customers, but this transactional approach can offer a high-quality product at a lower price for the user willing to accept the closed-ended nature of the deal. IBM made much of its reputation as a relational employer and a service-oriented supplier. Clearly, Gateway and IBM serve very different markets. Customer relations are largely a function of the way in which employees are trained and rewarded for treating those customers. The employment contract shapes the forms customer contracts may take.

The impact of relational employment contracts on customer service is largely a function of the cultural norms and values to which employees are committed. The relational employment contracts observed in Defenders can give rise to well-managed customer relations, especially when the norms of the Defender encourage cooperation and flexibility. Dennis Organ's (1990) research on organizational citizenship behavior provides evidence that employees who feel party to a good faith relationship with their employer are more likely "to go the extra mile" in providing service to both external as well as internal customers. However, if that relational contract includes tolerance of minimum levels of performance and a narrow definition of an individual's job (the popular image of the American and Canadian postal services), the result may be a secure individual with little reason, and little support, to fulfill customer needs. The extent to which relational contracts promote service is a function of

1. whether the organization's cultural values support service and
2. whether training and other resources are provided to support that service.

Relational contracts do not always guarantee service but can under the right conditions. Transactional employment arrangements tend to breed transactional customer relations. Having few long-term incentives and substantial pressure for immediate results, the short-term focus promotes limited involvement with customers and a desire to "close the deal." The transactional contract is in fact the best example of customer contracts directly paralleling employment ones. These contracts offer tremendous flexibility in the face of a changing market, but a pass-through employment system makes it difficult to engage in continuous improvement and in-depth learning. Suited to markets where existing products become rapidly obsolete, there may be little learning *within* the transactionally oriented firm. Top management must continually search the environment to identify what innovations they need to acquire rather than to develop them for themselves. Limited retention can lead to relatively low levels of organizational learning.

The question arises as to whether continuing to operate in a more transactional mode undercuts the stability and growth of a business in the long term (Davis-Blake & Uzzi, 1993).

In contrast, balanced contracts can make customer relations part of their terms of performance. Responsive organizations can have either relational or balanced contracts with customers. A balanced customer contract contains expectations for *customer* performance (e.g., participation in product design, information sharing). Such balanced contracts occur where customers perceive benefits from customization.

A relational contract has fewer specific requirements of customers than does a balanced one. A classic example of relational contracting with customers is LSI Logic, as described by Davidow and Malone in their book *The Virtual Corporation* (1992). Recognizing that the time it took to get customer contracts through its legal department prohibited quick delivery to customers, LSI Logic began shipping to its regular customers on verbal order, letting the paperwork follow. In this case, the company's willingness to trust its customers made responsiveness to customers possible.

Finally, in terms of the array of possible customer contracts, we need to consider the role of the "no guarantees" customer contract. Although used cars and "fly-by-night" operations come immediately to mind, no guarantees arrangements involve more than just exploitation of the unwary public. Organizations characterized by high instability both in the market as well as internally due to shifting strategies and personnel create customer relations involving uncertainty and variability regarding product or service quality. These low-trust customer relations can be a by-product of organizational transitions as well as the result of deliberate opportunism.

Industrial Marketing. The working partnerships of manufacturers and distributors have been widely studied using contract-related concepts. Anderson and Weitz (1992) observe that channel partners (e.g., equipment manufacturers and their industrial customers) who are motivated to develop a stable relationship demonstrate a willingness to make short-term sacrifices. They also maintain confidence in their relationship through frequent meetings and other forms of communication. Commitment created through these relationship-building activities is also enhanced through the use of pledges, which are actions undertaken by the customer-supplier channel members that demonstrate good faith. But more than simple declarations of good faith, pledges are specific actions binding a channel member to a relationship (Anderson & Weitz, 1992, p. 20). Two types of pledges Anderson and Weitz describe are

> idiosyncratic investments, such as training or personnel dedicated only to servicing a specific manufacturer's products, adopting a common order processing

system between the two firms, or building specialized facilities to handle a product line;

voluntarily constraining certain activities related to the relationship, such as exclusive distribution, limiting terminations in situations where substandard performance occurs, or establishing a termination notification requirement.

Pledges create self-enforcing arrangements because violating the agreement costs the pledge maker, which has weakened its own position (by reducing its ability to obtain other customers or suppliers). Trust is a critical feature in working industrial partnerships (Anderson & Narus, 1990). In these relationships, trust is defined as "the firm's belief that another company will perform actions that will result in positive outcomes for the firm, as well as not take unexpected actions that would result in negative outcomes for the firm" (p. 45). Here we see the contract features of voluntariness, benefits, reliance losses, and good faith. In practice, this trust is enhanced by joint annual planning detailing mutually defined performance objectives and the cooperative efforts required of each partner to attain these objectives: periodic communication on performance progress and a formal retrospective review of each partner's performance each year (Anderson & Narus, 1990, p. 56).

However, despite what has been referred to as the "partnership bandwagon" (Gross, 1989, as cited by Anderson & Narus, 1990), close, collaborative relationships are not always in the best interest of suppliers. Anderson and Narus (1990) describe what they refer to as the industry bandwidth of working relationships. Each bandwidth reflects the range of relationships pursued within a given industry. Ranging from pure transactional exchange to pure collaborative exchange, suppliers like employers find different degrees of benefit from types of exchanges depending on product value relative to the competition. Suppliers may participate in several kinds of relationships, though these tend to cluster within a range for the industry. When customers evaluate purchases solely on price and are unwilling to pay for added service, such accounts are more suited to limited, transactional exchanges. Where customization is valued and willingly paid for by the customer, relational exchanges are more likely. Anderson and Narus conclude that partnerships permit suppliers to leverage their limited resources through joint efforts with customers and gain benefits from customer ideas and higher profit margins on value-added services. More transactional arrangements offer the supplier the opportunity to streamline the product to compete more effectively on price. In effect, not all market segments or customers want the same working relationship. The result is likely to be different employment contracts in segments with different customer relationships.

Implications. In Chapter 4, four contemporary contract forms were proposed that have a variety of implications for organizations and their constituents (Table 7.3). Paradoxically, contract features that benefit one group (owners, workers, or customers) can under certain circumstances constrain another.

Examples of such paradoxes include the following:

- Relational contracts created to foster greater control over employees can actually reduce the firm's ability to influence their performance (secure employees may have limited motivation to do their jobs differently).
- Transactional contracts that give the organization its greatest flexibility regarding whom it employs also can reduce its ability to learn (people may move in and out of the organization so quickly that little organizational memory exists for new ideas or successful innovations).
- Arm's-length (transactional) relations with employees create limited relations with customers. On the other hand, paternalistic relations (relational contracts) with employees are no guarantee of quality service to customers.

The key feature in all these paradoxes is the slippage that can occur between the intended organizational strategy and that strategy actually realized through contracting with employees. If HR practices do not send messages compatible with the organization's goals, the firm's contracts with employees will not support those goals.

CONCLUSION

The futures of contracts mirror developments in business strategy. Relational agreements are likely in the more stable sectors of the economy, but balanced contracts (with their specific performance requirements) are likely where in-depth, technical, and customer/product knowledge is required to remain competitive. Transactional agreements serve the interests of entrepreneurs and those organizations in volatile industries such as entertainment or sports. Balanced employment contracts and more relational customer ones characterize the more notably successful firms in the 1990s. However, use of these contracts is largely predicated on top management's view of the organization's environment. High rates of unpredictable change in the future could move more firms toward the Prospector model, resulting in transactional contracts for employee and customer alike.

How well organizations implement their chosen strategy (and achieve their targeted relationship with customers) is affected considerably by their use of appropriate HR practices. An organization can elect a Responsive

TABLE 7.3 Contract Implications

	Transactional	*Relational*	*Balanced*	*No Guarantees*
Organization	High turnover Lower labor costs/less resources spent on developing employees Limited organizational learning/difficult to engage in continuous improvement and in-depth learning Tendency to have deep, narrow specialization of skills/services/products Well-defined contract terms Ability to create new contracts easily Flexibility to respond to changing market	Low rate of turnover Strong institutional memory but difficulty responding to new demands for learning Internal labor market Relatively homogeneous workforce Well-developed, distinct culture Resources spent on developing employees	Internally team-oriented Culture conducive to continuous learning and innovation High ability to influence member behavior Ability to renegotiate existing contracts Learning and organizational memory are a competitive advantage	Organization strategy is in transition Most likely, organization is moving toward transactional contracts
Employees	Little or no organizational loyalty Employees develop marketable skills Unstable employment Flexibility/easy exit Low intent to stay with organization long term Less willing to take additional responsibilities/ lower *scope* of contribution Reward system focuses on short term	High organizational loyalty Employees very dependent on organization Training: develop company-*specific* skills (less marketable) Stable employment Willing to commit to one company High intent to stay with organization Members highly socialized	Greater development opportunities (training/ lateral moves) Employees depend on coworkers for support (to deliver on promises) Mutual trust and respect among coworkers High commitment to organization Largest *scope* of contribution Participation expected	Absence of commitment from organization regarding future employment Demoralizing environment Terms of employment relationship (contracts) are *uninterpretable* Reluctant to trust organization and coworkers Relatively lower intent to stay with organization

Customer	Limited/focused relations with customers Predictable levels of performance from organization/predictable, discrete relationships Limited services (especially after sales are completed)	Stable customer relationships Organization has in-depth knowledge regarding customer preferences Quality of service/customer relations *depends* on organization norms and culture	Organization is highly customer responsive Involvement Customer has responsibilities and commitment to organization that must be kept so that organization can keep its end of the bargain High customer/organization interdependence Service is broader and more responsive Stable relations	Poor or *inconsistent* customer service/ relations/satisfaction Limited services

strategy *but,* by failing to align its human resource practices with that strategy, remain for all intents and purposes an Analyzer. Similarly, a would-be Analyzer can acquire a new business unit to bring in technological know-how that its Defender core lacks. But if it manages the new business as it does its Defender division, it will remain essentially a Defender.

The balanced contract has popular appeal (given the recent successes of General Electric, Square D, and others). Realistically, however, organizations in highly volatile environments will be hard pressed to manage people in ways consistent with that contract. Orsburn and his colleagues (1990) have detailed the many ways in which team building can go awry, one of the most common reasons being making commitments to team members and then laying some members off during tight economic times.[1] Part of the failure of People Express (PE) in the early 1980s is attributable to the failure of Don Burr, the CEO, to honor the contract made to employees. The challenging jobs that members were promised created expectations of participation in decisions and involvement in the growth of the company. Burr made choices to accelerate business expansion without consultation with PE employees whose workloads would be drastically affected by the change. The result was destruction of the team culture and breakdown in services. It is clearly better to create a deal one can keep than one at odds with business conditions or corporate strategy.

In managing the link between business strategy and contracts, several actions are critical:

- Align human resource practices and the business strategy (or else the result will be poor implementation including mixed messages to employees and customers).
- Identify the scope of appropriate customer service and consistently reflect this in employee recruiting, compensation, and development programs. Are in-depth relations with customers desired, perhaps even to the point of involving them in product design as part of the strategy? If so, a transactional contract will not provide sufficient organizational commitment on the part of employees to sustain such relationships. If, on the other hand, customers value very limited organizational relationships (if the product is a commodity), transactional arrangements may make the organization more cost competitive.
- Specify in understandable terms the performance terms required of current employees. If these are subject to change in the future, the contract conveyed during recruitment and in performance reviews should state the importance of flexibility and responsiveness.
- Maintain an honest and good faith relationship with employees. The quality of the relationship on which an employment contract rests has considerable impact on the ability to modify or renegotiate new contract features and terms.

New forms of employment arrangements, partnerships, and customer relations can be expected to follow emerging developments in organizational strategy. Each alters the nature of contracting for workforce members, network partners, and customers. Contracts between people and organizations can be either a constraint or a resource. In the future of contracts, we can expect considerable innovation and experimentation in contracting. Contracts are models of the future and their variety is increasing.

NOTE

1. Making commitments and then laying off people is not unique to team building. But this contract-related problem is a particular concern for those troubled organizations using team building as a last-ditch effort to change. When team building is implemented in the latter stages of economic difficulties, more realistic commitments are critical to the credibility of these efforts.

Trends in the New Social Contract

No snowflake in an avalanche ever feels responsible.

—S. J. Lee
(1968, as quoted in Bartlett's, 1980, p. 876)

Shifts in broad social understandings regarding employment contracts come about because of a critical mass of individual and organizational changes. Newspaper headlines announce: "Loyalty is dead." Help wanted ads in those same papers make fewer and fewer offers of a career path in the firm (Hirsch & Kreimelmeyer, 1993). Out of the media and our personal experiences, a new context is created for interpreting the meaning of employment. Once these new understandings become widespread, they affect the next generation of individuals and organizations and the contracts they make. This chapter deals with the implications of contract changes for the future, particularly the shifts contract change introduces in how people and their societies interpret such concepts as promises, commitments, employment, career, and organizations. It addresses the social context or ecology of contracts, forces for and against the continuation of employment contracts, the loss of voluntariness, and changing standards for fairness.

Changes affecting many individual contracts at the same time alter the context for future contract makers. In essence, an *ecology of contracts* exists in which today's contract performance changes tomorrow's contract terms. Ecology is the interaction of living things with their environment. Biologists tell us that the actions of life forms (e.g., oxygen-generating plants) contributed to the making of planet Earth, its atmosphere, crust, and weather (Lovelock, 1988). But, once created, atmosphere, crust, and weather shape subsequent life forms. Like ecological changes in nature, changes in contracts today can reshape the conditions under which subsequent contracts are made, judged, and performed. If enough individuals experience lateral moves rather than promotions, if few realize career options with their employer, and if good performers lose their jobs, such trends in individual contracts alter how "employment" and "career" are defined by society.

The ecology of contracts means that all behavior is relative to the setting in which it occurs.[1] Promise and commitment have no universal meaning but take on a character influenced to a great extent by the setting in which they occur. Features of contracts, such as long term, generous, flexible, or open, have little meaning out of context. Context gives meaning, and when context changes, meaning can change with it.

SHIFTS IN MEANING

Meanings change in three ways. Some concepts *cease to exist.* Terms such as *job security* or *permanent employee* have become abruptly obsolete in certain sectors of the economy. Second, new concepts are *created.* Concepts such as "core" and "peripheral employees" emerge to express newly created arrangements. But perhaps the most interesting form of change is when well-established concepts *shift in meaning.*

New uses for old terms signal a tacit acceptance of shifts in meaning (Rousseau & Wade-Benzoni, 1995; Table 8.1). Terms such as *employee* and *organization* have acquired meanings that reflect changing forms of worker-organization attachment. *Employee* used to signify a person with a job within an organization, full time, indefinitely. Now employees come in many different forms—core, peripheral, networked, outsourced, and so on. *Organization* traditionally referred to a legal entity with employees inside and an external market outside its boundaries. Now, however, an organization might not have a legal identity (e.g., a business unit or a professional service network). Boundaries are also becoming very blurry, particularly between organizations and customers. Concurrent engineering means that customers participate in new product design, often serving on a supplier's design committees. Quality systems can be adopted by organizations at the behest of their customers, who insist that suppliers integrate quality and information systems with their own. The meaning and nature of the organization is increasingly unclear. Even the term *management* has acquired new significance. It may now be less a role than an activity, as in *self*-management. Changes in meaning are symptoms of deeper shifts in the assumptions people make about work, workers, and organizations. These changes reflect cultural experiences that form the social contract.

TABLE 8.1 Organizational Constructs for Past and Future

Employee:	
Past	One employed by another for wages, same meaning for all who worked for the organization
Future	Include customers as "partial employees" due to their participation in service/production process
	Organization will have many different kinds of employees (core, contractors, part-timers, temps, partial employees, and so on)
Organization:	
Past	Legal entity with employees inside and an external market outside its boundaries
Future	Many forms, legal as well as enacted, some with inclusion of customer/ market inside boundaries, some with few employees within boundaries
Management:	
Past	Supervising and directing work of others
Future	Self-supervising employees, managers integrate work of others
Career:	
Past	Evolving sequence of work over time
Future	Different kinds of careers depending on employment status; part-timers and temps have jobs, not careers
	Boundaryless careers—not contained within one organization or even one industry or occupation

TRADITIONAL SOCIAL CONTRACTS AND CHANGE

Social contracts are the societal context for understanding the individual psychological contracts that employment creates. In his study of the steel industry, John Hoerr (1988) describes how a community in which a person lives can create a social contract shared by the community and its organizations:

> For many young men in the mill towns [in the 1950s], there was a tangible sense of having to make an implicit bargain with life from the outset. There were two choices. If you took a job in the mill, you could stay . . . among family and friends, earn decent pay, and gain a sort of lifetime security . . . in an industry that would last forever. You traded advancement for security and expected life to stick its bargain. Or you could spurn the good pay and long-term security, leave your family and the community and take a flyer on making a career in some other field. In a sense everybody growing up in America must decide whether to stay or move on . . . the very presence of the mill on the riverbank, its gates flung open . . . forced you to make this choice. (pp. 8-9)[2]

To force a choice means to direct activity without explicit consent. Practices that are the product of ongoing repetitive interactions, such as sons following fathers into an occupation, gradually take on a rulelike quality that makes them a social fact. Social contracts are not entered into by choice. Rather, they are "taken-for-granted" realities, assumptions people may not know they have until they are violated. The context is the contract, which here means agreement but not necessarily choice. Social contract features include (but are not limited to) the following:

- Societal-based work and family role expectations
- Entitlements and forms of Social Security
- Rights and responsibilities in the workplace supported by law and custom
- Culturally supported mobility patterns
- Patterns for distributing risk from occupational injuries, job loss, and other liabilities between employer and employee
- Pipelines between educational institutions and employment opportunities

Institutional theory contends that key features of the environment shape the structure of organizations and the behavior of people (DiMaggio & Powell, 1983). The broader societal setting comprises bundles of resources, communication patterns, and cultural elements—symbols of legitimacy and belief systems (Scott, 1983). Sources of belief systems include public opinion, educational systems, laws, courts, professions, ideologies, regulatory bodies, and governmental requirements. From the perspective of social contracts, pervasive beliefs involving employment include widespread social judgments regarding fair and appropriate conduct, entitlements (such as job property rights or owner authority over employees), and basic concepts of employment (permanent versus temporary) and how they are understood. At the societal level, these beliefs, both conscious (e.g., how linguistic terms are interpreted) and unconscious (e.g., the dynamics underlying entitlements), stem directly from the broader societal culture as well as indirectly through its impact on education, law, media, industry, and related institutions (Figure 8.1).

Societal Culture. Effects of social contracts are evident not only in the United States but in developing nations as well. For instance, in Mexico, the value placed on family is so strong that surveys indicate consistently that the major motivators in the Mexican workforce are to support one's family and to provide for the education of one's children (Abitia, 1986, 1991). In contrast, U.S. surveys typically indicate job challenge, autonomy, and advancement as the primary motivators of the American workforce (Kovach, 1987). Development of the Mexican economy is tied to business growth,

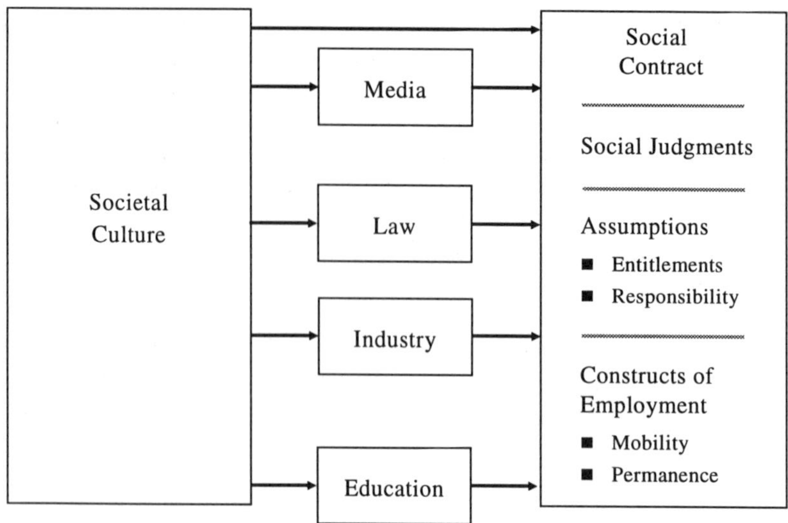

FIGURE 8.1. Social Contract Framework

expansion of the middle class, and development of Mexican managers. But a barrier to this development has been widespread reluctance of the population to move away from extended family ties. If career mobility and development require willingness to leave traditional roots, it may be slowed by fighting against the ties of culture and the prevailing social contract in which family dominates individual careers. Similar issues apply in other less industrialized parts of the world (Bhagat, Kedia, Crawford, & Kaplan, 1990), reflecting the incompatibility of many features of Western employment with the taken-for-granted social contract.

Education. Primary and secondary schooling is typically the pipeline through which careers are founded. Beliefs, behaviors, and skills acquired through schooling shape the organizations children ultimately join as adults. Japan provides an illustration of the substantive link between education, industry, and social contracts of employment. The pervasive emphasis in Japanese employment is that a good employee is a generalist, capable of playing whatever role is required without being differentiated from fellow group members. Specialization is not valued because it emphasizes difference as opposed to similarity. The emphasis on generalists is rooted in the high performance standards of the educational system. High competition weeds out those people not able to master broad academic disciplines, depriving them of the university admission critical to attaining professional roles in industry and government. The social contract in Japan inextricably ties lifetime career to successful performance in rigorous pre-university schooling (Huddleston, 1990). Any movement to alter work roles, careers, and skills in Japanese firms has powerful implications "upstream" for the educational institutions that provide the corporate labor force. Social contracts are cultural and, like culture, they evolve with the force of history, technology, education, and economics. The education system is a major socialization agent in any society's culture.

Media. Social interpretation of events occurs through the widely disseminated communiqués from television, radio, and newspapers. In recent comic strips, Dagwood quit his job (only for a short while, but with appropriate reactions from both Mr. Dithers and Blondie) and Dick Tracy was served with divorce papers. The media are both social reality's mirror and its driver. Pervasive stimuli create widespread responses and assimilation. As a source of pervasive information, advertising has been implicated in shifting societal perceptions and judgments.

Many social judgments change with time. One of the more significant shifts involves the interaction of the media and juries. In their research into temporal drift in social parameters, Nagao and Davis (1980) observe trends toward harsher judgments in jury trials for rape over a period of years using the same videotaped trial. Social decision processes need not have a constant effect over time. However, changes in social phenomena over time are often quite subtle and, as Nagao and Davis point out, difficult to evaluate. Rising concern over women's rights and greater attention given to crime victims in the press and television have shifted the focus of attention in juries and among would-be jurors. This trend in criminal trials contrasts with the increasingly tougher standards juries use in evaluating plaintiffs in civil suits ("U.S. Juries," 1994). In 1992, plaintiffs won 52% of personal injury cases decided by jury verdicts, down from 63% in 1989; awards have leveled off as well. At the heart of this shift are views about risk and responsibility. Advertising from the insurance industry is implicated as a possible cause of this shift.

Our thinking about employment relations is centered on risk and responsibility as well. How the media portray corporations, the labor force, and their respective problems in the face of change can influence social judgment. Shifts in social judgment affect which laws are passed and how they are interpreted. Just as parameters juries use change in conjunction with other social forces, including advertising and recent events, so too can social contracts change regarding risks, responsibilities, and entitlements. Popular media can alter how events are interpreted.

Law. Employee job property rights and entitlement to due process in termination are the norm in many nations (see Brunstein, 1992, for France, and Watcher & Stengelhofer, 1992, for Germany). The United States has been the exception until recently. Although at-will employment practices have in thc past made terminations easier in the United States than in most of the industrialized world, entitlements are now expanding particularly with regard to due process (Edelman, 1990; Selznick, 1969). Union avoidance is only a minor motivator in the expansion of corporate due process, despite being frequently cited in the academic literatures (e.g., Freeman & Medoff, 1984; Montgomery, 1979).

Edelman (1990) argues that the legal definitions of fair governance tend to interact with cultural understandings of workplace justice. Her event-history analyses of personnel practices show that civil rights mandates of the 1960s created a normative environment that threatened the legitimacy of arbitrary organizational governance. This precipitated widespread use of formal grievance procedures for nonunion employees. Since the 1960s, courts have become noticeably less sympathetic to arbitrary dismissals. Recognizing employer duties to treat employees fairly, albeit under limited circumstances, courts also have reinforced the employer's principal means of demonstrating fair treatment. Courts have begun to reinforce due process protections, specifically the institution of grievance procedures. The process of diffusion is self-perpetuating because, as due process protections become more prevalent, the cost of nonconformity, specifically the legal costs, increases (Edelman, 1990, p. 1412). A further analysis of the issues using an expanded database supported Edelman's conclusions (Sutton, Dobbin, Meyer, & Scott, 1994). Expanding their analyses to differences between states, Sutton and his colleagues observed that adoption rates for due process practices were higher among California employers, who operate under a legislative and judicial regime that is more assertive toward employee rights (p. 966). As they put it: "Our evidence suggests that concepts of employee rights, citizenship, and due process have become powerful metaphors of governance among organizations in some societal sectors" (p. 967).

Industry. Industries themselves have their own cultural beliefs and values that shape employment relations within particular sectors. An illustration of historical shifts in social contracts associated with employment is the broad redistribution of employment-related risk in American manufacturing since the nineteenth century. Consider the case of occupational health and safety. Until the early twentieth century, injuries on the job were essentially problems workers dealt with themselves with little legal recourse or compensation. Injuries were thought to "just happen." Employers were not responsible for such "random" events and had little obligation—even if a worker were killed or permanently disabled. Because accidents were not attributed to the nature of the job, the prevailing belief was that nothing could be done about them. No industrial safety departments existed. No government inspectors visited to ensure that plants were safe. Prevailing beliefs shaped organizational and governmental actions, and employees absorbed the risk themselves. Since the turn of the century, new perspectives regarding accidents generally and occupational injuries specifically have emerged. Injuries are now seen as preventable and organizations are increasingly held responsible for them. Government regulation, technological improvements, and increasingly closer worker-manager relationships both result from and fuel the belief that accidents are at least to some extent controllable and therefore preventable. A broad social entitlement to a safe workplace replaced the laissez-faire nineteenth-century view.

Trends toward enhancing employer responsibility reflect a 100-year-long cultural shift. Early industrialization focused on output and labor availability. Although factory workers were outnumbered by farmworkers, organizations had few responsibilities toward their workers, and workers had few rights or claims against the company in case of accident or complaint. But as industrial labor became dominant, employment corporations become the focal point for labor. Owners took new responsibilities for workers, such as for their benefits, hours, working conditions, and employment relationships, including "scientific management" (Burack, 1993). The more time people spent at work, the less time they had to make arrangements such as insurance or retirement plans for themselves. Increasingly, company officials assumed more responsibility for their employees.

Societal changes affect industry culture and thus can also alter how well particular employment arrangements function. Practices that work well in one era break down in another.[3] Union-management agreements from the 1930s to the 1960s structured work and responsibilities, fostering employee and organization welfare. Fast growing and productive manufacturing organizations typically were unionized. However, by the 1970s and 1980s, unionization had institutionalized mistrust and conflicting interests (Kochan et al., 1986). Why the change? The reasons revolve around the changing nature of trust and social distance between worker and managers.

Historically, unions helped to bridge the social distance between people who labored and those who managed by creating means for bargaining and managing disputes. Their presence in organizations was associated with efficiency and coordination between labor and management. The decline in unionization coincides with a trend in many industries toward greater trust between management and labor (Miles & Creed, 1995). This trust has occurred because workers are more skilled and need less monitoring, because socioeconomic differences between management and labor are smaller today than they were generations ago, and because labor can aspire to management positions, thus experiencing less social distance. The weakening position of unions in this country can also be attributed to some extent to poor union responsiveness to their constituents (Hoerr, 1988). Hoerr argues that in the steel industry, organized labor became an insider in the organization by accepting a broad class of management prerogatives (work scheduling, operational decision making) that were protected from union interference. Unions, relegated to filing grievances for disciplinary actions or job assignments, took no responsibility for making the workplace more productive or for gaining a voice for their members in operations.

Improved relations between workers and managers, especially in nonunionized settings, weaken a union's ability to organize. The failure of white-collar unions to replace traditional industrial blue-collar ones can in large part be attributed to the identification of white-collar workers with their managers. Enhanced employee control over work and participation (Miles & Creed, 1995) reduces the social distance between labor and management. Managers look, talk, and act in many ways like their subordinates, and some of these subordinates stand a reasonable chance of becoming managers. However, it should be noted that neither worker-manager identification nor career advancement are traditional features of blue-collar work settings.

Conclusion. Work restructuring has given many employees the task of managing their own work, placing traditional managerial concerns in the purview of rank-and-file members. Widespread changes in education levels and work-related values regarding autonomy and responsibility have occurred in conjunction with restructurings (Miles & Creed, 1995). From the perspective of an individual's contract, these role changes can sometimes blur old boundaries. But the stronger these relationships become, the more they will rely on implicit understandings rather than on formal controls to govern actions. With their similarities as great as they may ever have been, workers and managers also share something else: a vulnerability and a sense of risk. Formerly, the rules of the game were clear (Lashinsky, 1993). People now work long, hard, and scared, according to Mirvis and Hall (1994), regardless of rank.

Environment shapes social contracts, constraining their terms and coloring their interpretations. However, broad institutional factors are not the primary cause of contracting for individuals and organizations. Events occurring within the relationship as well as individual and social cognitions are the major factors that shape how individuals understand their contracts. Nonetheless, the "facts of the situation," to quote Herbert Simon (1951), do include the broader context in which relationships occur.

CONTRACTS IN TRANSITION: THE THREATS TO CONTRACTING

In times of transition, there may be conflicts between prevailing and emerging social contracts. Debates concern entitlements, how losses are distributed, and rights and responsibilities. Broad social, economic, and technological forces work against creating contracts along the lines of past arrangements, but others provide conventional contracts continued momentum.

The following are contemporary features threatening the existence of familiar contract forms:

- *Increased monitoring,* including surveillance technology, drug testing, and expanded information systems, can alter the nature of the employment relationship by signaling lack of trust (Frey, 1993). Drug testing can extend conditions of employment into people's personal lives (constraining even legal behaviors such as smoking and alcohol consumption). Increased performance measurement (e.g., computer measurement of keystrokes, call counts, and other performance minutia) can focus attention on limited behaviors rather than on flexibility or innovation, signaling a more transactional employment arrangement.
- *Expanded use of temporaries* by organizations that also employ core workers can change the nature of the career path, shared cultural values, and relational norms (Castro, 1993). Use of temporaries can create more career options for core workers (Davis-Blake & Uzzi, 1993; Handy, 1989). However, they can also limit the amount of high-quality work available to a large segment of the workforce as well as diminish the coordination, learning, and shared values manifested between various work groups. Use of temporaries not only signifies limited commitment between workers and the firm but can also erode the confidence of the firm's nontemporary workers in their own relationship with the employer (Pearce, 1993). Presence of temporaries changes the ecology of contracting for all workers in the organizations.
- *Greater worker mobility* creates opportunities elsewhere that might affect both employee and employer commitments (Booth & Chaterji, 1989). There is little reason to invest heavily in people who will shortly leave; similarly, there is little reason for an employee to go the extra mile in an employment relationship he or she knows will end soon.
- *Dynamic and unpredictable environments* undermine the ability to predict what will be needed in the labor force, often even in the short term. Organizations can formally avoid making commitments by outsourcing many types of work or hiring temporary workers. However, many firms respond to this unpredictability by inconsistencies in top management's

messages to its workforce, signaling in effect that there is no strategy—and therefore no real contract to be relied on for either direction or support.

These factors make organizations less able to specify clear performance terms required of employees and make both parties less willing to make commitments. When good performers are terminated, the remaining valuable employees feel insecure. But of all the forces that operate against contracting today, two are the most critical: the rise of downsizing and the loss of voluntariness.

Downsizing. The planned elimination of positions or jobs as a widespread business practice has hit with cataclysmic force. According to Wayne Cascio (1993), counting only jobs held for at least 3 years, 5.6 million people lost permanent jobs from 1987 to 1991. The major reason appears to be overhead reduction (particularly staff and white-collar jobs, which include staff and white-collar salaries). By definition, downsizing does not include poor performers or normal departures due to retirement or voluntary resignations. It is firm-related factors and not employee-related ones that account for the terminations. The most likely candidates are firms struggling with high debt (in the aftermath of mergers and acquisitions or construction and development efforts). Firms in the 1990s carry more debt than they did in the previous two decades. Servicing debt often means drastic steps to ensure the needed cash. Firms that didn't take on debt, including foreign competitors, can gain significant market share. Meanwhile, loss of market share stimulates more downsizing for debt-ridden firms (Cascio, 1993).

Does downsizing cut costs? Recent studies indicate that *fewer than half* of downsized companies report that cuts reduced expenses significantly, because of costly overtime needed to replace people who were dismissed. *Less than a third* say that profits or shareholder returns increased as expected. Survivors typically are less loyal and less willing to provide service to customers and support for fellow employees. Despite evidence that downsizing fails to achieve most goals set for it, companies that reduce staffing levels typically do not try other cuts first (e.g., cuts in pay, shorter workweeks, vacations without pay; Cascio, 1993). One must ask the question, then, if it doesn't work, why have organizations taken to downsizing so readily?

The most likely cause is a shift in taken-for-granted beliefs about how organizations should be managed. What stockholders and owners willingly entertain as their options in dealing with employees have changed strikingly, even in the space of a few years. CEOs report finding it easier and easier to use downsizing as a cost-cutting strategy (Lawler, personal communication). What began as the private trauma of a few individuals in the early years of corporate restructuring has become part of the cultural experience of American labor (Hirsch, 1987). Downsizing has proliferated as a tactic for reducing costs, streamlining operations, or changing culture and structure. Yet there is little systematic research on its effects, especially in the long term. And reasons behind its use have changed. Evidence exists that those first firms to use large-scale downsizing did so due to immediate business pressures. But firms who adopted downsizing later did so in part to imitate their competitors and peers. Haunschild (1993) observes that business strategies such as acquisitions escalate when firms' executives serve on boards of directors whose other members are associated with organizations that have previously chosen this strategy. If imitation accounts for a large proportion of the acquisitions that occur, imitation also may account for the widespread use of downsizing. Because downsizing is a frequent aftermath of acquisition, a "me too" quality is probably not surprising.

Keeping up with the competition is a different motivation for altering the contract than is the need to respond to a crisis or severe business downturn. As we discussed in Chapter 6, external justification in the form of business-related reasons is critical to fairness in contracting. But we have reason to believe that rationales acceptable today would have been unacceptable a short time ago. Recall the paragraphs from Chapter 6 in which the photocopy shop owner reduces the wage of an employee after a factory in the area closes and the going wage declines. In the 1980s, people had a consistent answer when asked whether the photocopy shop could justify a wage reduction. Respondents overwhelming said "no." But in the 1990s, representative answers have shifted:

> "Yes, if it makes the shop more competitive."
>
> "It depends on your point of view. Maybe it's not fair to the worker but the owner should be free to set the wage based on the market."
>
> "No, but if the business takes a downturn, yes."

Opinion often differs depending on the industry and the level of the person answering the question. In a group of more than 50 CEOs, 47% said it was fair to cut the wage because it would be better for the business to pay less, regardless of the health of the company. Middle managers in a more traditional industry (i.e., meat packing) argued it was still unfair even today (92%). Context affects our view of commitments—and many features of that context are in flux. We suspect that strategic drift and inchoate searchings for new understandings of the business and the marketplace have left many managers virtually rudderless. When organizations do not know what to do, there is pressure to try anything that produces tangible results. Downsizing does generate immediate results: "On the day that the announcement is made, stock prices generally increase, but then there usually begins a long slow slide" (Cascio, 1993, p. 98). Nonetheless, in one study, two years after downsizing, 10 of 16 stocks were trading below the market by 17% to 48% and 12 were below comparable firms in their industries by 5% to 45% (Dorfman, 1991).

Downsizing begs for more downsizing. The reasons given for downsizing have become less concrete in recent years. In the 1980s, firms downsized to be able to pay huge debt services acquired following an acquisition. Recently, firms have begun to downsize "in anticipation" of continuing competition. Conventional wisdom includes downsizing as an effective management tactic, and changing societal standards support its use. Firms are managing workers as they manage inventories of unsold goods—trying to keep both sets down (Cascio, 1993), an approach termed *kanban employment.* The Japanese term *kanban* refers to just-in-time delivery with no stockpiling or inventorying of resources. Kanban employment, then, redefines the resources labor offers in limited monetizable terms (Friedman, 1988). The reasons given for downsizing signal something about the terms of employment. Cuts taken to save a business can be construed to protect the organization and its people. However, cuts taken simply to better position a firm undercut the value of labor and trivialize the contributions of members. Moreover, they erode the firm's ability to demand high performance contract terms in the future. Fundamental shifts in contracting follow from the proliferation of downsizing.

Loss of Voluntariness. Much emphasis is placed on the freedom of contracts, the rights of individuals and of organizations to enter into agreements of their choosing. In times of great change, when contract breach is more likely, we risk loss of that freedom. Restructurings in organizations result in a loss of voluntariness when the jobs employees are left with are not the ones they chose to accept. We have discussed how contract change requires acceptance, which is promoted by an emphasis on choice. But in unstable climates there may be little choice.

Adult-adult relationships are based on choice, commitments freely offered and accepted. But in transitions, it is likely that many employment arrangements do not have the force of a contract, because changes may take place without the consent of those affected by them. Terms of employment are created without the possibility of the employee leaving the firm when those conditions are altered so as to become undesirable.

Loss of voluntariness at work is likely to cause people to seek broader fulfillment outside of organizations. The "organization man" William Foote Whyte (1956) described may no longer be exclusively male or particularly organizational. Traditional models of employment supported by a society are intertwined with beliefs about what constitutes a successful life, lifestyles, and opportunities. Many people have resisted letting go of the seeming ideal of lifetime work with one employer (Mirvis & Hall, 1994). As a consequence, when moved laterally, laid off, or retired early, they experience a loss of status or employment in relational terms (seduced, betrayed, jilted, and abandoned). This disillusionment slides into cynicism (Kanter & Mirvis, 1989). In the future, they lower expectations and commitments to an employer, keep their emotions in check, and in this manner shield themselves from disappointment and avoid getting "burned" again. Families and friends witness the toll (Williams, 1989). One move has been toward the boundaryless career in which loyalty is to one's work and/or coworkers but not to the organization. Many consultants, for instance, already pursue these careers. Others may have reached their limit in their quest for stimulation at work and now seek satisfaction in other areas of life (Mirvis & Hall, 1994).

In many organizations within certain industries in particular (e.g., oil, telecommunication), the arrangements that exist between organizations and members hardly resemble a contract at all. Protracted changes in structure and personnel over a period of years can occur when business strategy is itself in transition and top management has as yet no workable model of the future. The telecommunication industry, particularly former AT&T affiliates, has been in transition for over a decade after the breakup of that corporation. Local operating companies and the new organizational forms emerging continue to struggle with the new competition. New performance demands in the 1980s followed by waves of early retirements and downsizings have left many units with a transitional contract in which no real performance terms exist to guide employee effort.

As one information systems manager in a telecommunication firm put it:

> We have been solving the same set of problems over and over every few years . . . cut costs, consolidate activities. Now they tell us the trend in the industry is to outsource IS (information systems). But we're still here. What's next? I'd just like to know what I should be doing.

The new transitional contract is a quasi contract. No employee volunteered to be part of the deal, and no performance terms exist, specific or otherwise. Rising cynicism about organizations and employment opportunities results from

1. Erosion of rewards and incentives derived from employment
2. Escalating losses (e.g., security, information, control)
3. Inconsistent messages from erstwhile contract makers
4. No clear model of the future

OUT OF TRANSITION: TRENDS TO NEW CONTRACTING

There are signs of a new motivation in the workforce. Maccoby (1988) describes the "self-developer" who wants not only to master a skill but also to explore and play; he or she seeks knowledge but also balance between work and other life pursuits. Mirvis and Hall (1994) hypothesize that people's core identities may be enlarged by incorporating a commitment to their *life's work,* which reflects not only job and career but also work as a spouse, parent, and community member. Social networks may be more a focus for identification than organizations are. Though voluntariness in organizations has been lost for many, the desire for control and participation remains and finds new forms of exercise.

At the individual level, there are several features that continue to promote contracting despite a turbulent environment:

- *Development in the workforce:* Higher education levels, especially the increased professionalization of the workforce, create individuals who themselves initiate contract making. Individuals who have expectations and skills for self-determination are better able to negotiate their employment conditions both with organizations at hire and with their superiors and colleagues on the job. Graen and Scandura (1987) demonstrate that managers supervise highly skilled and well-motivated workers differently than their less able counterparts, an indicator that active individual contract making is at work among the highly qualified segment of the workforce.
- *Self-determinism:* To the extent that work takes places outside of traditional organizational roles, particularly in the form of independent contracting arrangements (Office of Technology Assessment, 1985; Rousseau & Wade-Benzoni, 1994), individuals need to develop their own idiosyncratic contracts with those parties (other individuals as well as firms) who employ their services. Individuals working outside of traditional organizations will become more skilled contract makers to substitute for their loss of internal organizational contract makers.
- *Increasingly complex work/family demands:* The expansion of the female workforce has created tremendous concern regarding the issues surrounding workers as parents. Organizations are often more willing to make accommodations to working parents who are female than they are for their male counterparts (Klein, 1994). Women lawyers requesting flexible schedules to accommodate child care receive more supportive reactions than do men, thus creating more idiosyncratic employment arrangements for these working women. The merger of one set of social expectations (women as

primary child care givers) with another (responsible employee) may create more current options for women than men. Of course, an emerging social change emphasizing joint parenting could extend to males the trend toward family-based idiosyncratic work arrangements.

- *Ongoing needs for predictability, control, and voice:* Contracts as a basis for social relationships occur in societies where individual autonomy and self-expression are valued. Despite upheavals at work, many social beliefs regarding the self and personal agency remain unchanged. Too, in times of great uncertainty, arrangements for achieving greater control, predictability, and voice have their greatest value. Individual workers will continue to seek benefits through contracting and perhaps more frequently will assert themselves to have greater say in creating idiosyncratic contract terms.

Those organizations that depend on internalized employee values to yield a high rate of service or innovation cannot function without a committed workforce. Workable contracts are the bedrock of commitment. In these respects, there are several *organizational trends* that promote contracts:

- *Competitive advantages in recruiting and retention:* To be an employer of choice for the most skilled and therefore most sought after workers involves offering more opportunities and benefits over longer terms than one's competitors (Gerhart & Milkovich, 1992). Handy (1989) describes the advantages to organizations of a stable, highly skilled, culturally integrated workforce of "core" employees. Employment provisions also offer core workers greater development, autonomy, and benefits than typically available to their peripheral counterparts.
- *Emphasis on service-oriented cultures:* Those sectors of the economy valuing close customer relations and substantial service functions will require employees socialized into service-oriented norms and values, with deep expertise and knowledge to respond flexibly to customer demands. More elaborate contracts with implicit as well as explicit terms are required to provide service.
- *Recognition of labor-management tension in the postmerger and acquisition era* manifested by government, business, and academic leaders: In 1994, the Commission on the Future of Worker-Management Relations created by President Bill Clinton proclaimed a crisis (stagnant wages, high unemployment, and lax response to global competition) and called for a new framework for worker-management relations ("A Call," 1994) to create more trust, innovation, and efficiency. Whether or not government succeeds in creating a new worker-management framework, organizations are recognizing the need.

■ *Expanded legal rights* that uphold or clarify obligations of employee and employer (Voluck & Hanlon, 1987): Recognition of job property rights in many states gives legal standing to relational contract terms. Plant closing laws, though seldom enforced, give moral standing to good faith and fair dealing principles.

Together, these trends give rise to additions and amendments to collective understandings of what employment involves. Burack (1993, pp. 151-154) argues for trends in what is an increasingly shared new contract. Its provisions between responsive, successful corporations and their members include the following:

- Customer/client needs as driving force of company actions
- Balance between short- and long-run considerations
- Flexibility as essential to being a learning organization
- Employee-employer relations built on adult-adult attitudes and responsibilities as a basis for a trustful, cooperative relationship

Such widespread contract terms are likely to be linked to specific industries (e.g., consumer products, professional service firms) and related professions (e.g., marketing) where discretionary behavior on the part of employees creates competitive advantage.

CHANGING THE RULES: NEW CRITERIA FOR FAIRNESS

Changes in social contracts alter the standards by which events are gauged (Figure 8.2). If risks are now more equally distributed between workers and organizations (their owners or stockholders), people generally might develop different views of what employees are entitled to during economic downturns or under escalating competitive pressures. Losses that previously were unacceptable, such as threats to job security and a stable income, might be more tolerable or, better put, tolerated. Shifting social contracts also create a new frame of reference for those firms that would be an "employer of choice" for the best qualified candidates. Firms offering development and advancement may be less common and therefore they can stand out among their competition. Changing standards have different implications for the experiences of individuals and groups as well as for witnesses and outside observers. Victims and observers each use distinct metrics for evaluating what is fair.

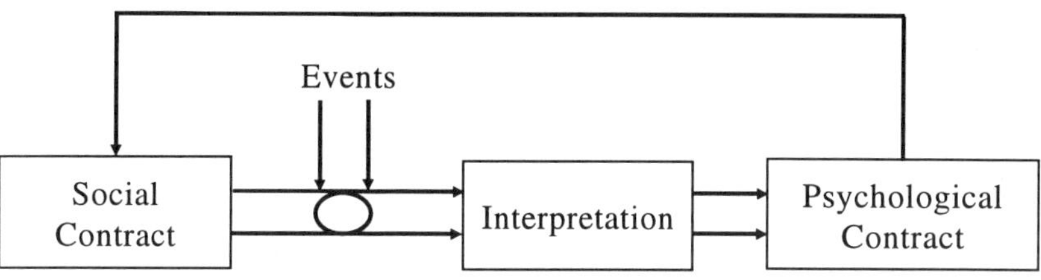

FIGURE 8.2. Linking the Social and the Psychological Contracts

When contracts change, fairness is difficult to evaluate because there are not necessarily single outcomes. Changing promotion requirements to emphasize faculty research in a traditionally teaching-oriented university can generate very different reactions. The decision may seem fair and reasonable to new faculty recruited from major research institutions and also fair to members of the broader academic community outside this university who compare this school's practices with those of their own. But most current faculty at this university may resent its new demands, particularly if their teaching requirements remain substantial and the support they receive for research is minimal (e.g., no released time from teaching for research activities or little funding). Some outcomes are valued (at least by some people): enhanced university reputation and career opportunities for highly trained research faculty. Other outcomes are not: higher work load, poor performance on new criteria, lower esteem and peer regard, and frustration in adjusting to changing standards. Multiple outcomes can yield divergent points of view regarding what is fair. In the psychological contracts of individuals, the normative contracts of groups, and the implied contracts of outsiders, fairness is defined differently.

Psychological Contract. The saying "what is past is prologue" applies in individual-level psychological contracting. We make predictions regarding what will happen in the future based on past experience. Because the contracts individuals hold are a present image of the past, recent events, especially salient and memorable ones, can redefine past experience. New interpretations for old terms are a primary consequence of the changing context of contracts. Precedent (what other similar persons and firms have done) changes standards by altering expectations regarding the probability of events. Because of changing standards, old contract terms have new meanings;

long term could be 20 years or 20 months. Losses involved in changes can also appear to be smaller when they are less of a surprise. Thus a person's second layoff may not involve the same psychological costs as the first one did. Even the economic costs might be lower if the laid-off person has learned to set money aside "just in case." Even if the victim didn't think to do this, third parties might think he or she was foolish not to do so. In sum, psychological contracts held by individuals are shaped by past experience, and criteria of fairness shift with changes in interpretation.

Normative Contract. Normative contracts are schemas that connect people and give them a common understanding of events (Resnick, 1991). When group members hold common beliefs, they tend to see what they expect to see ("believing is seeing"; Weick, 1992). Based on social consensus, such beliefs are likely to be highly resistant to change, even under dramatically new circumstances. Normative contracts lead groups to filter out information that doesn't fit existing beliefs and to organize new information in stereotypical ways. When shared expectations are realized in group perceptions, the confirmation bias exists (e.g., Buckhout, 1982). Confirmation bias, the propensity to affirm prior interpretations and discount, ignore, or reinterpret evidence counter to those interpretations, tends to keep groups from exploring alternative possibilities. Normative contracts are likely to develop in work groups with longer histories, more stable and homogeneous memberships, higher outcome interdependence, and greater cohesion.

Change in the criteria by which group members gauge the normative contract is likely to come about under conditions similar to those associated with cultural change: the addition of new members and the disruption of existing social networks. The entry of recruits different than traditional incumbents causes the normative contract to change. An influx of new members can erode established contracts and create new interpretations for organizational events. Introducing new members whose contracts differ from those of veterans can erode the consensus that creates normative contracts. Similarly, changes that move people away from traditional roles and relationships shift the networks in which they are embedded and alter the way information is socially processed. Normative contract change is likely when new networks are created, often the case after downsizing and restructuring (Pradhan Shah, 1994).

Implied Contract. The social construction outsiders make of the agreement between the employee and employer is the implied contract. Third parties looking into an employment relationship tend to use externalities as a benchmark. What is typical, representative, or precedent setting? New precedents redefine the rules for fairness groups, communities, and society in general. We know that socially processed information takes forms different than individual interpretations. Being an outsider rather than a principal to a relationship makes available different information to use in formulating judgments. The new rules outsiders use, as members of juries or the general public, will be based on available precedent not only in the specific employment relationship gauged but also in their own circumstances and as portrayed in vividly available information on "typical" situations. When terms like *disposable worker* and *free agent* become cultural motifs, they shape both legislative and case law as well as broader social notions of what is "reasonable to expect" (Bok, 1978). As implied contracts come to be understood differently, by juries or by the public, fairness criteria shift for contracts in general.

RESTORING VOLUNTARINESS: NEW CONTRACT MAKING

Organizational upheavals are typically transitions between one equilibrium and another. Contemporary writers caution that change is becoming a way of life (Davis, 1987; Kanter, 1989). The legacy of a decade of downsizing, restructuring, and protracted strategic drift may be a critical mass of workers who place little faith in would-be organizational contract makers. Creating contracts that yield value-adding worker behavior and appropriate organizational support is one mechanism for creating or restoring a sense of confidence, competence, and common purpose.

Despite forecasts of unending turbulence, some sort of new balance in employment relations is needed for organizations to innovate, learn, and serve their constituents. When organizations can build contracts, they are able to add value, retain knowledge, and engender willingness to contribute. A workable contract creates wealth (Schleifer & Summers, 1988). We have made a case for ways in which contract *terms* might change. But fundamentally organizations must enhance their *contracting capability,* that is, their ability to make and keep strategically appropriate psychological contracts with their workers. We need new contract making. To make new contracts, voluntariness must be brought back into organizations.

Voluntariness means there are choices. The striking feature of contemporary employment relations is their *variety.* Not only do we now differentiate between core and peripheral employment (Handy, 1989) but we see consultants (some once "retired"), freelancers, and networked workers, working parents who align their day with their children's, and people who stay home to care for kids or write a novel. Employment in any given organization increasingly suggests a very big tent covering a variety of loose/tight, broad/focused forms of involvement. Voluntariness derives from using this variety to the advantage of both the people and the organization. Unfortunately, many organizations have become more explicitly coercive, urging their employees to take it or leave. Greater participation in generating and choosing between assignments, schedules, and distributed responsibilities can help both organization and individual deal with changing demands.

Upheavals have not only rewritten organization-related views of employment. Individuals, in large numbers, have reexamined their model of career success. Reexamining career aspirations causes people to look to other sources of psychological success or else risk feeling disappointment and a sense of failure (Mirvis & Hall, 1994). Findings from a recent survey showed that a majority of American workers rate the effect of a job on their personal and family life as "very important" in making employment decisions—far more so than wages, benefits, and even job security (Galinsky & Friedman, 1993). But setting new standards of success can be complicated for working people asked to do more at work while simultaneously striving for personal development and being pressed by the demands of change, family, home, and community. What must become clearer is the array of choices possible. At present, identifying the scope of these decisions is complicated by a dearth of role models.

Rather than encourage a lonely life of reading self-help books and taking self-assessment tests, we look to the notion of new schemas for careers and relationships that offer opportunities, stimuli, involvement, and networks that people can use to remake themselves and redefine their standards for personal success. As old assumptions are unfrozen, we can fuel the transition by voicing the questions they raise, about critical skills, meaningful work, interdependence with colleagues and clients, and readiness for the future.

For organizations, a critical question is how to create a culture more open to alternative career paths (Hall, 1993). Hall offers a number of recommendations. Engaging top management in the examination of the required career culture is a first step. In a related vein, top management benchmarking can be persuasive, given that executives learn new ideas from exposure to board members from different organizations. Experimenting with alternative career path moves on a trial basis can open up possibilities. This is especially effective if the first people given the opportunity for nontraditional moves are viewed by the organization as high performers. The human resource (HR) department could provide better support in creating alternatives by using an HR information system to monitor employee interests in alternatives. The HR department could also assess the impact of alternatives on individual performance and organizational results.

For individuals, Mirvis and Hall (1994) suggest several possibilities: substituting work and work group loyalty for organizational identification, having several careers over a lifetime, taking career breaks for family or personal development. They argue that new career options opening up boundaries around work also open up boundaries of identity. The frequently asked question at parties in middle-class America, "Who do you work for?" may be replaced by the question, "What's going on in your life?" reflecting a recognition that answers to that question will change, and often. A boundaryless career in a shamrock organization might have an individual working in core areas for a time, taking a job with a supplier company or consulting firm, followed by a stint as an individual contractor on selected projects, and then finally returning to the fold as a senior core contributor and mentor.

We expect that individuals with more complete knowledge of their valued skills will assume more responsibility for managing their employment contracts. Rather than defer the contract-making process to recruiters and managers, individuals will foster more workable contracts through personal initiative and feedback seeking, thus creating broader trust and a zone of acceptance on the part of their employer.

IMPLICATIONS

All contracts are gauged by the standards of their time (Atiyah, 1981). Societal values give rise to the meaning of promises (binding commitments or "mere words"). In a broad sense, society shapes contracting through the entitlements and responsibilities incumbent on its members. Etzioni (1993) argues that there is no such thing as a right (e.g., freedom of speech) without responsibility (e.g., to not do harm).[4] A contract is in essence an agreement to be bound to both rights and responsibilities. Debates about how the risk of doing business should be distributed or how personal, family, and professional life intertwine will always take place in the context of contract making and change.

What we need to do now is to use the concept of contract more realistically. To do so, we must further develop and apply a behavioral understanding of contracts. Much of the difficulty in understanding how contracts operate in everyday work settings has come from exaggerating the apparently objective features of contracts and undervaluing how contract parties actually think and behave. Contracts, we have seen, are rich in assumptions as well as facts, uncertainty as well as predictability. Balancing these makes it possible for organizations and persons to operate more effectively. Contracts are a way for both groups to know and create the future.

NOTES

1. A good deal of contract theory is undersocialized; that is, it ignores the context in which exchanges are made (consistent with Granovetter's, 1985, critique of transaction cost economics). Institutionalists have an oversocialized view, that forces in the environment are inevitable causes of individual and organizational experiences (see Davis & Powell, 1992, for a review). In the present development of a behavioral theory of contracts, we seek a balance.

2. Reprinted from *And the Wolf Finally Came: The Decline of the American Steel Industry*, by John P. Hoerr, by permission of The University of Pittsburgh Press. © 1988 by University of Pittsburgh Press.

3. Christopher Jencks (1993) implicates the changing labor market, both its shrinking and the type of employment available, for the rising homelessness. Jencks recalls the 1950s when flophouses were still in business. Inhabitants could stand on a corner and be picked up to do a day's work. "You can't wait for Ronald McDonald to pick you up," he said of the abundance of fast-food restaurant jobs requiring workers to be present consistently ("Housing Not," 1993, p. 164). Here the demise of a particular type of employment relationship (unskilled day labor) contributed to a pervasive societal problem.

4. However, there can be very loose connections between what entitlements and the efforts of recipients offer. When entitlements are not contingent on responsibilities, one-sided obligations result and risks are distributed unequally with returns. When entitlements are closely tied to fulfillment of membership conditions and performance terms, there may be more stability. Current debates about welfare and workfare wrestle with aspects of the social contract and how closely tied rights and responsibilities might be.

References

Abitia, E. A. (1986). *Los valores de los Mexicanos* (Vol. 1). Mexico City: Banamex.

Abitia, E. A. (1991). *Los valores de los Mexicanos* (Vol. 2). Mexico City: Banamex.

A call for easing labor-management tensions. (1994, May 30). *New York Times,* pp. 33, 34.

Alchian, A. A., & Demsetz, H. (1972). Production, information costs, and economic organization. *American Economic Review, 62,* 777-795.

Allen, R., & Keaveny, T. (1981). Correlates of faculty interests in unionization: A replication and extension. *Journal of Applied Psychology, 66,* 582-588.

Ancona, D. G., & Caldwell, D. F. (1992). Bridging the boundary: External activity and performance in organizational teams. *Administrative Science Quarterly, 37,* 634-666.

Anderson, E., & Weitz, B. (1992). The use of pledges to sustain commitment in distribution channels. *Journal of Marketing Research, 29,* 18-34.

Anderson, J. C., & Narus, J. A. (1990). A model of distribution and firm working partnerships. *Journal of Marketing, 48,* 62-74.

An end to a law firm that defined a type. (1994, February 7). *New York Times,* pp. A1, B4.

Argyris, C., & Schön, D. (1978). *Organizational learning: A theory of action perspective.* Reading, MA: Addison-Wesley.

Arthur, M. (1994). The boundaryless career: A new perspective for organizational inquiry. *Journal of Organizational Behavior, 15,* 295-306.

Ashford, S. J. (1986). Feedback seeking as an individual adaptation: A resource perspective for creating information. *Academy of Management Journal, 29,* 465-487.

Ashford, S. J., & Cummings, L. L. (1983). Feedback as an individual resource: Personal strategies of creating information. *Organizational Behavior and Human Performance, 32,* 370-398.

Atiyah, P. S. (1981). *Promises, morals and law.* Oxford: Clarendon.

Barksdale, K., & Shore, L. M. (1993). *A comparison of the Meyer and Allen and O'Reilly and Chatman models of organizational commitment* (Working paper). Atlanta: Georgia State University.

Barnard, C. (1938). *Functions of the executive.* Cambridge, MA: Harvard University Press.

Bartlett's familiar quotations (6th ed.). (1980). New York: Little, Brown.

Bartunek, J. M. (1988). The dynamics of personal and organizational reframing. In R. E. Quinn & K. S. Cameron (Eds.), *Paradox and transformation: Toward a theory of change in organization and management* (pp. 137-162). Cambridge, MA: Ballinger.

Bartunek, J. M., Gordon, J. R., & Weathersby, R. P. (1983). Developing complicated understandings in administration. *Academy of Management Review, 8,* 273-284.

Bartunek, J. M., & Moch, M. K. (1987). First order, second order, and third order change and organization development interventions: A cognitive approach. *Journal of Applied Behavioral Science, 23,* 483-500.

Baxter, L., & Wilmot, W. (1984). Secret tests: Social strategies for acquiring information about the state of relationships. *Human Communication Research, 11,* 171-201.

Bazerman, M. H. (1985). Norms of distributive justice in interest arbitration. *Industrial and Labor Relations Review, 38,* 558-570.

Belous, R. (1989, March). How human resource systems adjust to the shift toward contingent workers. *Monthly Labor Review,* pp. 7-12.

Bettis, R. A., Bradley, S. P., & Hamel, G. (1992). Outsourcing and industrial decline. *Academy of Management Executive, 6,* 7-22.

Bhagat, R. S., Kedia, B. L., Crawford, S. E., & Kaplan, M. R. (1990). Cross-cultural issues in organizational psychology: Emergent trends and directions for research in the 1990s. In C. L. Cooper & I. T. Robertson (Eds.), *International review of industrial and organizational psychology* (Vol. 5, pp. 59-98). New York: Wiley.

Bies, R. J., & Moag, J. S. (1986). Interactional justice: Communication criteria of fairness. In M. H. Bazerman, R. Lewicki, & B. Sheppard (Eds.), *Research on negotiations in organizations* (Vol. 1, pp. 43-55). Greenwich, CT: JAI Press.

Bies, R. J., & Shapiro, D. L. (1993). Interactional fairness judgements: The influence of causal accounts. *Social Justice Research, 1,* 199-218.

Bies, R. J., & Tyler, T. R. (1993). The "litigation mentality" in organizations: A test of alternative psychological explanations. *Organization Science, 4,* 352-366.

Birnbaum, M. H. (1983). Perceived equity of salary policies. *Journal of Applied Psychology, 68,* 49-59.

Bok, S. (1978). *Lying: Moral choice in public and private life.* New York: Random House.

Booth, A., & Chaterji, M. (1989). Redundancy payments and firm-specific training. *Econometrika, 56,* 505-521.

Bradshaw, D. A., & Deacon, L. V. M. (1985, November). Wrongful discharge: The tip of the iceberg. *Personnel Administration,* pp. 74-76.

Bridges, W. (1991). *Managing transitions: Making the most of change.* Reading, MA: Addison-Wesley.

Brockner, J. (1988). The effects of work layoffs on survivors: Research, theory, and practice. *Research in Organizational Behavior, 10,* 213-255.

Brown, C., & Medoff, J. (1989). The employer size-wage effect. *Journal of Political Economy, 97,* 1027-1053.

Brown v. Safeway Stores, Inc., 190 F. Supp. 295 (1960).

Brunstein, I. (1992). Human resource management in France. *Employee Relations, 14*(4), 53-70.

Buckhout, R. (1982). Eyewitness testimony. In U. Neisser (Ed.), *Memory observed: Remembering in natural contexts* (pp. 116-125). San Francisco: Freeman.

Bull, C. (1987). The existence of self-enforcing implicit contracts. *Quarterly Journal of Economics, 102,* 147-159.

Burack, E. (1993). *Corporate resurgence and the new employment relationships.* Westport, CT: Quorum.

Buroway, M. (1979). *Manufacturing consent: Changes in the labor process under monopoly capitalism.* Chicago: University of Chicago.

Cameron, K. S., Freeman, S. J., & Mishra, A. K. (1991). Best practices in white collar downsizing: Managing contradictions. *Academy of Management Executive, 5*(3), 57-73.

Capelli, P., & Scherer, P. D. (1990). Assessing worker attitudes under a two-tiered wage plan. *Industrial and Labor Relations Review, 43,* 225-244.

Carruth, G., & Ehrlich, E. (Eds.). (1988). *The Harper book of American quotations.* New York: Harper.

Carter, J. (1977, January 20). [Inaugural address]. Washington, DC.

Cascio, W. (1993). Downsizing: What do we know? What have we learned? *Academy of Management Executive, 7,* 95-104.

Castanzias, R. P., & Helfat, C. E. (1991). Managerial resources and rents. *Journal of Management, 17,* 115-171.

Castro, J. (1993, March 29). Disposable workers. *Time, 141*(13), 42-47.

Clark, M. S., & Reis, H. T. (1988). Interpersonal processes in close relationships. *Annual Review of Psychology, 39,* 609-672.

Cowherd, D. M., & Levine, D. I. (1992). Product quality and pay equity between lower-level employees and top management: An investigation of distributive justice theory. *Administrative Science Quarterly, 37,* 302-320.

Davidcw, W., & Malone, M. (1992). *The virtual corporation.* New York: Harper.

Davis, G. F., & Powell, W. W. (1992). Organization-environment relations. In M. Dunnette & L. Hough (Eds.), *Handbook of industrial and organizational psychology* (Vol. 3, pp. 315-375, 2nd ed.). Palo Alto, CA: Consulting Psychologists Press.

Davis, S. (1987). *Future perfect.* Reading, MA: Addison-Wesley.

Davis, S. M., & Lawrence, P. R. (1977). *Matrix.* Reading, MA: Addison-Wesley.

Davis-Blake, A., & Uzzi, B. (1993). Determinants of employment externalization: The case of temporary workers and independent contractors. *Administrative Science Quarterly, 29,* 195-223.

Dickson, D. (1974). *The politics of alternative technology.* New York: Universe.

Dienschen, R. M., & Liden, R. C. (1986). Leader-member exchange model of leadership: A critique and further development. *Academy of Management Review, 11,* 618-634.

DiMaggio, P. J., & Powell, W. W. (1983). The iron cage revisited: Institutional isomorphism and collective rationality in organizational fields. *American Sociological Review, 48,* 147-160.

Dorfman, J. R. (1991, December 10). Stocks of companies announcing layoffs fire up investors: Best prices often wilt. *Wall Street Journal,* pp. C1, C3.

Edelman, L. B. (1990). Legal environments and organizational governance: The expansion of due process in the American workplace. *American Journal of Sociology, 95,* 1401-1440.

Etzioni, A. (1993). *The spirit of community: Rights, responsibilities and the communitarian agenda.* New York: Crown.

Farrell, D. (1983). Exit, voice, loyalty and neglect as responses to job dissatisfaction: A multi-dimensional scaling study. *Academy of Management Journal, 26,* 596-607.

Fiske, S. T., & Taylor, S. E. (1984). *Social cognition.* Reading, MA: Addison-Wesley.

Florida, R., & Kenney, M. (1991). Transplanted organizations: The transfer of Japanese industrial organizations to the U.S. *American Sociological Review, 56,* 381-398.

Foa, U. G., & Foa, E. B. (1974). *Societal structures of the mind.* Springfield, IL: Charles C Thomas.

Folbre, N. R., Leighton, J. L., & Roderick, M. R. (1984). Plant closings and their regulation in Maine, 1971-1982. *Industrial and Labor Relations Review, 37,* 195.

Folger, R. (1977). Distributive and procedural justice: Combined impact of "voice" and improvement on experienced inequity. *Journal of Personality and Social Psychology, 35,* 2253-2261.

Folger, R., & Bies, R. J. (1989). Managerial responsibilities and procedural justice. *Employee Rights and Responsibilities Journal, 2,* 79-90.

Forbes, F. S., & Jones, I. M. (1986). A comparative, attitudinal, and analytical study of dismissals of at-will employees without cause. *Labor Law Journal, 37,* 157-166.

Frank, R. H., Gilovich, T., & Regan, D. T. (1993). Does studying economies inhibit cooperation? *Journal of Economic Perspectives, 7,* 159-171.

Freeman, R. B., & Medoff, J. L. (1984). *What do unions do?* New York: Basic Books.

Frey, B. S. (1993). Does monitoring increase work effort? The rivalry with trust and loyalty. *Economic Inquiry, 31,* 663-670.

Friedman, D. (1988). *The misunderstood miracle: Industrial development and political change in Japan.* Ithaca, NY: Cornell University Press.

Galinsky, E., & Friedman, D. (1993). *National study of the changing workforce.* New York: Families and Work Institute.

Gerhart, B., & Milkovich, G. T. (1990). Organizational differences in managerial compensation and performance. *Academy of Management Journal, 33,* 663-691.

Gerhart, B., & Milkovich, G. T. (1992). Employee compensation: Research and practice. In M. D. Dunnette & L. M. Hough (Eds.), *Handbook of industrial and organizational psychology* (pp. 481-569, 2nd ed.). Palo Alto, CA: Consulting Psychologists Press.

Getman, J., Goldberg, S., & Herman, J. (1976). *Union representation elections: Law and reality.* New York: Russell Sage.

Gioia, D. (1986). The state of the art in organizational social cognitions: A personal view. In H. P. Sims Jr. & D. A. Gioia (Eds.), *The thinking organization: The dynamics of organizational social cognition* (pp. 336-356). San Francisco: Jossey-Bass.

Goffman, E. (1974). *Frame analysis.* Cambridge, MA: Harvard University Press.

Gomez-Meijia, L. R., & Balkin, D. B. (1989). Effectiveness of individual and aggregate compensation strategies. *Industrial Relations, 28,* 431-445.

Goodman, P. S. (1979). *Assessing organizational change.* New York: Wiley.

Goodman, P., & Salipante, P. (1976). Organizational rewards and the retention of the hard-core unemployed. *Journal of Applied Psychology, 61,* 12-21.

Gouldner, A. W. (1960). The norm of reciprocity. *American Sociological Review, 25,* 165-167.

Graen, G., & Scandura, T. (1987). Toward a psychology of dyadic organizing. In L. L. Cummings & B. M. Staw (Eds.), *Research in organizational behavior* (Vol. 9, pp. 175-208). Greenwich, CT: JAI Press.

Granovetter, M. (1985). Economic action and social structure: The problem of embeddedness. *American Journal of Sociology, 91,* 481-510.

Greenberg, J. (1992). *Creating unfairness by mandating fair procedures: The hidden hazards of a pay-for-performance plan.* Unpublished manuscript, Ohio State University, Columbus.

Greenberg, J., Bies, R. J., & Eskew, D. E. (1991). Establishing fairness in the eye of the beholder: Managing impressions of organizational justice. In R. A. Giacalone & P. Rosenfeld (Eds.), *Applying impression management: How image making affects organization* (pp. 111-135). Newbury Park, CA: Sage.

Greenwald, A. G. (1980). The totalitarian ego: Fabrication and revision of personal history. *American Psychologist, 35,* 603-618.

Gundry, L. R., & Rousseau, D. M. (1994). Communicating culture to newcomers. *Human Relations, 47,* 1068-1088.

Guzzo, R. A., & Noonan, K. A. (1994). Human resource practices as communications and the psychological contract. *Human Resources Management, 33,* 447-462.

Guzzo, R. A., Noonan, K. A., & Elron, E. (1994). Expatriate managers and the psychological contract. *Journal of Applied Psychology, 79,* 617-626.

Hall, D. T. (1993, March). *The "new career contract": Alternative career paths.* Paper presented at the Fourth German Business Congress on Human Resources, Cologne.

Handy, C. (1989). *The age of unreason.* Cambridge, MA: Harvard Business School Press.

Harrison, B. (1984, June). Plant closures: Efforts to cushion the blow. *Monthly Labor Review,* pp. 41-43.

Harvard Business School. (1990). *Peter Browning and Continental White Cap (A)* (Case No. 9-486-090). Cambridge, MA: Author.

Haunschild, P. R. (1993). Interorganizational imitation: The impact of corporate acquisition activity. *Administrative Science Quarterly, 38,* 564-592.

Heilbrun, C. (1973). *Toward a recognition of androgyny.* New York: Knopf.

Heskett, J. L., Sasser, W. E., & Hart, W. L. (1990). *Service breakthroughs: Changing the rules of the game.* New York: Free Press.

Hirsch, P. M. (1987). *Pack your own parachute.* Reading, MA: Addison-Wesley.

Hirsch, P. M. (1994). Undoing the managerial revolution? Needed research on the decline of middle management and internal labor markets. In R. Swedberg (Ed.), *Economic sociology.* New York: Russell Sage.

Hirsch, P. M., & Kreimelmeyer, W. (1993). *Changing labor markets.* Unpublished manuscript, Northwestern University, Department of Sociology.

Hirschhorn, L., & Gilmore, T. (1992, May-June). The new "boundaryless" company. *Harvard Business Review,* pp. 104-115.

Hirschman, A. O. (1970). *Exit, voice, and loyalty.* Cambridge, MA: Harvard University Press.

Hoerr, J. P. (1988). *The wolf finally came: The decline of the American steel industry.* Pittsburgh, PA: University of Pittsburgh Press.

Housing not a key factor in homelessness. (1993, March 11). *Pioneer Press,* p. 164.

Huddleston, J. N., Jr. (1990). *Gaijin Kaisha: Running a foreign business in Japan.* Tokyo: Tuttle.

Huseman, R., Hatfield, J., & Miles, E. (1987). A new perspective on equity theory: The equity sensitivity construct. *Academy of Management Review, 12,* 222-234.

Hussey, D. E. (1985). Implementing corporate strategy: Using management education and training. *Long Range Planning, 18*(5), 28-37.

In her majesty's service, but without free soap. (1993, October 2). *New York Times,* p. 6.

Jackson, S. L., Schuler, R. S., & Rivero, J. C. (1989). Organizational characteristics as predictors of personnel practices. *Personal Psychology, 42,* 727-786.

Jencks, C. (1993). *The homeless.* Cambridge, MA: Harvard University Press.

Kahneman, D., Knetch, J. L., & Thaler, R. H. (1986). Fairness as a constraint of profit-seeking: Entitlements in the market. *American Economic Review, 76,* 728-741.

Kahneman, D., & Tversky, A. (1979). Prospect theory: An analysis of decision under risk. *Econometrika, 47,* 263-291.

Kanfer, F. H., Cox, L. E., Griner, J. M., & Karoly, P. (1974). Contracts, demand characteristics and self control. *Journal of Personality and Social Psychology, 30,* 605-619.

Kanfer, F. H., & Karoly, P. (1972a). Self-control: A behavioral excursion into the lion's den. *Behavior Therapy, 3,* 398-416.

Kanfer, F. H., & Karoly, P. (1972b). Self-regulation and its clinical application: Some additional considerations. In R. C. Johnson, P. R. Dukecki, & O. H. Mowrer (Eds.), *Conscience, contract and social reality.* New York: Holt, Rinehart & Winston.

Kanter, D. L., & Mirvis, P. H. (1989). *The cynical Americans.* San Francisco: Jossey-Bass.

Kanter, R. M. (1977). *Men and women of the corporation.* New York: Basic Books.

Kanter, R. M. (1989). *When giants learn to dance.* New York: Simon & Schuster.

Kaufmann, P. J., & Stern, L. W. (1988). Relational exchange norms, perceptions of unfairness, and retained hostility in commercial litigation. *Journal of Conflict Resolution, 32,* 534-552.

Kearns, D. T., & Nadler, D. A. (1992). *Prophets in the dark: How Xerox reinvented itself and beat back the Japanese.* New York: HarperCollins.

Kelly, M. R., & Harrison, B. (1992). Unions, technology, and labor-management cooperation. In L. Mishel & P. B. Voos (Eds.), *Unions and economic competitiveness* (pp. 247-286). New York: M. E. Sharpe.

Kerr, S. (1975). On the folly of rewarding A while hoping for B. *Academy of Management Journal, 18,* 769-783.

Klein, K. (1994). *A policy capturing study of implied contracts.* Unpublished manuscript, University of Maryland.

Kochan, T., Katz, H., & McKersie, R. (1986). *The transformation of American industrial relations.* New York: Basic Books.

Kovach, K. A. (1987, September-October). What motivates employees? Workers and supervisors give different answers. *Business Horizons,* p. 61.

Kozlowski, S. W. J., Chao, G. T., Smith, B. M., & Hedlund, J. (1993). Organizational downsizing: Strategies, interventions, and research implications. In C. Cooper & I. Robertson (Eds.), *International review of industrial and organizational psychology.* New York: Wiley.

Lashinsky, A. (1993, March 8). When the bond breaks: A generation of managers face job cuts. *Crain's Chicago Business,* pp. 15, 17-18.

Latham, G. P., & Saari, L. M. (1979). Importance of supportive relationships in goal-setting. *Journal of Applied Psychology, 64,* 151-156.

Levine, J. M., & Moreland, R. L. (1987). Social comparison and outcome evaluation in group contexts. In J. C. Masters & W. P. Smith (Eds.), *Social comparison, social justice, and relative deprivation: Theoretical, empirical and policy perspectives* (pp. 105-127). Hillsdale, NJ: Lawrence Erlbaum.

Levinson, H. (1962). *Organizational diagnosis.* Cambridge, MA: Harvard University Press.

Levinthal, D. (1988). A survey of agency models of organizations. *Journal of Economic Behavior and Organization, 9,* 153-185.

Levitan, S. A., & Conway, E. (1988). *Part-time employment: Living on half rations.* Washington, DC: George Washington University, Center for Social Policy Studies.

Lind, E. A., & Tyler, T. R. (1988). *The social psychology of procedural justice.* New York: Plenum.

Locke, E. A. (1978). The ubiquity of the technique of goal setting in theories and approaches. *Academy of Management Review, 3,* 594-601.

Locke, E. A., Shaw, K. N., Saari, L. M., & Latham, G. P. (1981). Goal setting and task performance. *Psychological Bulletin, 90,* 125-152.

Lovelock, J. (1988). *The ages of Gaia.* New York: Bantam.

Lucero, M. A., & Allen, R. E. (1994). Employee benefits: A growing source of psychological contract violations. *Human Resource Management, 33,* 425-446.

Macaulay, S. (1963). Noncontractual relations in business: A preliminary study. *American Sociology Review, 28,* 55-69.

Maccoby, M. (1988). *Why work.* New York: Simon & Schuster.

Macneil, I. R. (1985). Relational contract: What we do and do not know. *Wisconsin Law Review,* pp. 483-525.

MacNeil, N. (1970). *Dirksen: Portrait of a public man.* New York: World.

Major, D. A., Kozlowski, S. W., Chao, G. T., & Gardner, P. O. (1992, May). *Newcomer expectations and early socialization outcomes: The moderating effects of role development factors.* Paper presented at the Society for Industrial and Organizational Psychology Conference, Montreal.

March, J. (1971, May). The technology of foolishness. *Civil o Konomen* (Copenhagen), *18*(4).

Martin, J. (1992). *Cultures in organizations: Three perspectives.* New York: Oxford University Press.

McLean Parks, J., & Schmedemann, D. (1994). When promises become contracts: Implied contracts and handbook provisions on job security. *Human Resource Management, 33,* 403-424.

Mellers, B. A. (1982). Equity judgment. *Journal of Experimental Psychology, 111,* 242-270.

Miles, R. E., & Creed, W. E. D. (1995). Organizational forms and managerial philosophies. In L. L. Cummings & B. Staw (Eds.), *Research in organizational behavior* (Vol. 17). Greenwich, CT: JAI Press.

Miles, R. E., & Snow, C. C. (1984, Summer). Designing strategic human resources systems. *Organizational Dynamics,* pp. 36-52.

Miles, R. E., & Snow, C. C. (1986). Network organizations: New concepts for new forms. *California Management Review, 28*(3), 62-73.

Milkovich, G., & Newman, J. (1990). *Compensation.* Homewood, IL: BPI/Irwin.

Miller, G. (1956). The magical number seven, plus or minus two: Some limits on our capacity for processing information. *Psychological Review, 63,* 81-97.

Miller, V. D., & Jablin, F. M. (1991). Information seeking during organizational entry: Influences, tactics, and a model of the process. *Academy of Management Review, 16,* 92-120.

Miner, A. S. (1987). Idiosyncratic jobs in formalized organizations. *Administrative Science Quarterly, 32,* 327-351.

Mirvis, P. H., & Hall, D. T. (1994). Psychological success and the boundaryless career. *Journal of Organizational Behavior, 15,* 365-380.

Montgomery, D. (1979). *Workers' contract in America: Studies in the history of work, technology, and labor struggle.* Cambridge, NY: Cambridge University Press.

Nadler, D. A. (1977). *Feedback and organization development: Using data-based methods.* Reading, MA: Addison-Wesley.

Nagao, D. H., & Davis, J. H. (1980). Some implications of temporal drift in social parameters. *Journal of Experimental Social Psychology, 16,* 479-496.

Navy women bringing new era on carriers. (1994, February 21). *New York Times,* pp. A1, A14.

Near, J., & Miceli, M. (1986). Retaliation against whistleblowers: Predictors and effects. *Journal of Applied Psychology, 71,* 137-145.

Nicholson, N., & Johns, G. (1985). The absence culture and the psychological contract: Who's in control of absence? *Academy of Management Review, 10,* 397-407.

Office of Technology Assessment. (1985). *Automation of America's offices.* Washington, DC: Government Printing Office.

Orbell, J. M., van de Kraft, A. J. L., & Dawes, R. M. (1988). Explaining discussion-induced cooperation. *Journal of Personality and Social Psychology, 54,* 811-819.

Organ, D. W. (1990). The motivational basis of organizational citizenship behavior. In L. L. Cummings & B. M. Staw (Eds.), *Research in organizational behavior* (Vol. 12, pp. 43-72). Greenwich, CT: JAI Press.

Orsburn, J. D., Moran, L., Musselwhite, E., & Berger, J. H. (1990). *Self-directed work teams.* Homewood, IL: Business One.

Ostroff, C., & Kozlowski, S. W. J. (1993). Organizational socialization as a learning process: The role of information acquisition. *Personnel Psychology, 45,* 849-874.

Partnow, E. (Ed.). (1993). *The new quotable woman.* New York: Meridian.

Pearce, J. L. (1993). Toward an organizational behavior of contract laborers: Their psychological involvement and effects on employee co-workers. *Academy of Management Review, 36,* 1082-1096.

Perloff, L. S., & Fetzer, B. K. (1986). Self-other judgements and perceived vulnerability of victimization. *Journal of Personality and Social Psychology, 50,* 502-510.

Pfeffer, J., & Baron, J. N. (1988). Taking the workers back out: Recent trends in the structuring of employment. In B. Staw & L. L. Cummings (Eds.), *Research in organizational behavior* (Vol. 12, pp. 257-303). Greenwich, CT: JAI Press.

Pradhan Shah, P. (1994). *The impact of social structure on employee behavior.* Unpublished dissertation, Northwestern University, Kellogg Graduate School of Management.

Promises don't pay off. (1993, February 16). *Daily Northwestern,* pp. 1, 8.

Rajan, M. N., & Graham, J. L. (1991). Nobody's grandfather was a merchant: Understanding the Soviet commercial negotiation process. *California Management Review, 33,* 40-57.

Resnick, L. B. (1991). Shared cognition: Thinking as social practice. In L. B. Resnick, J. M. Levine, & S. Teasley (Eds.), *Perspectives on socially shared cognitions* (pp. 1-20). Washington, DC: American Psychological Association.

Riley, D. W. (Ed.). (1993). *My soul looks back 'less I forget: A collection of quotations by people of color.* New York: HarperCollins.

Robertson, L. S. (1977). Car crashes: Perceived vulnerability and willingness to pay for crash protection. *Journal of Community Health, 3,* 136-141.

Robinson, S. L. (1992). *Responses to dissatisfaction.* Unpublished dissertation, Northwestern University, Kellogg Graduate School of Management.

Robinson, S. L., Kraatz, M. S., & Rousseau, D. M. (1994). Changing obligations and the psychological contract: A longitudinal study. *Academy of Management Journal, 37,* 137-152.

Robinson, S. L., & Rousseau, D. M. (1994). Violating the psychological contract: Not the exception but the norm. *Journal of Organizational Behavior, 15,* 245-259.

Roloff, M. E. (1987). Communication and reciprocity in intimate relationships. In M. E. Roloff & G. R. Miller (Eds.), *Interpersonal processes* (pp. 11-38). Newbury Park, CA: Sage.

Ross, M., & Sicoly, F. (1979). Egocentric biases in availability and attribution. *Journal of Personality and Social Psychology, 37,* 322-336.

Rotchford, N. L., & Roberts, K. H. (1982). Part-time workers as missing persons in organizational research. *Academy of Management Review, 7,* 228-234.

Rousseau, D. M. (1989). Psychological and implied contracts in organizations. *Employee Rights and Responsibilities Journal, 2,* 121-139.

Rousseau, D. M. (1990a). Assessing organizational culture: The case for multiple methods. In B. Schneider (Ed.), *Organizational climate and culture* (pp. 153-192). San Francisco: Jossey-Bass.

Rousseau, D. M. (1990b). New hire perceptions of their own and their employer's obligations: A study of psychological contracts. *Journal of Organizational Behavior, 11,* 389-400.

Rousseau, D. M. (1993). *Teamwork: Inside and out.* New York: Business Week Advance.

Rousseau, D. M., & Anton, R. J. (1988). Fairness and implied contract obligations in terminations: A policy-capturing study. *Human Performance, 1,* 273-289.

Rousseau, D. M., & Anton, R. J. (1991). Fairness and obligations in termination decisions: The role of contributions, promises, and performance. *Journal of Organizational Behavior, 12,* 287-299.

Rousseau, D. M., & Aquino, K. (1993). Fairness and implied contract obligations in job termination: The role of remedies, social accounts, and procedural justice. *Human Performance, 6,* 135-149.

Rousseau, D. M., & Greller, M. (1994). Human resource practices: Administrative contract makers. *Human Resource Management, 33,* 385-401.

Rousseau, D. M., & McLean Parks, J. (1993). The contracts of individuals and organizations. In L. L. Cummings & B. M. Staw (Eds.), *Research in organizational behavior* (Vol. 15, pp. 1-43). Greenwich, CT: JAI Press.

Rousseau, D. M., Robinson, S. L., & Kraatz, M. S. (1992, May). *Renegotiating the psychological contract.* Paper presented at the Society for Industrial Organizational Psychology meetings, Montreal.

Rousseau, D. M., & Wade-Benzoni, K. A. (1994). Linking strategy and human resource practices: How employee and customer contracts are created. *Human Resources Management, 33,* 463-489.

Rousseau, D. M., & Wade-Benzoni, K. A. (1995). Changing individual-organizational attributes: A two-way street. In A. Howard (Ed.), *Changing nature of work.* San Francisco: Jossey-Bass.

Rusbult, C., Farrell, D., Rogers, G., & Mainous, A. (1988). Impact of exchange variables on exit, voice, loyalty and neglect: An integrative model of response to declining job satisfaction. *Academy of Management Journal, 31,* 599-627.

Rynes, S. L., & Boudreau, J. W. (1986). College recruiting in large organizations: Practice, evaluation, and research implications. *Personnel Psychology, 39,* 729-757.

Salancik, G. R., & Pfeffer, J. (1978). A social information processing approach to job attitudes and task design. *Administrative Science Quarterly, 23,* 224-253.

Schleifer, A., & Summers, L. H. (1988). Breach of trust in hostile takeovers. In A. J. Auerbach (Ed.), *Corporate takeovers: Causes and consequences* (pp. 33-67). Chicago: University of Chicago Press.

Schlenker, B. R. (1980). *Impression management: The self-concept, social identity, and interpersonal relations.* Belmont, CA: Brooks/Cole.

Schneider, B. (1987). The people make the place. *Personnel Psychology, 40,* 437-453.

Scholtes, P. (1988). *The team handbook.* Madison, WI: Joiner.

Scott, W. R. (1983). The organization of environments: Network, cultural, and historical elements. In J. W. Meyer & W. R. Scott (Eds.), *Organizational environments: Rituals and rationality.* Beverly Hills, CA: Sage.

Seabright, M., Levinthal, D., & Fichman, M. (1992). Role of individual attachments in the dissolution of interorganizational relationships. *Academy of Management Journal, 35,* 122-160.

Selznick, P. (1969). *Law, society, and industrial justice.* New York: Russell Sage.

Shanteau, J., & Harrison, P. (1991). The perceived strength of an implied contract: Can it withstand financial temptation? *Organizational Behavior and Human Decision Processes, 49,* 1-21.

Shore, L. M., & Wayne, S. J. (1993). Commitment and employee behavior: A comparison of affective commitment and continuance commitment and perceived organizational support. *Journal of Applied Psychology, 18,* 774-780.

Simon, H. A. (1951). A formal theory of the employment relation. *Econometrika, 19,* 293-305.

Simon, H. A. (1976). *Administrative behavior.* New York: Macmillan. (Original work published 1958)

Sims, H. P., & Gioia, D. A. (1986). *The thinking organization.* San Francisco: Jossey-Bass.

Skinner, B. F. (1969). *Contingencies of reinforcement: A theoretical analysis.* New York: Appleton-Century-Crofts.

Snow, C. C., Miles, R. E., & Coleman, H. J. (1992, Winter). Managing 21st century network organizations. *Organizational Dynamics,* pp. 5-20.

Social Security won't be subject to freeze, White House decides. (1993, February 9). *New York Times,* pp. A1, B3.

Sutton, J. R., Dobbin, F., Meyer, J. W., & Scott, W. R. (1994). The legalization of the workplace. *American Journal of Sociology, 99,* 944-971.

Sutton, R. I., Eisenhardt, K. M., & Sucker, J. V. (1985). Managing organizational decline: Lessons from Atari. *Organizational Dynamics, 14,* 17-29.

Taylor, S., & Brown, J. (1988). Illusion and well-being: A social psychological perspective on mental health. *Psychological Bulletin, 103,* 193-210.

Thompson, J. D. (1967). *Organizations in action.* New York: McGraw-Hill.

Thurow, L. C. (1980). *The zero-sum society.* New York: Basic Books.

Toyota to hire designers on a contractual basis. (1994, January 22). *New York Times,* p. A39.

Tyler, T. R., & Lind, E. A. (1992). A relational model of authority in groups. In M. P. Zanna (Ed.), *Advances in experimental social psychology* (Vol. 25, pp. 115-192). New York: Academic Press.

Uhnak, D. (1977). *The investigation.* New York: Simon & Schuster.

U.S. juries grow tougher on plaintiffs. (1994, June 17). *New York Times,* pp. A1, B9.

Uzzi, B. (1991). *The network effect: The structural embeddedness of organizational decline and deindustrialization.* Unpublished manuscript, State University of New York at Stonybrook, Department of Sociology.

Van Buren, A. (1988, August 1). Court makes a turkey of a decision. *Chicago Tribune.*

Venkatesh, A., & Vitalari, N. P. (1992). An emerging distributed work arrangement: An investigation of computer-based supplemental work at home. *Management Science, 38,* 1687-1706.

Voluck, P. R., & Hanlon, M. J. (1987). Contract disclaimer in policy documents. *Personnel Journal, 66,* 123-131.

Vroom, V. (1964). *Work and motivation.* New York: Wiley.

Wade-Benzoni, K. (1993). *Humiliation in the workplace.* Unpublished manuscript, Northwestern University, Kellogg Graduate School of Management.

Wakbayashi, M., & Graen, G. (1984). The Japanese career progress study: A seven year follow-up. *Journal of Applied Psychology, 69,* 603-614.

Wanous, J. P. (1980). *Organizational entry: Recruitment, selection and socialization of newcomers.* Reading, MA: Addison-Wesley.

Wanous, J. P. (1992). *Recruitment, selection, orientation and socialization of newcomers* (2nd ed.). New York: Addison-Wesley.

Wanous, J. P., Keon, T. L., & Latack, J. C. (1983). Expectancy theory and occupational organizational choices: A review and test. *Organizational Behavior and Human Performance, 32,* 66-85.

Watcher, H., & Stengelhofer, T. (1992). Human resource management in a unified Germany. *Employee Relations, 14*(4), 21-37.

Weber, A. R., & Taylor, D. P. (1963). Procedures for employee displacement: Advance notice and plant shutdown. *Journal of Business, 36,* 302-315.

Weick, K. E. (1979). *Social psychology of organizing.* Reading, MA: Addison-Wesley.

Weick, K. E. (1992). Agenda setting in organizational behavior: A theory-focused approach. *Journal of Management Inquiry, 1,* 171-182.

Weinstein, N. D. (1980). Unrealistic optimism about future life events. *Journal of Personality and Social Psychology, 39,* 806-820.

Welch, J. (CEO), & Hood, E. (President). (1992, February 14). To our share owners. In *General Electric Annual Report.* Fairfield, CT: General Electric.

Whyte, W. (1956). *Organization man.* New York: Simon & Schuster.

Williams, R. C. (1989). *The trusting heart.* New York: Times Books.

Williamson, O. (1979). Transaction-cost economics: The governance of contractual relations. *Journal of Law and Economics, 3,* 233-261.

Wilson, J. A., & Elman, N. S. (1990). Organizational benefits of mentoring. *Academy of Management Executive, 4*(4), 88-94.

Wolfe Morrison, E. (1991). *Newcomer information seeking: An investigation of types, modes, and sources.* Unpublished manuscript, New York University, Stern School of Business.

Wolfe Morrison, E., & Bies, R. (1991). Impression management in the feedback seeking process: A literature review and research agenda. *Academy of Management Review, 16,* 522-541.

Wolfe Morrison, E., & Cummings, L. L. (1992). The impact of feedback diagnosticity and performance expectations on feedback seeking behavior. *Human Performance, 5,* 251-264.

Yoder, D., & Staudohar, P. D. (1985, Summer). Management and public policy in plant closure. *Sloan Management Review, 26*(4), 45-58.

Index

About the Author

Denise M. Rousseau is Professor of Organizational Behavior at Carnegie-Mellon University. She holds degrees in industrial/organizational psychology and anthropology from the University of California at Berkeley. She has been a faculty member at Northwestern University, the University of Michigan, and the Naval Postgraduate School at Monterey, California. Her research addresses the impact of work group processes on performance and the changing psychological contract at work. Her research has appeared in prominent academic journals, such as the *Academy of Management Review, Administrative Science Quarterly, Human Relations, Journal of Applied Psychology,* and *Journal of Organizational Behavior.* Her books include the *Trends in Organizational Behavior* series with Cary Cooper, *Developing an Interdisciplinary Science of Organizations* with Karlene Roberts and Charles Hulin, and *The Boundaryless Career* with Michael Arthur. Active in executive training and development, she has taught in executive programs at Northwestern (Kellogg), Cornell, Carnegie-Mellon, and Chulalongkorn University (Thailand). Her writings for managers have appeared in *Business Week Advance, Kellogg World,* and *Human Resource Management.* She is a Fellow in the American Psychological Association and the Society for Industrial/Organizational Psychology and serves on the Board of Governors for the Academy of Management. She is Associate Editor of the *Journal of Organizational Behavior.*